The Curse of The Great Train Robbery

For his second book, *The Curse of The Great Train Robbery*, Jon Fordham, a retired building society general manager and county cricket executive director, investigates the impact the Great Train Robbery was to have on the lives not only of the robbers themselves, but also on their families, on the railway and post office workers who were on the train that night, the police officers who worked tirelessly to bring the robbers to justice and on some of the people who, through no fault of their own, suddenly found themselves involved in what was described at the time as the Crime of the Century.

D1340700

The Curse of The Great Train Robbery

Jon Fordham

Arena Books

Copyright © Jon Fordham 2016

The right of Jon Fordham to be identified as author of this book
has been asserted in accordance with the Copyright, Designs and Patents Act 1988.

First published in 2016 by Arena Books

Arena Books
6 Southgate Green
Bury St. Edmunds
IP33 2BL

www.arenabooks.co.uk

Distributed in America by Ingram International, One Ingram Blvd., PO Box
3006, La Vergne, TN 37086-1985, USA.

Jon Fordham

The Curse of The Great Train Robbery

British Library cataloguing in Publication Data. A catalogue record for this
book is available from the British Library.

ISBN-13   978-1-909421-73-8
BIC classifications:- BTC, BGH, JKV, JKVF, JKVM.

Printed and bound by Lightning Source UK

Cover design
by Jason Anscomt

Typeset in
Times New Roma

PREFACE

The interest in the Great Train Robbery continues to be as strong as ever, even though it is over fifty years since it took place.

2013 saw the passing of three of the train robbery gang - Bruce Reynolds, Ronnie Biggs and John Daly - and the number of surviving gang members, known to have been at the scene of the crime on 8 August 1963, can now be counted on the fingers of one hand.

There have been quite a few books written about the robbery over the years, so you may well wonder why I decided to add to the number. The latest book to be written has the advantage of being the most up to date, but you would think that everything worth writing about a crime that was committed over five decades ago has already been covered.

However this is not the case and there are still questions to be answered and riddles to be solved. For example, as recent as September 2014 gang member Gordon Goody, then aged 84, gave an interview to *The Observer* during which he revealed that the man previously known only as the 'Ulsterman', and one of the principle instigators of the robbery, was in fact a post office worker by the name of Patrick McKenna. Goody followed up the interview with the publication of his book in November 2014 which he titled '*How to Rob a Train.*'

Another unknown surrounds the mystery of who coshed Jack Mills, the train driver of the Glasgow to London overnight mail train. There are a number of people who could have struck the blow that felled Mr Mills, but his true identity has never been revealed.

But the main reason why I decided to write this book is that, at the time, many people regarded The Great Train Robbery as a victimless crime since the money stolen belonged mainly to the big banks of the day, including Midland Bank, Bank of Scotland, Westminster Bank and Barclays Bank.

However, this completely overlooks the lasting effects the robbery had not only on Jack Mills, but also on a host of other men, women and children, who were not directly involved in the crime, but whose lives were changed irrevocably because of the actions of others.

On reading this book you may disagree with some of those I have suggested were victims to 'The Curse of the Great Train Robbery'.

If you do, and I'm sure many who read this book will, I challenge you to write the next book about the crime which was described at the time it was committed as the 'Crime of the Century.'

'The people who paid the heaviest price for the Great Train Robbery are the families. And that is the families of all the people involved with the Great Train Robbery. The Robbers' families, the families of Old Bill, the families of the rail men and the post office workers, and even the families of the people that have helped us over the years. All have paid a price, one way or another, for our collective involvement in the robbery - a very heavy price, in the case of my family. For that I do have my regrets, but it still has been a life well worth living'.

Ronald Arthur Biggs

For the love of money is a root of all kinds of evil. Some people, in their eagerness to get rich, have wandered away from the faith and caused themselves a lot of pain.

1 Timothy 6:10

'I felt choked when I saw her. She had been through so much in her life, like all the Train Robbers' wives – the years of absent husbands, the endless round of prison visits, struggling to cope on their own.'

Bruce Richard Reynolds

CONTENTS

THE STORY

THE VICTIMS

THE END OF THE LINE

INTRODUCTION

It is over 50 years since 'The Great Train Robbery' captured the imagination of the British public and the fascination with the events of 8 August 1963 shows no sign of abating.

When news broke that a large gang of robbers had hijacked a Royal Mail train on route from Glasgow to London, they became instant folk heroes and modern day Robin Hoods in the eyes of many. After all, they reasoned, the money stolen was the property of the banks and didn't belong to anyone in particular.

This perception was further embellished as reports of the amount of cash stolen steadily increased during that first day, finally settling at an astonishing £2,631,784 – equivalent to around £47million today. Each member of the gang walked away with suitcases and holdalls packed with around £150,000 in banknotes.

To put this amount of money into perspective, when Vivian Nicholson became famous overnight in 1961 for scooping the largest ever win on Littlewoods Pools, she banked £152,319. Her winnings would be equivalent to around £2.8million in 2015, significantly more than the average £2million prize pocketed by today's National Lottery winners. As they looked on at the vast piles of cash in front of them, the train robbers must have felt like they had also won the pools.

Another slant on public opinion was that the robbers had given a Churchillian two finger salute to the Establishment – an Establishment already struggling to cope with the fall out caused by the 'Profumo Affair' which led to the resignation of Prime Minister Harold Macmillan in October 1963, and which would ultimately mean defeat for the Conservatives at the general election the following year.

Initially, the gang was faceless and nameless. But over the days and weeks following the robbery, the police, led by Detective Chief Superintendent Tommy Butler of the Scotland Yard Flying Squad, released the names of those they wished to interview and who, they said in the time honoured tradition, could help them with their enquiries. In no time at all, the names and faces of the robbers became familiar to the British public throughout the land.

When Viv Nicholson won the Pools in 1961, she told reporters that she would 'spend, spend, spend'. However, within a couple of years her husband had been killed in a car crash and the money had all but evaporated.

Despite telling reporters later in her life that, given the chance, she would do exactly the same again, there must have been times when Nicholson deeply regretted the pools win that had changed her life forever.

In the same way, and for similar reasons, most, if not all of the Great Train Robbers who were caught must have regretted being part of what was, at that time, the biggest robbery in the country's history.

The events of 8 August 1963 changed forever the lives not only of the robbers and their accomplices, but also many of their family and friends, as well as the British Railways and Post Office employees who were just going about their job on the English Electric Type 4 diesel-electric locomotive D326 that left Glasgow Central at 6:50pm on Wednesday 7 August 1963, but which never arrived at London Euston at 3:50am the following morning as scheduled.

THE STORY

CHAPTER 1
The Planning

The BOAC Robbery

On 27 November 1962, security staff delivering wages to the admin offices of the British Overseas Airways Corporation (BOAC) at London Airport were attacked and relieved of £62,000 by a gang the media called either 'the City Gents Gang' or 'the Bowler Hat Gang', due to the fact that some of them were wearing smart suits and bowler hats and, in some instances, carrying rolled up umbrellas fitted with iron bars.[1]

Amongst the gang were Charlie Wilson, Ronald 'Buster' Edwards, Roy James, Bruce Reynolds, Bill Jennings and Gordon Goody, all of whom would be part of the 'firm' that robbed the mail train on 8 August 1963. A 7th member of that firm, Jimmy White, allowed the City Gents Gang to use his flat in Norbury, South London as a meeting place after the BOAC robbery, where the others were able to count and share out the money.[2]

The attack on the two security staff was a fairly vicious one. Both were coshed to the ground, one courtesy of a whack from a specially adapted brolly. Two BOAC clerks hit the ground without being ordered to, whilst a third, apparently paralysed with fear, was smashed on the head with a cosh wielded by Edwards. '*His skull seemed to split open and he fell to the floor with blood flowing from his scalp*', wrote Piers Paul Read in his book '*The Train Robbers, Their Story*'.[3]

In the 1988 film '*Buster*', directed by David Green, Edwards was played by singer songwriter Phil Collins who portrayed him as a 'likeable rogue'. However, this would seem to be somewhat at odds with the real life Buster Edwards.

With the way cleared of any opposition, in a flash the gang and the money were in the two getaway cars, both Jaguars, one of which was driven by Roy James.

The choice of James to drive one of the 'Jags' was a 'no-brainer'. At that time, he was showing real promise as an up and coming racing driver, holding his own when racing against contemporaries such as Mike Hailwood and Jackie Stewart. His skill behind the wheel was put to the test several times during the getaway - on one occasion swerving and stopping in front of traffic to give the second Jag a chance to run a red light.

After abandoning the cars, the gang made their way separately to Jimmy White's flat. There was an air of disappointment when they counted the cash as they had expected a significantly bigger pay-day.

The sheer nerve of the gang, and the brutality of the robbery, had both the local CID and the Flying Squad scurrying around looking for some early arrests. The Flying Squad had a fairly good idea who was involved – particularly who the getaway drivers were as few wheel men could have handled a car the way Roy James had.

Within 24 hours, Wilson, Goody, James and Mickey Ball (the other getaway driver) had been arrested and put into an identity parade. However, as none of the four were picked out by witnesses, they were all released without charge.

At another identity parade a couple of weeks later, Mickey Ball was wrongly picked out by a witness who thought he was Bill Jennings. As Jennings had been involved in the violent attack on the security staff, Ball owned up to being one of the getaway drivers as he knew this would mean a shorter sentence. He was subsequently sent to prison for five years.

Immediately after dividing up the cash, Bruce Reynolds and his wife Frances went abroad, first to Paris and then on to Tangier, leaving their young son with friends. Reynolds remained out of the UK for some time, during which his name was taken off the list of suspects for the BOAC job by a friendly police contact – although it cost Reynolds £1500.

The police remained determined to convict Goody, James and Wilson, although ultimately they were unable to get sufficient evidence to put James away, and so he too was in the clear. However, a third identity parade was arranged, and this time witnesses identified Goody and Wilson. Both were then charged with the robbery.

A few months before the BOAC robbery, Gordon Goody had met Brian Field in a Soho nightclub.[4] Field was a solicitor's clerk working for James & Wheater, a legal practice owned by sole practitioner John Wheater. Field and Wheater had both spent time in the British Army where the latter was said to have served his country with distinction.

Field had previously acted for Buster Edwards, and he and Goody struck up a working relationship whereby Field would supply Goody with occasional information about the contents of the country homes of some of his clients.[5]

Goody made bail thanks to Field, whilst some of Wilson's associates greased a few palms so that he too was granted bail.

At his trial, Wilson was acquitted on the instructions of the presiding judge when two prosecution witnesses swore they had seen him at the scene of the robbery, but in two different places at the same time.

Goody, however, was made to sweat for his acquittal. The alibi that Field and he had concocted failed to convince anybody at the trial as it was so obviously contrived, and the future was beginning to look pretty bleak. In desperation, Goody turned to his 'Plan B' – bribing one of the jury.

Despite the fact that the juror Goody targeted turned down the offer of £400, the jury was unable to come to a unanimous decision and the judge was left with no option other than to order a retrial.[6] At the retrial, Goody and Field came up with a strategy that was far more subtle than simply 'nobbling' the jury.

The crux of the prosecution case was a witness who said that during the robbery he had been assaulted by the man in a checked cap, and that the cap had come off during the struggle and that Goody was the man in the checked cap. The cap in question had been found at the scene and was in the possession of the police. However, for a payment of just £200, a sympathetic police officer switched the cap for one three sizes larger.

When counsel for the defence cross examined the prosecution witness, he got him to agree that if Goody was wearing the cap, then the cap obviously had to be the same size as Goody's head.[7] The cap was then given to Goody and when he put it on it covered both his ears and eyes. Inevitably, the jury acquitted Goody and he walked out of court a free man, much to the chagrin of the police.

Robbing trains – a softer option

As the banks became more security conscious out of necessity, and safe manufacturers made their products more difficult to crack, criminals in the early 1960's inevitably began to look at softer targets elsewhere.

In his book 'The Autobiography of a Thief', Bruce Reynolds wrote that he and his associates had begun sizing up the chances of robbing trains sometime prior to the BOAC robbery. 'The firm's collective knowledge, which consisted of half-truths, rumours and exaggerations, all pointed to the railways as being especially vulnerable' wrote Reynolds.

At this stage, their ideas about robbing trains did not include how to stop them.

The first potential target identified was a train carrying money from William Hill's betting shops in the Midlands to their Central London offices. This plan was shelved when Reynolds found out that the train would be carrying mainly cheques rather than cash.

They then turned their attention to the Irish Mail Train, a passenger train operating out of Paddington station, which Buster Edwards had discovered often transported the wages of railway workers to Swindon. Loading the wages at Paddington was carried out under tight security, so the only realistic option was to carry out the robbery while the train was in motion and then stop it by pulling the communication cord. A practice run with Edwards, Bill Jennings and Gordon Goody went smoothly – in stark contrast to the robbery itself.

On the day of the robbery, when the train had reached Ealing, Reynolds, Goody and Charlie Wilson made their way to the guard's van and smashed their way in. When the train passed the Hayes signal box, Edwards pulled the communication cord – but nothing happened. Jennings had a go and still nothing happened. By this time, the train was approaching West Drayton where a getaway van was waiting.

Edwards and Jennings ran down the train and joined the others; Edwards found a control wheel which he turned and the train began to slow down, but by the time it had stopped completely it was a good mile away from West Drayton.

The gang jumped out and sprinted back towards the waiting van. Their haul was just £700 and they left behind them a railway guard who had been beaten and tied up with nylon stockings, and a ticket collector who had been coshed and left unconscious with blood streaming down his face. [8 & 9]

When Reynolds returned to the UK after the dust had settled on the BOAC robbery, he and the gang started to look at the possibility of robbing trains once again.

The first under consideration was a weekly shipment of gold from South Africa which was put onto a train at Southampton and then met by a large police presence when it arrived at Waterloo station. The strength of the welcoming committee ruled out any chance of the gang getting their hands on the gold.

The second train, which they nicknamed 'the Money Train', appeared to offer a better chance of success. The Money Train ran from Bournemouth to Waterloo in the early hours of the morning collecting bags of cash on route. The train's last stop before Waterloo was at Weybridge in Surrey. Here it was met by a two car police escort and the cash bags were then taken to Weybridge Post Office.

Surveillance had revealed that the Tuesday morning train usually carried the largest number of bags, and so the gang began to put together a plan which involved an ambush when the bags were being taken from the train to the waiting police cars.

However, the plan never got off the ground. Two Jaguars had been stolen to be used as getaway cars, and these had been stowed away in garages being rented by Jimmy White, together with some other equipment needed during the planned ambush. Ironically, White's garages were broken into, and the thieves got away with both cars and all the equipment the gang had stored. The plan to rob the Money Train was postponed indefinitely.

The Travelling Post Office

Having helped Gordon Goody to be acquitted of the BOAC robbery, solicitor's clerk Brian Field contacted Goody towards the end of February 1963 and arranged to meet him at the Old Bailey the following day.

Field told Goody that he had been contacted by someone who had detailed information on the movement of large sums of cash across the country, who had asked him to sound out a firm which would be interested in making use of this information.

As expected, Goody told Field he was interested and the following day he and Buster Edwards met Field at his office in New Quebec Street, not far from Marble Arch tube station. Field introduced the pair to a middle aged man who called himself Mark. From Field's office, Mark took Goody and Edwards to Finsbury Park in North London where they were introduced to another middle aged man. However, no names were exchanged at this point and the man would become known as the 'Ulsterman' because of his thick Northern Irish accent.

The identity of the Ulsterman remained a secret for over 50 years until Goody named him as Patrick McKenna in an interview with the *Observer* newspaper published at the end of September 2014. Aged 43 at the time Goody first met him, McKenna was a Belfast born post office worker living in Islington, North London.

In the *Observer* interview, Goody revealed that he discovered the identity of the Ulsterman when he picked up a glasses case, with the name Patrick McKenna inside, whilst the post office worker had gone off to buy some ice creams. [10]

At this first meeting, the Ulsterman told Goody and Edwards about the trains known as 'Travelling Post Offices' (TPO's) and specifically the train that ran overnight from Glasgow Central station to London Euston. This train was usually about a dozen coaches long and all but one of the coaches contained normal mail which post office workers sorted while the train was on the move.

It was the contents of the other coach that was of particular interest to the Ulsterman as it carried mail bags containing cash, with the train picking up additional bags at stops on route. The cash came from provincial banks and according to McKenna, the amount of cash on the train at any one time could run to several million pounds.

When Goody asked about the source of the information, the Ulsterman told them it was from a relative (brother or step-brother) who worked for the Post Office.

At the end of the meeting, Goody and Edwards told the Ulsterman they were definitely interested, and agreed to meet him again.

After discussing the proposition with Bruce Reynolds at his flat in Putney, it was agreed that a meeting would be arranged with the other regular members of the firm. A few days later Edwards, Goody, Wilson, Reynolds, Bill Jennings, Roy James, Jimmy White and Alf Thomas (a friend of White) met at Edwards's flat in Twickenham.

By then, Goody had met the Ulsterman for a second time and was able to tell the others that the first coach behind the diesel engine on the TPO carried parcels only and would be unmanned. Next was the HVP (High Value Packages) coach where the bags of cash were held. In this coach would be four or five post office sorters. Behind this would be up to 10 other coaches containing mail, and in total there would be around 70 post office sorters spread between the third and the twelfth coach.

The train normally left Glasgow Central at 6:50pm and would arrive at London Euston just before 4:00am, making several stops along the way where additional mail bags were taken on board.

After it was agreed that any robbery couldn't take place whilst the train was at any of the stations, the main discussion concentrated on how and where to stop it during its 400 mile journey.

Where to stop the train

Having ruled out hitting the train at either Glasgow or Euston due to heavy security at both stations, it seemed the only option was to find a suitable place to stop it during its journey.

It was agreed that the train should be stopped as close to London as possible as the firm's thinking at this stage was to be back in the capital long before the police began setting up road blocks in the immediate aftermath of the robbery. The other proviso was that the robbery should take place somewhere remote to avoid anybody witnessing it.

According to Bruce Reynolds, the following day he and his brother in law John Daly (known as 'Paddy') caught a northbound train from Euston to get a feel of the terrain outside London. [11 & 12]

Once the train had gone through Tring in Hertfordshire, Reynolds noticed an area around Leighton Buzzard that looked promising. At around 40 miles from Euston, with open countryside on either side of the track, it seemed a real possibility. On the return journey, Reynolds noticed a point on the B488 where the road curved and ran under the railway track.

The following night, the firm met again at Edwards's flat and Reynolds reported back. It was agreed that Roy James would drive up to this point on the B488 and work out the best and quickest route back to London should this be the place they eventually decided to stop the train.

There is some confusion as to who actually found the location first, since Buster Edwards stated that he and another gang member had taken a drive out from London and tried to follow the railway track by road. This they did, but couldn't find anywhere suitable to stop the train. Having drawn a blank, on their return to London the pair got hold of some ordnance survey maps and found, on paper at least, the perfect spot – quiet, isolated and with a bridge where the road – the B488 - went beneath the railway line. [13, 14 & 15]

According to Edwards, he and Bruce Reynolds drove up to have a look at the spot the next day.

In his autobiography, Reynolds, when discussing his train journey, wrote '*I wouldn't have been surprised to see Buster, Gordon, Charlie and Roy, done up in some guise. They would be out as well, ducking and diving, discreetly digging for inspiration and information'.*

Whichever is the correct version, the facts of the matter are that the perfect location for the robbery had been found. This was at a place called Bridego Bridge in the Parish of Mentmore, in the county of Buckinghamshire – 2 miles from Leighton Buzzard and 38 miles from Euston.

How to stop the train

Having more or less decided on where the train could be stopped, the next problem facing the firm was how to go about stopping it. At a brainstorming session the best suggestion was that a red signal would always force a train to stop, and as this was a fairly common occurrence, it wouldn't unduly alert the driver.

There was also some concern that the Ulsterman had told them there could be at least 70 post office workers on the train, leaving the firm seriously outnumbered if things got a bit out of hand.

To minimise any potential opposition, someone raised the possibility of uncoupling the engine and the first two carriages, separating them from the other 10 carriages where the bulk of the post office sorters would be. Bruce Reynolds was certain that it could be done, but at that point had no idea how.

During the discussion, Buster Edwards mentioned that a mate of his, Tommy Wisbey, had been working with a South Coast firm who had been robbing trains on the Brighton line. He had also heard that one of them knew how to stop trains.

It was agreed that Edwards would speak to Wisbey and, the following day, Edwards met him at a club at the Elephant and Castle owned by Bobby Welch, also a member of the South Coast firm. Welch was initially suspicious and more than a little bit miffed that Edwards seemed to know so much about their activities. However, thanks to Wisbey, who had known Edwards since the 1950's when they had both worked for Freddie Foreman, an associate of the Kray twins, Welch knew that Edwards was 'sound' and he agreed to set up a meeting with their man Roger Cordrey who could stop trains.

A couple of days later, Edwards met Wisbey and Cordrey at Waterloo station where he outlined the train job to the two men, and in particular the need to stop the train and then separate the engine and the first two coaches from the rest of it.

Having listened intently to Edwards, Cordrey confirmed that he could stop the train. However, if they wanted his help, it would come with one condition – the rest of the South Coast firm, comprising Wisbey, Welch, James Hussey and Frank Munroe, would have to be part of the team that carried out the robbery.

When Edwards reported back to the rest of the gang, Cordrey's terms were at first greeted with derision and a degree of animosity. However, when they had all calmed down, they realised that it was 'Hobson's Choice' – if they couldn't stop the train, it was game over before it had started. And, as Gordon Goody pointed out, the additional 'muscle' might well come in handy.

A few days later Reynolds took Cordrey to Bridego Bridge for a recce and it was then that Cordrey really bought into the plan. He agreed that Bridego Bridge was the ideal point to unload the mail bags from the train. But to stop it, Cordrey needed to tamper with signals which meant stopping the train at the first set of signals before the Bridge.

Reynolds and Cordrey walked up the line and came to a set of signals at a place called Sears Crossing. It was here that Cordrey explained how he could stop the train. It was both childishly simple and a stroke of genius.

The back plate of the signals would be removed and the green light covered with a glove. The red light would then be disconnected from the main power supply and connected to a six volt Ever Ready battery. Job done!

There was also a dwarf signal at ground level a few hundred yards further up the line which would also need to be fixed so it showed an amber light warning the driver to slow down in time for the train to stop at the Sears Crossing lights. The dwarf signal only had two lights – amber and green.

Whilst Cordrey could stop the train, Reynolds knew that there were still two other problems to overcome – how to uncouple the train, and how to get the engine and the remaining two coaches from Sears Crossing to Bridego Bridge where the mail sacks could be unloaded.

The South Coast Raiders

The next meeting also took place at Buster Edwards's flat, but this time it included the South Coast firm, or the South Coast Raiders as the press referred to them.

The first to put in an appearance was Cordrey who arrived on his own. Then, arriving together were Wisbey, Welch, Hussey and Munroe.[16]

The South Coast Raiders had begun life with fairly low key activities such as opportunist snatches from guard's vans whilst the guard was being distracted. On one occasion, a member of the gang pretended to have a seizure just as the train was pulling into a station. Whilst the guard was trying to administer some first aid, other members of the gang were rifling through the packages in the guard's van.

However, it didn't take long for the Railway Police to wise up and alert the guards to what was going on, and the gang realised that they had to diversify.

It was then that Cordrey came up with the idea of stopping trains by tampering with the signals which enabled him to stay trackside whilst the others, with balaclavas covering their faces, would storm the guard's van, tie up the guards and take any bags which contained cash.

By this time, railway guards were refusing to work on the Brighton line without adequate protection, so British Railways agreed to fit bolts, chains and locks that could only be opened from the inside, to the guard's van on all Southern Region trains. However, this only brought about a temporary halt to the activities of the South Coast Raiders as the gang came up with ways to counter these measures and normal business was soon resumed.

On one occasion, Frank Munroe pretended to be a disabled passenger with Tommy Wisbey as his male carer. As was the practice at that time on non-corridor trains, wheelchair bound passengers always travelled in the guard's van.

As soon as Cordrey had stopped the train between stations just outside London, the disabled passenger miraculously regained use of his legs; the guard was knocked unconscious and within minutes Wisbey and Munroe were in a getaway car with the mail bags safely stashed in the boot.

However, not long after this, Cordrey received a visit from the police. He spent a night in a cell and was then put into an identification parade. As he hadn't been part of the robbery itself, no one picked him out and he was allowed to go home. But he had been unnerved by this experience, and for some time after, Cordrey kept a low profile and stayed away from the rest of the Raiders.

Eventually, when they did meet up again, they agreed to keep away from the Brighton line and decided to target the Irish Mail train instead. Also known as the Irish Express, this Midland Region mail train ran out of Euston bound for Holyhead, Fishguard and Dublin. It was rumoured that the train would be carrying valuable diamonds.

On the 20 February 1963, Cordrey set off for the spot the gang had decided was ideal to stop the train, whilst the rest of them bought tickets and settled down in a compartment close to the guard's van.

Soon after the train got underway, the gang descended on the guard's van and attacked both the guard and ticket inspector – but it was at this point that things began to go a bit pear-shaped.

Hearing the commotion, a group of soldiers piled into the guard's van, only to be met by a ferocious attack from the gang who dished out a liberal dose of medicine with their coshes.

Someone pulled the communication cord as the train went through Watford, and thinking that they had arrived at the point where Cordrey was to stop the train, the gang opened the door and jumped out, expecting to see the Hertfordshire countryside. What they saw instead were the lights of Hemel Hempstead train station. The gang scattered – they had no alternative and it was a case of every man for himself.

In an interview for the *Daily Post* in December 2013, Howel Owen, the guard on the Irish Mail train that day, relived the attack by the South Coast Raiders that left him and ticket collector Tom John Thomas beaten, bloodied and tied up. According to Owen, one of the gang told the two '*don't try anything silly, I've got a gun*'.[17]

However, mistakenly, Mr Owen attributed the attack to Bruce Reynolds, Jimmy White and Ray (not Roy) James, and not the actual attackers on the day who were Wisbey, Welch, Hussey and Munroe. He told the *Daily Post* that Bruce Reynolds was probably the man who tied him up, Jimmy White acted as lookout, and 'Ray' James was one of the men he saw in the guard's van.

Ironically, White and James were the least likely of any of the train robbers to be involved in such a violent attack. As Piers Paul Read stated in his book 'The Train Robbers – Their Story', '*Jimmy White...like Roy* (James), *Bill* (Jennings) *and John Daly, preferred not to take part in the violence which might be involved in the other aspects of the job.*'[18]

In his interview for the *Daily Post*, Mr Owen continued '*The robbers weren't chancers; they knew what they were looking for. They thought the train was carrying diamonds from Amsterdam to Dublin and that there was a consignment of £5 notes going to Ireland. They got away with about £3,000.*

'*Where I think they got their plans wrong is that they hadn't counted on there being so few passengers on the train and they didn't expect us back in the guard's van so soon.*'

Eventually, the South Coast Raiders managed to make their way back to Bob Welch's club empty handed.

It was while they were considering their next move that Buster Edwards paid his visit to Bob Welch and Tommy Wisbey, and it was probably just at the right time for the Raiders, hence the full turn out at Edwards's flat – the first full meeting of the firm that was to commit what was to become known as the Great Train Robbery.

The back-up train driver

After the introductions, Reynolds took to the floor and gave a brief summary of the progress that had been made since the previous meeting. The need to find someone to uncouple the train was solved when Roy James volunteered to find out how it could be done.[19] As well as uncoupling the train, the vacuum to operate the train's braking system also needed to be disconnected, as well as the tubes that carried steam to heat the coaches. Bill Jennings said that he was happy to help James and Jimmy White offered to become first reserve.

However, there was still the question of moving the train from Sears Crossing to Bridego Bridge, and whilst the general feeling was that the driver would be 'encouraged' to do it, they knew that it would be dangerous to depend on this and not have a contingency. There was therefore a consensus that a back-up driver would be needed on the night, just in case.

At the end of the evening, Reynolds suggested that the next meeting should be on Wimbledon Common where they could have a kick about with a football, so as not to look too suspicious.

The need for an experienced train driver on the night of the robbery continued to cause concern for some time. Roy James, as well as volunteering to do the uncoupling, was also pretty confident that he would be able to move the train the short distance from Sears Crossing to Bridego Bridge.

Masquerading as a school teacher who wanted to tell his pupils how modern trains worked, he had persuaded a train driver he had befriended to let him into the cab when he next moved his train from Euston station into a siding. The driver explained all the controls to James who, as a more than promising motor racing driver, had the ability to absorb how mechanical things worked very quickly.

However, on the actual night, he would also be uncoupling the train, and as he couldn't be in two places at once, the search for an experienced back-up driver continued. As it happened, a solution to the problem fell into Bruce Reynolds's lap when he least expected it.

Deciding that he needed an evening out and a break from planning the robbery, Reynolds took his wife Frances, and their son Nick, to Redhill in Surrey to visit Ronnie Biggs, an old friend he first came across in Borstal many years earlier. As a criminal, Biggs was not in the same league as Reynolds or the majority of the firm. However, Reynolds enjoyed his company, and Frances seemed to hit it off with Biggs's wife, Charmian.

At that time, Biggs had a small carpentry business and during the course of the evening mentioned to Reynolds that he was doing some work on a bungalow for an old chap who had promised to take Biggs's son Nick for a ride on his train.

As casually as he could, Reynolds probed Biggs with a few questions until he asked him if he thought the old boy would be interested in doing something on the wrong side of the law, and that there would be a good 'drink' in it for him.

Sensing that there could also be something in it for him, Biggs began to pump his old friend for some more information.

Reynolds gave him a brief outline of the proposed robbery, and Biggs agreed to speak to the old train driver on condition that he (Biggs) would also become a full member of the firm. This seemed like divine intervention for Biggs as, at that time, he was having some serious cash flow problems, and at some stage in the evening had intended to 'tap up' his old friend for a loan.

Despite Reynolds's attempts to persuade Biggs to accept a decent finder's fee for the introduction, Biggs was adamant that if he wasn't in, he wouldn't speak to the old boy. Reynolds agreed to speak to the rest of the firm about the proposition, and told Biggs he would get back to him in a few days.

As Reynolds feared, the reaction to the suggestion that Biggs come on board as a full member of the firm was pretty negative. Roy James in particular resented that a train driver was being hired since he was still confident that he would be able to drive the train himself, and having Biggs involved, and taking a full share of the cash as well, was adding insult to injury.

And what if the robbery didn't go totally according to plan? If the old boy was caught and subjected to a grilling from the police, would he be able to keep his mouth shut for long? That was highly unlikely, so in reality he represented a major and unnecessary security risk.

But in the end, it came down to making sure all the bases were covered and that there was someone on hand who could move the train, once it was in the control of the gang, if the driver and his assistant refused to cooperate.

A few days later, Reynolds and Buster Edwards travelled down to Redhill and met up with Biggs and the train driver.

The train driver's true identity has never been revealed, and there is also confusion as to the name he was known by. In his book *The Train Robbers, Their Story*, Piers Paul Read calls him Stan Agate, [20] whereas in *The Autobiography of a Thief*, Bruce Reynolds refers to him as Peter. [21]

And in *The Great Train Robbery, The Definitive Account*, Nick Russell-Pavier & Stewart Richards state that the gang generally called him 'Pop'. [22]

Finally, to add to the confusion even further, in the 2013 BBC drama *The Robber's Tale*, which was inspired by Robert Ryan's book *Signal Red*, the driver was called Alf. However, given that he was a generation older than the rest of the gang, I suspect that many would have referred to him as Pop, and I have used that nickname from here onwards.

When Reynolds and Edwards met with Biggs and Pop, they found he was in his late fifties/early sixties and thought he seemed a bit 'away with the fairies', as if he didn't quite realise what he was getting himself in to. He also didn't inspire a tremendous amount of confidence when he told Reynolds and Edwards that he had never driven one of the D-type diesels that would be pulling the mail train on the night.

However, he told the pair that it wouldn't be a problem for an experienced driver and anyway, he was going to cadge a ride in the cab of a D-type with an old railway mate – so job done.

A few days later, Biggs told Reynolds that all had gone well with Pop, and it seemed that almost all of the pieces of the jigsaw were now in place.

Leatherslade Farm

The final decision for the firm was to agree on where they would go in the immediate aftermath of the robbery.

Roy James was all for a quick return to London in a convoy of Jags especially adapted with their rear seats removed to make room for the mail bags. He had done the journey from Bridego Bridge several times, and in the early hours of the morning when they would be on the road, he knew that it could be done in well under the hour.

However, as a driver, James was in a league of his own and, in reality, he would be back in South London well before anyone else.

James's idea also meant that the mail bags would be split up with no-one knowing how much money was in each bag. As Shakespeare put it in Henry IV Part One; *'Eight yards of rough road is like seventy miles to me, and these hard-hearted crooks know it. It stinks when there's no honour among thieves.'*

Almost certainly, it was their mutual distrust of each other that drove the decision to remain in the area for a few days after the robbery – in fact when it was put to a vote, James was the only one against, and he accepted the majority view with good grace.

So, the remaining question was where could they hide up while they waited for the dust to settle?

Wherever it was, it needed to be out of the way and isolated, a fair distance from the site of the robbery, with outbuildings to hide the various vehicles, and large enough for at least 16 people to rest up for a few days without being seen.

Bruce Reynolds and John Daly scanned the property pages of the local newspapers and eventually found a farm being advertised by Midland Marts, a local firm of estate agents.

Midland Marts were one of three agents marketing the property, and were advertising it as *'a smallholding between Bicester and Thame. Valuable freehold holding of five acres, elevated position, well set off the road, detached four bedroomed house, two reception rooms and large kitchen, adjoining two bedroomed cottage, mains water, septic tank drainage, useful outbuildings. Price £5500.'*

1963 was almost thirty years before the advent of the Property Misdescriptions Act which *'prohibited the making of false or misleading statements about property matters in the course of estate agency business and property development business'*, and in reality, this property had been allowed to become run-down. The outbuildings were dilapidated; the five acres of land were as uncared for as the main building, and to top it off, there was no mains electricity – power was provided by a generator.

This was the infamous Leatherslade Farm, and when Reynolds and Daly had taken a look at the property on the outside they agreed that it would suit their needs perfectly, particularly as a large screen of trees hid it from the road.

Reynolds then made the mistake of knocking on the door and speaking to the vendors, Bernard and Lily Rixon. By doing this he was creating a potential link between himself and the crime. [24]

After Gordon Goody and Buster Edwards had also taken a look at the outside of the farm, it was decided to go ahead with the purchase, and the matter was referred to Brian Field so that the transaction could be handled by James & Wheater, the law firm Field worked for.

A couple of days later, Brian Field called on the Rixons accompanied by Leonard Field, (no relation to Brian), and the pair were shown around the property by Mrs Rixon.

Leonard Field, a merchant seaman, was the brother of Harry Field who had been a client of James and Wheater when he was charged with horse doping and robbing a bank in Stoke. For the last offence he was sentenced to five years in prison.

Possibly not the sharpest tool in the box, Leonard agreed to allow the purchase of Leatherslade Farm to proceed in his name, so that the true identities of the purchasers could remain hidden. In return, Brian told him he would receive a £12,000 'drink'. According to Leonard, he believed the farm was going to be used to store stolen cigarettes.

After looking over the property, Brian Field told Mrs Rixon to instruct their solicitor to send the legal contract of sale to Mr John Wheater of James & Wheater as Mr Leonard Field was ready and willing to sign it straight away.

When John Wheater spoke to Mrs Rixon, he was told that another prospective purchaser had also made an offer. Wheater upped the offer on behalf of Leonard Field to £5750 not wishing to be gazumped or to become involved in a contract race. However, the other purchaser subsequently withdrew, and the sale price was eventually agreed at £5550.

A 10% deposit was provided by Leonard Field as when his brother Harry was convicted and imprisoned for the bank robbery, Leonard had been appointed Power of Attorney over Harry's financial affairs, and the deposit was raised from Harry's capital.

According to the report prepared for the Home Secretary by HM Chief Inspector of Constabulary on 6 October 1964; *'The owner...understood that a deposit of £555 (10%) had been paid to the agents and agreed with the solicitors that the purchaser could have possession of the premises when full settlement was made. He was later given to understand that full settlement could not be made until 13 August 1963, because the purchaser's money would not be available until that date. The purchaser still wished to take possession of the premises by 29 July 1963, and finally it was agreed he could take over on that date, providing he paid 7% interest on the balance outstanding to cover the mortgage on the new property the owner was buying.'* [25]

On 29 July 1963, Mr and Mrs Rixon vacated Leatherslade Farm and Brian Field advised Bruce Reynolds that he and the gang were free to move in as soon as they wanted.

The last piece of the jigsaw was now in place.

Final preparations

Gordon Goody and Buster Edwards had their last meeting with Patrick McKenna, the Ulsterman, and the date for the robbery was set for the early hours of 7 August. This was just after the August Bank Holiday and expectations for a bumper pay day were high. Goody and Edwards agreed to meet the Ulsterman at Brian Field's house, near Pangbourne, a few days after the robbery to hand him his share of the cash. The Ulsterman also gave Goody a telephone number to ring on the evening of 6 August to confirm that everything was good to go.

By now, Brian Field had collected the keys to Leatherslade Farm and passed them to Reynolds. The plan was for the firm to arrive at the Farm on the 5/6 August in small groups so as not to arouse any suspicions.

The full roll call was Bruce Reynolds, Charlie Wilson, Gordon Goody, Buster Edwards, Roy James, Bill Jennings, John Daly, Jimmy White, Alf Thomas, Roger Cordrey, James Hussey, Bob Welch, Tommy Wisbey, Frank Munroe, Ronnie Biggs and Pop, the engine driver.

Each one had a specific job to do.

Reynolds would be up track so he could radio through to the others the moment he could see the approaching mail train. His brother-in-law, John Daly, would be at the dwarf signal changing the green light to amber as Roger Cordrey had shown him. Cordrey himself would be at the signals at Sears Crossing ensuring the light was showing red. Roy James would also be at the signals and it was his job to cut all telephone wires in the vicinity.

As soon as the train stopped at the lights, James, Bill Jennings and Jimmy White were in charge of uncoupling the engine and the first two coaches from the rest of the train. They would approach the train from the east side of the track, along with Alf Thomas and Bob Welch.

Approaching the train from the west side of the track, so they could deal quickly with the driver and his assistant would be Charlie Wilson, Tommy Wisbey, Gordon Goody, Frank Munroe, James Hussey and Buster Edwards. In the background, until the train driver had been removed from his cab, would be Pop and Ronnie Biggs. The plan was well rehearsed and everyone was full of confidence.

As there was an army camp in the vicinity at Bicester, Reynolds had come up with the idea that the gang should be dressed as soldiers since the locals would be quite used to seeing small convoys of military vehicles in the area from time to time.

An ex-army lorry and a Land Rover were bought at auction by White and Thomas, and a second Land Rover was stolen by White from Leicester Square in London. These were given a paint job to make sure they resembled army vehicles.

Jimmy White also acted as the firm's quartermaster and, with help from Roy James and Charlie Wilson, supplied each member of the firm with a uniform bought from army surplus stores. These were to be worn on the journey to Sears Crossing, and then from Bridego Bridge back to Leatherslade Farm.

On arrival at Sears Crossing, dark blue overalls were to be put on over the uniforms so that passengers on any passing train would take them for railway workers.

Reynolds had organised his own uniform which was that of a British army major. He also wore a beret with the winged dagger badge of the SAS, which had been sown on by his wife Frances. Reynolds liked to think of himself as the youngest major in the British army, despite having done only six weeks of his two year National Service before absconding.

Reynolds and John Daly had also brought white overalls with them as they were going to be the first to arrive at Leatherslade Farm, and hoped to pass themselves off as decorators should there be any unexpected callers.

The lorry and the Land Rovers were used to transport the equipment and food needed by the gang during their stay at the farm.

The food included a sack of potatoes and a box of fruit from the greengrocer father-in law of Charlie Wilson, tins of tomatoes, Heinz and Star baked beans, Heinz and Campbell's soup, peas, fruit salad, condensed milk, creamed rice, Senior's pork luncheon meat, Fray Bentos corned beef, Dairylea cheese spread, packs of butter, sugar and salt, catering sized jars of Maxwell House coffee, Lyon's coffee, packets of tea, eggs, bacon and cans of beer.

There was also a good supply of toilet rolls and candles together with mugs, plates and sets of cutlery plus a chess set, Ludo, Snakes and Ladders and the John Waddington board game Monopoly.

Included amongst the equipment taken to the farm were torches and torch batteries, 6 volt batteries to switch the lights on the two signals, four walkie-talkies, two Hitachi VHF radios, sleeping bags, air beds, blankets and air cushions, axes, coshes, a pair of handcuffs, pickaxe handles, saws, hacksaws and blades, wire cutters, bolt cutters, screw drivers and tins of paint. [26, 27]

As Bruce Reynolds went through everything in his mind for the umpteenth time, he knew that they were ready for anything.

CHAPTER 2
The Robbery

The arrival

Once Frances Reynolds had sewn the SAS badge onto his beret, Bruce Reynolds said his goodbyes to her and their young son Nick, and then set off in one of the Land Rovers to pick up John Daly. They then collected Ronnie Biggs and Pop who had told their wives they were off to Wiltshire on a tree-felling job.

The four arrived at Leatherslade Farm at lunchtime and tucked into some of the food that had already been dropped off. Reynolds and Daly then changed into their white decorator's overalls, and it was just as well that they had as not long after there was a sudden knock at the front door.

The caller was a neighbour who introduced himself as Mr Wyatt when Reynolds opened the door. Wyatt said he was calling to speak to the new owner about continuing the arrangement he had had with Mr Rixon who had allowed him to rent one of his fields. Reynolds told him that he was only a decorator, but that he would pass a message on to the new owner who was a Mr Fielding from Aylesbury.

Next to arrive were Jimmy White and Alf Thomas in the lorry, which they parked in one of the outbuildings. They then took the Land Rover so they could return to London and pick up Roger Cordrey, Frank Munroe, Bobby Welch and Tommy Wisbey. Cordrey was noticeably quiet – understandable since he had returned home to Brighton a couple of days earlier to discover that his wife had left him for another man, and had taken their children with her.

By the time they arrived back at Leatherslade, they found that Roy James, driving the second Land Rover, had already arrived along with Buster Edwards, Charlie Wilson, Bill Jennings and James Hussey. The lone absentee was Gordon Goody.

Goody had flown to Belfast on 2 August along with his mother and a friend called Jack Knowles who bore more than just a passing resemblance to Goody. The three of them stayed with Goody's uncle in Lisburn.

However, Goody returned to the UK three days later, arranging for his friend to send out postcards on 6, 7 and 8 August, which Goody had written out before he left.

With the adrenaline flowing, many of the gang were becoming decidedly edgy. They just wanted to get going and the later it got, the more uptight they were becoming.

Goody eventually surfaced, having been given a lift to Leatherslade by Brian Field. Their relief at seeing Goody was tempered by his news – he'd spoken to McKenna, the Ulsterman, on the phone at Field's house and had been told that the job would have to be postponed for 24 hours. McKenna had received information that the expected post Bank Holiday cash surplus wasn't going to be loaded onto the mail train until the following night.

As Bruce Reynolds put it – *'we were all mightily pissed off: another 24 hours of waiting.'* [1]

It's on!

The engine and the first five coaches of the Travelling Post Office left Glasgow Central at 6:50pm on 7 August 1963. It arrived at Carstairs station in South Lanarkshire at 7:32pm where it added four more coaches. These had arrived from Aberdeen.

The engine, now pulling 9 coaches, left Carstairs at 7:45pm, arriving at Carlisle at 8:54pm, where it picked up a further three coaches bringing it up to its full complement of a D-type diesel engine and 12 coaches.

At Carlisle, the guard was relieved and his replacement, 61 year old Thomas Miller, remained with the train for the rest of its journey.

The train then left Carlisle at 9:04pm and arrived at Preston at 10:53pm where it stayed for 10 minutes before setting off for Warrington, where it arrived at 11:36pm as scheduled. The next stop was Crewe, arriving at 12:12am where the driver and his assistant were relieved. They were replaced by driver Jack Mills and his assistant David Whitby, who were both due to remain with the train until its scheduled arrival at London Euston some four hours later.

After leaving Crewe at 12:30pm, the train stopped at Tamworth at 1:23am, and at Rugby at 2:12am before passing through Bletchley at 2:53am. At this point it was just 10 minutes away from Sears Crossing.

After a day spent kicking their heels playing cards, solitaire and Monopoly, the gang had learnt earlier that evening that they were in business. Gordon Goody had slipped out to ring Brian Field from a nearby call box. The Ulsterman had given Field the nod that the mail train had left Glasgow on time, and it looked like it would be carrying a full load of mail bags. [2]

This was it. No more waiting, no more dress rehearsals. This was it for real. The disappointment of the previous day was forgotten as the gang began their final preparations for the crime that, for most of them, would change their lives forever.

On the train

On the train were 77 post office employees who spent the entire journey sorting letters by hand. The sorters job was both repetitive and tedious, and the railway coaches were noisy and claustrophobic.

The only window space was a line of small rectangular windows above head height – not as though there was anything to see as the bulk of their journey was completed at night. And anyway, with the post office demanding a 98%

accuracy rate, the sorters had little spare time to look at the outside world speeding by.

In overall charge from Carlisle to Euston was Frank Fuggle, a Post Office inspector who based himself in the 5th coach. He was aided by Thomas Kett, an assistant inspector whose duties on the night were supervising the staff in the second, third and fourth coaches. There was nobody in the first coach since it contained parcels that had been pre-sorted.

The HPV coach was situated between the parcel van and coach three, and in this coach, apart from Kett, were post office workers Frank Dewhurst, Leslie Penn, John O'Connor and Joseph Ware.

Both O'Connor and Ware had joined the train at Tamworth, and were working in other coaches until just before 3:00am when they were ordered to report to the HVP coach. [3]

Both men used the corridor that ran through the train from the 12th coach to the second coach. There was no access to the first coach which could only be entered when the train was stationary. And, since there was no access from coach one to coach two, the driver and his assistant were totally isolated from the rest of the train when it was on the move.

None of the railway staff, or any of the post office workers, had ever received any training as to what to do in an emergency. Safety Bulletins informing staff of the dangers of their working environment and giving tips on manual handling and health and safety, were not introduced on the Travelling Post Offices until the 1970's.

And, amazingly, with the train transporting a fortune in bank notes each day, there were neither guards nor British Transport police on board. Why should there be – after all, no-one would ever dare rob one of Her Majesty's mail trains!

Ready and waiting

After receiving the news from Goody that it was all systems go, preparations for the night ahead began in earnest. At 11:00pm everyone began changing into their uniforms, checking their watches every few minutes. Time began to drag, they were all anxious to get on the road. It was about an hour's drive from the farm to Bridego Bridge along the country lanes, and arriving too early could only increase the risk of being seen.

Eventually, at around half an hour past midnight, on a warm and clear night, Reynolds gave the order they had all been waiting for and the small convoy of three vehicles slowly made its way down the farm track and then turned right onto the B4011 Thame Road.

The lead vehicle was a Land Rover driven by John Daly with Reynolds at his side. Next came the lorry driven by Alf Thomas with Jimmy White beside him. Bringing up the rear was the second Land Rover with Roy James at the wheel.

So wrapped up was Ronnie Biggs in getting prepared for the departure, that he had completely forgotten that when the clock ticked past midnight, it was his 34th birthday. It was to be a birthday like no other.

The convoy maintained a steady speed throughout the journey, not wishing to alert anyone to their nocturnal activities. They were seen by a couple of people who thought nothing of it at the time, but who would remember it a few days after the robbery.[4] The VHF radios were tuned into the police frequency and they remained reassuringly quiet throughout the journey.

The three vehicles arrived at Bridego Bridge on the dot of 1:30am. This was the first time many of the gang had seen the bridge at first hand, and several took the opportunity to climb up the bank and look towards the signals in the direction the train would be coming from. A marker, a piece of a white sheet attached to a couple of poles, was knocked into the ground so that Pop would know exactly where to stop the train when the time came.

The lorry was backed up towards the bank, ready to take the bags of cash once the HVP coach had made the short journey from Sears Crossing.

Roy James, probably the fittest of the train robbers, climbed up the nearest telegraph pole to cut the overhead wires. James would also cut the telephone lines to the nearest farmhouses before taking up his position at Sears Crossing.

Reynolds, Daly and Cordrey took one of the Land Rovers and drove to the dwarf signal, just up the line from Sears Crossing. Cordrey quickly went to work on the signal. When he had finished, both the amber and green lights were on. All Daly had to do was to put a glove over the green light as soon as word was given that the train was approaching.

Reynolds and Cordrey then drove back to Sears Crossing so Cordrey could repeat the procedure on the overhead signals.

As Reynolds took up his place as the look-out for the train, the bulk of the gang made their way up the track from Bridego Bridge to Sears Crossing, more than ready to do whatever was necessary to secure the train.

Reynolds had a pair of binoculars with him and from his position would be able to see the train from about two miles distance. He looked at his watch for the umpteenth time and then spoke into his walky-talky to make sure that everyone was in the proper place. They were ready and waiting.

Going to work

'*This is it! This is it! This is it!*' shouted Reynolds into his walky-talky.[5]

It was just before 3:00pm when he picked up the lights of the oncoming mail train. With those words, Reynolds set in motion the events that would dominate the front pages of newspapers all over the world for the next week or so.

As planned, Jack Mills, the driver, slowed down when he saw the dwarf signal on amber, and came to a complete stop just a few yards from the gantry signal which was showing red.

Both Mills and David Whitby could see that a signal further down the line was at green. They would have expected this signal to also be showing red, and suspecting that there may be a fault somewhere, Whitby got down from the engine and went to the telephone by the gantry to call the nearest signal box, which was at Leighton Buzzard.

Despite finding the wires cut, Whitby wasn't unduly alarmed. Nor did he think anything was up when he caught sight of someone (Buster Edwards) in overalls standing between the second and third coaches, and he called out to attract his attention as he started to walk towards him.

As Whitby got to within touching distance, Edwards grabbed him by the arm, and pushed him down the embankment where the fireman found himself staring at two other men brandishing coshes. One of them told Whitby '*If you shout, I'll kill you*'.

Meanwhile, Jack Mills was completely unaware of what had happened to his assistant. He had also noticed two men coming from the embankment who he assumed to be a couple of linesmen there to repair the signal. These may well have been Roy James and Jimmy White moving into position to uncouple the train between the second and the third carriages.

Thinking that they would be on the move again shortly, Driver Mills released the brake lever and started building up the pressure needed to release the brakes.

At the sound of this, there was real concern that the train was about to move off. If it did, the robbers would be left high and dry. Fearing this was about to happen, one of the gang launched himself up the steps to the driver's cabin. Simultaneously, Mills turned towards the doorway and, instead of David Whitby, he was confronted with the top half of a man in a balaclava wielding a cosh. Bravely, Mills began to kick out.

At the same time, someone else came into the cab from the other side and Jack Mills was struck a blow to the head which left him bloodied and dazed, and as he fell he hit his head on the curved steel dashboard that ran under the driver's window.

In that state, he was easily overpowered and his cab quickly became crowded with other members of the gang.

Mills was taken to the passage outside the engine's fan room and handcuffed to David Whitby who had been brought up to the engine from the bottom of the embankment. It was now Pop's big moment – the only reason why he was there – to move the train the short distance to Bridego Bridge.

However, by now the train had also been uncoupled, and when doing this Roy James and Jimmy White had inadvertently caused the train's braking system to lose pressure, and a failsafe mechanism had automatically locked the brakes making it impossible to move the train without the vacuum pressure being restored.

As Pop took the driver's seat he caught sight of Jack Mills who was still bleeding from his head wound. This undoubtedly unnerved the old chap, and being surrounded by half a dozen burly figures watching his every move did him no favours whatsoever.

Pop turned the handle to release the brakes – but without any vacuum, they remained locked.

'*What's the problem*?' he was asked.

'*I'm waiting for the brake pressure to build*' was his reply.

'*Get him out of here and get the driver*' shouted someone, probably Gordon Goody. [6]

Despite his protests, Pop was hauled out of the driver's seat. Jack Mills had his handcuffs removed and was led back to his cabin and told to move the train or '*he would get some more stick*'. [7]

Mills quickly realised that the brakes were locked and that the train wouldn't move unless the vacuum was restored.

Whilst all this was going on, Jimmy White, having realised that the lack of vacuum was possibly caused when he and Roy James had uncoupled the train, ran to the back of the HVP coach and gave the air pressure valve a kick to close it properly. [8]

Immediately, the pressure began to build and Mills was able to slowly move the train forward towards the marker that had been set up earlier at Bridego Bridge, leaving the rest of the train, ten coaches in total, marooned back at Sears Crossing.

Hitting the jackpot

The train eased forward until it was level with the marker. Just before the assault on the HVP coach began, Bruce Reynolds told Ronnie Biggs to take Pop to one of the Land Rovers and make sure that he stayed put. Even though Reynolds hadn't witnessed the events in the driver's cabin, he sensed that the old man was deeply affected by his apparent failure to do the one job he was there to do.

At the same time, Jack Mills and David Whitby, once again handcuffed together, were led along the embankment and told to lay face down.

As the gang began the assault on the HVP coach, someone allegedly shouted '*Get the guns*!' to frighten the five post office workers inside.

Windows were shattered and doors smashed by iron bars and a pick axe during a short-lived but ferocious attack and, in a matter of seconds, gang members were inside subduing any threat of resistance. Several of the post office workers were hit with coshes as they were pushed to the front of the coach where they were made to lie down and close their eyes. Worker Frank Dewhurst said that he was struck 5 or 6 times, and assistant inspector Thomas Kett received at least two blows to the head. [9]

The mail bags, in a cage at the back of the coach, were now completely at their mercy and a single blow with an axe made short work of the padlock on the door. Someone took one of the bags and slit it open with a knife. It was packed tight with bundles of banknotes – the stuff of their dreams.

The first bags were pulled out of the cage and a human chain was formed going from the HVP coach and down the embankment to the rear of the lorry, where they were thrown into the back. The bags were heavy and the work was hard going, but the thought of all that cash spurred each of them on.

They had lost valuable time with the failed attempts to move the train to Bridego Bridge, and whilst the bags were being moved from the train to the lorry, Bruce Reynolds continually checked the time on his watch. He knew it was vital that they made it back to Leatherslade Farm before daylight to avoid being seen.

At 3:30pm Reynolds shouted out that it was time to pack up and go, and despite shouts back from those at the front of the chain that there were still a few bags left in the cage, everyone did as they were told and made their way back to the lorry and the Land Rovers for the drive back to the farm. The overalls they had worn during the robbery were discarded and the gang once again looked like an army detail on manoeuvres.

By now, Jack Mills and David Whitby were in the HPV coach alongside the five post office workers, and before the last of the gang left for the drive back to Leatherslade, he told them not to move for half an hour as they were leaving someone behind to make sure they did as they were told.

The drive back was dictated by the speed of the lorry. In total the mail bags weighed over two tons, a hefty load even for an Austin Loadstar, and it was fairly slow going.

Ronnie Biggs was given the VHF radio and told to listen out for any reports of the robbery from the Buckinghamshire Constabulary on the police wavelength.[10]

However, it was eerily quiet – so quiet that someone asked Biggs if he was tuned in properly. It was, of course, just the lull before the proverbial storm.

Stranded at Sears Crossing

When the mail train had slowed down and then stopped at Sears Crossing, none of the 70 odd post office workers thought anything of it initially. It had been a long shift and the train was just under an hour's journey to the final stop at London Euston.

After the train had been stationary for a few minutes, Stanley Hall, a higher-grade postal worker, opened the door of coach three and saw what he thought were two railwayman walking towards the engine.

Assuming them to be sorting out the reason for the stoppage with the driver and his assistant, he closed the carriage door. Even when he saw steam escaping from the back of the HVP coach, and then, through the window of the communicating door, saw the coach moving slowly away, he still didn't think that there could be anything seriously wrong.

Another higher-grade postman, Dennis Jefferies, also saw the HPV coach pulling away, but like his colleague he wasn't particularly concerned.

Meanwhile the guard, Thomas Miller, at the rear of the train, had noticed that the train's vacuum pressure gauge had dropped to zero as the front of the train was being uncoupled by Roy James and Jimmy White. Whilst this was unusual, he didn't think too much about it at first. However, as the minutes passed without the train moving, he decided to walk back down the train to find out what the problem was.

At the ninth coach he bumped into Post Office Inspector Frank Fuggle who had left his base in the 5th coach to find Miller. Miller decided to get out of the train to speak to the driver and find out what the problem was and how long it was going to take to fix it. In the back of his mind was the risk that the stationary train posed to other London bound trains that might be due to pass through Sears Crossing.

As the track was dead straight at that point, Miller couldn't see the front of the train from the embankment and still didn't think anything serious had happened. That all changed when he got to where the engine and the first two coaches should have been.

Standard operating procedures stated that detonators be placed some distance back from the train so as to warn any other trains using the same track. [11]

This Miller proceeded to do, unaware that Thomas Wyn-de-Bank, the signalman at the Leighton Buzzard signal box, had already received a call from the Cheddington signalman, Len Kinchen, asking where the TPO train was. Wyn-de-Bank could see that the train had passed through Sears Crossing, but an indicator showed that the approach line to it was still engaged. This suggested that either part of the train had been left behind or that there was a track failure in addition to the signal fault. [12]

Wyn-de-Bank told Kinchen that he was arranging for a colleague, Frank Mead, to go to Sears Crossing to investigate. He also contacted the Control Office at Euston that he was closing the line to any further trains until he had heard back from Mead.

Once he had laid the detonators, Thomas Miller made his way back to Sears Crossing where he discovered that the telephone line had been cut, so he was unable to speak to the signalman. He then spoke to Frank Fuggle and told him that he was going to go for help and started walking in the direction of Bridego Bridge.

Within 10 minutes or so, Miller arrived at the missing engine and carriages where he found driver Jack Mills and his assistant David Whitby still handcuffed together, and three of the five post office workers. The other two, Thomas Kett and Leslie Penn, had already gone off to seek help. Between them, the five men told Miller what had happened, and he decided to head for

Cheddington station as fast as he could to raise the alarm and to get urgent medical attention for Jack Mills.

On his way to Cheddington, Miller flagged down a train going northbound in the opposite direction, quickly told the guard what had happened and asked him to give some first aid to Mills.

Miller then continued on to Cheddington, and a few minutes later flagged down a train going southbound on an adjacent line. When he spoke to the driver, he found out that he had been told by the Leighton Buzzard signalman, Thomas Wyn-de-Bank, to examine the line and then report back on the location of the TPO.

The driver gave his fireman the first aid box, told him to walk back to Bridego Bridge and then drive the train and the two coaches to Cheddington station. It didn't occur to the driver, his fireman or Thomas Miller that the police would have wanted the train to stay exactly where it was at Bridego for a full forensic examination. There was the very real possibility of vital clues to the identity of the robbers being either contaminated or destroyed.

The train carrying Miller arrived at Cheddington at 4.15am, and the first report to the police was at 4:24am and made to the information room at Scotland Yard. It came from the Control Office at Euston where they had received a call from the Cheddington signal box asking for the police and an ambulance to attend a break in at Cheddington station. That request was passed on to Buckingham Constabulary HQ at 4:25am. The hunt for the robbers of the mail train had just begun, almost an hour after the gang had left the scene.

CHAPTER 3
The First Few Days

Counting the cash

Six minutes after the call was made to Scotland Yard by Euston Control, at exactly 4:30am by Bruce Reynolds's watch, the three vehicles drew up outside the farmhouse of Leatherslade Farm.[1]

The two Land Rovers were parked in sheds whilst the lorry was backed up to the farmhouse. The mail bags were unloaded and stacked in one room. There were 120 bags in total containing packets of five pound, one pound and 10 shilling notes. Some of the notes were old-style fivers which had been officially withdrawn in March 1961, although they were still regarded as legal tender.

Shed of its load, the lorry was driven into an adjacent barn so it couldn't be seen from the air, and the cash count began. Any Scottish and Irish banknotes were put into a separate pile.

Not everyone joined in the count. Roy James said he needed to catch up on lost sleep and went for a lie down and it wasn't long before Reynolds followed suit.

John Daly and Gordon Goody took up positions in an upstairs bedroom with binoculars and a VHF radio – their role was to watch for any signs of police activity on the ground and from the skies. Whilst the police didn't have their own helicopters, the RAF had been used in the past to back up police searches.

However, if the police should come calling, the robbers were more than prepared to meet them head on. The coshes used during the robbery were hung up on a row of hooks by the front door alongside several pick axe handles. [2]

It took the gang several hours to open up the mail bags and slit open the packets of money before passing the banknotes to Charlie Wilson and Roger Cordrey, the self-appointed accountants.

Police initially reported that the cash stolen was in the region of £100,000. Whether this was a genuine error is not certain. However, there were far too many people that knew how much money had actually been on the train for the police to stick to this story.

Reynolds had been asleep for several hours when he was awoken by Buster Edwards. The final count had come to £2,631,784. Each of the robbers would be walking away from Leatherslade Farm with around £150,000, the equivalent to around £2.7million by today's standards (2015).

There were the sounds of celebration coming from downstairs and Reynolds knew that he should be down there enjoying the moment with the rest of the gang.

However, something didn't feel quite right and in his autobiography he wrote that '*Deep inside, I could already feel an emptiness, a sense of anti-climax. So we've got it; what do I do now.*'

The police response – the first day

Having received the request for police and an ambulance to attend a break in at Cheddington station at 4:25am, the first patrol car arrived at the station at 4:36am with two police constables on board, PC's Atkins and Milne.

Realising immediately that this was not just another routine call-out for a burglary, they relayed what information they had at that time to Bucks Police HQ. By 4:50am Detective Superintendent Malcolm Fewtrell had arrived at HQ, and forty minutes later he set off for the scene of the crime accompanied by Assistant Chief Constable George Wilkinson.

One of the first things the police did was to send a constable to the Royal Bucks Hospital in Aylesbury with a handcuff key as Jack Mills and David Whitby were still handcuffed together. However, the key failed to unlock the cuffs as they were of American origin, and it took a hacksaw to separate the two men. Whilst being released from the handcuffs, Whitby had told the police officer that he thought the robbers had used an army truck, and that at least one of them had had a cockney accent.

Mills was examined and treated by a senior house surgeon. He had a number of lacerations to his head and needed 14 stitches. He was kept in hospital under observation for 48 hours and was discharged on 10 August.[3]

Fewtrell and Wilkinson were logged as arriving at Cheddington Station at 6:17am. Two officers from the Bucks Police Fingerprint and Photographic Department joined them at 6:30am and immediately began to examine the engine and the HVP coach which had been moved again, this time to the Aylesbury loop line at Cheddington.

They interrupted their examination of the train to go to Sears Crossing where they spent time examining the batteries, wires and other bits and pieces that had been used to stop the train by tampering with the lights. At this point, Fewtrell realised that a number of items had been left behind by the robbers including a heavily blood-stained cloth, a couple of pick axe handles, an iron bar, string and a man's black leather glove. He immediately appointed an Exhibits Officer to take charge of collecting and logging every item – a list that would eventually grow to epic proportions.

Sometime after 10:00am, Fewtrell showed the Chief Constable of Buckinghamshire, Brigadier John Chaney, around the scene. Post Office Investigation officers and British Railway Transport Police had also arrived at the station.

At 10:33am a message was sent to Scotland Yard and to the chief constables of the neighbouring counties which read: '*At approximately 02:45 hours today, a mail train robbery occurred between Leighton Buzzard and Cheddington, Bucks. 120 mail bags containing a very considerable sum of money are missing. It is thought that persons responsible may have hidden up and will attempt to get away by mingling with normal morning traffic. Observation and frequent spot checks of traffic vehicles is requested.*'

A dedicated incident room was set up at Bucks Police HQ to keep the mail train robbery investigation separate from all other police matters and it wasn't long before it began receiving calls from both the media of the day and the general public.

At some stage during the morning Brigadier Cheney rang George Hatherill, the Commander at Scotland Yard, asking that the Yard be represented at a meeting at the GPO Headquarters at King Edward Building, in Newgate Street, London, scheduled to take place at 3:00pm.

This meeting was chaired by Clifford Osmond, Controller of the GPO Investigation Branch and amongst the 30 or so people present were Hatherill and a number of other officers from Scotland Yard, Malcolm Fewtrell and Brigadier John Cheney from Buckinghamshire Police and senior officials from British Transport Police, British Railway and the Post Office.

Fewtrell and Cheney told the group what action had been taken by the Buckinghamshire force so far, and what they intended to do over the next 24 hours. It was at this point that they revealed that the theft had possibly netted the robbers in the region of two and a half million pounds.

It was agreed during the meeting that Scotland Yard would send Detective Superintendent Gerald McArthur and Detective Sergeant Jack Pritchard to Aylesbury to help Buckinghamshire Police with their investigation.

Before they arrived, Police HQ received a message timed at 6:00pm from Linslade sub-division that three vehicles in close convoy had been spotted in the area at about 1:20am. They were described as '*a small vehicle, an army-type lorry, large wheels exposed, and a light Land Rover.*' [4]

When they eventually arrived at Aylesbury shortly after 10:00pm, McArthur and Pritchard were brought up to speed with the latest information, and arranged for road checks to be put in place from 2:00am to 4:00am the next morning which might jog the memory of any regular early morning travellers in the area.

They also spoke to local farmers and, using an Ordnance Survey map, familiarised themselves with the immediate vicinity of the robbery – in particular any deserted farms, outbuildings and former RAF and Army Camps that could possibly be used by the robbers as a hideaway.

Change of plan

Just 9 hours after the robbery had taken place, the midday news on the radio generated some concern amongst those listening at Leatherslade Farm. The announcer said it was thought that army vehicles may have been used by the gang that raided the mail train.

This meant an immediate change of plan since the robbers had intended to use the Land Rovers and the lorry for their return to London once the initial post robbery police activity and press interest had died down. The three vehicles could now not be used again.

The original intention had been to stay at the farm until Sunday (11 August), but Bruce Reynolds reluctantly agreed that the robbers would leave the following day (Friday). However, the only form of transport that could be used was a bicycle that Roger Cordrey had brought with him.

The gang had to make contact with someone on the outside, and Cordrey decided to cycle into Oxford, a journey of around 10 miles. Once in Oxford, he stopped at the first public telephone box and called Brian Field who agreed to drive to the farm later in the evening.

Cordrey then called Mary Manson, a friend of Bruce Reynolds, who agreed to meet Reynolds in Thame, a market town around 6 miles from Leatherslade Farm, the following day. [5] He also called a bank manager contact in London who he had used before to launder money through his bank account. However, far from being pleased to hear from him, the bank manager let Cordrey know, in no uncertain terms, that he never wanted to hear from him again.

Rattled by this, Cordrey bought an evening newspaper. The robbery dominated the pages and at that moment he suddenly realised the enormity of the crime they had committed earlier that day. Needing time to think, Cordrey booked himself into a hotel for the night.

Meanwhile, having made the decision to quit the farm, the gang spent the rest of the day clearing out and cleaning up the farmhouse. All surfaces were wiped down, clothes and shoes worn during the robbery were burnt on a bonfire and a large hole was dug. However, when they tried to burn some of the empty mail bags, they sent a large pall of dark smoke into the air. Desperate not to bring any attention on the farm, the rest of the bags were put into the hole.

Brian Field was good as his word and arrived at Leatherslade Farm, accompanied by his German born wife Karin, just as dusk was approaching. He came with both good news and bad news.

The good news was that on the short drive from their Oxfordshire home, the Fields had seen no sign of any road blocks or general police activity. The bad news, as Roger Cordrey had discovered, was the level of publicity the robbery was already attracting.

After a brief discussion, the consensus was that Field should take Roy James to London so he could organise some alternative transport ready for use the following day.

An hour or so later, Brian and Karin Field dropped James off at an address in Bayswater. There was little else that could be done for the time being and the rest of the gang were to endure a fairly sleepless night.

The police response – the second day

Early on Friday morning, Detective Superintendent Malcolm Fewtrell took Detective Superintendent Gerald McArthur to Cheddington station, so the Scotland Yard man could see the engine and the two coaches, only to discover that the engine and parcel van had already been returned to normal service.

Whilst McArthur was looking over the HVP coach, an irate Fewtrell managed to locate the diesel engine at Crewe, and the parcel van at Windermere. However, it was not until the following day that these were returned to Cheddington.

When the two detectives returned to Aylesbury, along with McArthur's Scotland Yard colleague Jack Pritchard, they went through the witness statements. All of these mentioned that one of the robbers had told them not to move for thirty minutes as somebody would be watching them.

The three men decided that the thirty minutes might represent the time the robbers had allowed for their journey back to their hideaway. And if this was the case, they could be anywhere between 15 to 30 miles away.

This meant a search area of over 2,800 square miles – an area so large that even with maximum resources applied to the search, the robbers would have plenty of time to destroy any evidence they couldn't take with them and still be long gone before their hideaway was discovered.

However, the three detectives agreed that going public might well flush out the robbers if they were still in the area, and make them leave their hideaway in a hurry, before they were ready.

A press conference was called and an announcement made that the search for the robbers would be widened to cover a 30 mile radius from the scene of the crime and that police would focus on all isolated farms and buildings. A request was also made asking members of the public to report any suspicious activities within their local area. [6]

Whilst the BBC broadcast both the detail of the press conference and the request for public assistance, no road blocks were actually put in place to back this up. It can only be assumed that this was down to the sheer size of the area to be searched.

Later in the day, a conference was held at police headquarters in Aylesbury between the GPO Investigation Branch and British Transport Police, where it was agreed that the GPO IB would take statements from the post office workers who were in the ten coaches left stranded at Sears Crossing, whilst the Transport Police would interview all staff employed on the line where the robbery took place.

Going their separate ways

Early on Friday morning, the gang heard the radio announcement that police would be concentrating their search on isolated farms and buildings within a 30 mile radius of the scene of the robbery. What they didn't know is that the search would begin from the crime scene outwards, rather than from 30 miles inwards, so they probably had more time than they realised. However, this news had the desired effect and greatly increased the anxiety levels at Leatherslade Farm. Even though the decision had already been made to quit the farm, as far as the gang were concerned, the threat of road blocks backing up the police search was now a distinct possibility.

Bruce Reynolds left the farm early on Friday morning and hitched a lift into Thame. As arranged, he met up with Mary Manson who had brought along a friend for company. The two women had driven up in a furniture van and while they stayed in Thame, Reynolds drove the van back to the farm where he picked up John Daly and their shares of the money.

They then drove back to Thame, and handed the van keys to the women who were going to drive it back to Manson's house in Mitcham, Surrey. Reynolds and Daly then caught a Greenline bus to London Victoria where they picked up a taxi which took them to Manson's place so they could collect their money.

From there, they took it to a garage Reynolds was renting and hid it under some stacks of furniture.[7]

Shortly after Reynolds and Daly had left the farm, a car came racing up the driveway. Thinking that this could be the start of a police raid, coshes and pick axe handles were grabbed, only to discover that the car driver was Roger Cordrey, who had ditched his bike and bought a used Wolseley in Oxford.

He had some of the morning newspapers with him to show the others the extent of the publicity the robbery was attracting. Despite this, Cordrey told them that he hadn't seen any signs of police activity in the vicinity.

Whilst at the farm, Frank Munroe asked Cordrey to look after his share of the money and this was loaded into the boot of the Wolseley along with Cordrey's own share. Cordrey then set off for Oxford with Jimmy White in the passenger seat. On reaching Oxford the pair first headed for Cordrey's lodgings at 28 Edith Road, which he had organised prior to the robbery, before driving to a nearby village where Cordrey bought a Rover 105R.

Cordrey and White then swapped cars and White returned to the farm in the Wolseley to collect Alf Thomas and with their shares of the cash in the boot, as well as Frank Munroe's, they headed off to London.

After leaving the Wolseley with Thomas, White then bought an Austin Healey from a garage in the King's Road, Chelsea under the name John Steward, paying £900 cash for it.

Whilst his autobiography suggests that his day's excitement ended when he and John Daly hid their cash under the furniture in his garage, it is more than probable that Reynolds continued to duck and dive. Around 4:00pm, according to a car salesman at the Chequered Flag Garage in Chiswick, Reynolds agreed to buy a black Austin Healey for £835. He returned a couple of hours later with Mary Manson who paid for the car in five pound notes.

Then Reynolds in his Austin Healy, Manson in her black Ford Cortina and Daly in a van, drove back to Leatherslade Farm where they left the van for those still at the farm to use.

Reynolds then returned to London with Ronnie Biggs who he dropped off at Redhill, whilst Daly and Pop the train driver hitched a ride with Mary Manson. Little did he know at the time that it would be over 28 years before Reynolds and Biggs would again set eyes on each other.

Twenty four hours earlier, Brian and Karin Field had given Roy James a lift into London so he could try and organise transport for those of the gang that still needed it. As afternoon gave way to early evening there had been no word from James.

Eventually, Brian Field arrived at the farm driving a Commer van, followed by his wife in their Jaguar. Using the van left behind by Bruce Reynolds, the remaining members of the gang – Gordon Goody, Charlie Wilson, Buster Edwards, Bill Jennings, Bob Welch, Tommy Wisbey, James Hussey and Frank Munroe - were at last able to leave Leatherslade Farm to spend the night at the Field's Oxfordshire home. [8]

There is a degree of uncertainty surrounding the whereabouts of Roy James on that Friday. The most likely scenario is that he arrived back at the farm mid-afternoon driving a van which was then part of the convoy that set off for Field's home later in the day.

Another scenario has him falling asleep at his London flat and, being dead tired, not waking up until it was almost 11:00pm. He is then said to have driven his Jaguar at high speed to the farm, only to discover that by then everyone else had already left.

Whatever happened to James, the fact is that less than 48 hours after committing one of the major crimes of the 20th century, the gang that robbed the mail train of more than £2.6million had left their hideaway far earlier than planned. Most of the gang were to regret that hasty departure for the rest of their lives.

The ticking bomb

The gang realised that by quitting the farm at such short notice they were leaving behind a lot of their equipment, provisions and general detritus from the robbery itself, as well as the two Land Rovers and the lorry.

Before they left, they wiped down all surfaces and anything else that they may have inadvertently handled when not wearing the gloves Bruce Reynolds had given them when they had first arrived at the farm.

However, whether or not cleaning the farm after their departure was part of the overall planning process is uncertain. According to Ronnie Biggs, whilst waiting for their transport the day after the robbery, there was a discussion about cleaning the farm then and there and the consensus was that the best way to sanitize it was to burn it to the ground. [9]

This suggests that that there were no specific plans in place.

Yet, in her book 'The Robbers' Tale', Peta Fordham (no relation) states that a close associate of the robbers (William Still) had been hired to clean the farm. However, a brush with the police, prior to the robbery taking place, meant that he was under surveillance and so unable to fulfil his contract. [10]

In Signal Red, a fictionalised account of the robbery written by Robert Ryan, the name Tony Fortune is given to this character. [11]

However, the most likely scenario is that Brian Field was responsible for making sure that the farm was cleaned. With James & Wheater handling the legal formalities of the purchase, and having called at the farm a couple of weeks prior to the robbery with Leonard Field, a direct link connecting him to the robbery had been established.

Brian Field was well aware of this and that he could also be identified by Mrs Rixon who had shown the pair around the property.

The person contracted by Field to clean the farm was the man known only as Mark, who Gordon Goody and Buster Edwards had first met in Field's office and who had then taken the pair to their first meeting with Patrick McKenna, the Ulsterman.

On the Monday after the robbery, Charlie Wilson contacted Field to make sure that Mark had done the business. Despite receiving Field's reassurances, Wilson was less than convinced.

Field was summoned to an urgent meeting with Wilson, Reynolds, Edwards, Daly and James the following day when he admitted that Mark had let him down and hadn't yet cleaned the farm as agreed. The five robbers decided that their only option was to do the job themselves, despite the risks this entailed. However, before they could set off, news came that the police had found Leatherslade Farm.

The ticking time bomb had just exploded.

The police response – the third, fourth and fifth days

From Saturday 10 August to Monday 12 August, the police had no tangible successes despite the amount of resources being thrown at the investigation.

On the Saturday, the head of the Flying Squad incident room met with members of Buckinghamshire CID to receive a progress report. In return he briefed them on the efforts being put into the investigation back in London.

At the same time, Detective Superintendent Maurice Ray of the Fingerprint Branch at Scotland Yard was able to examine the engine and the parcel van which had been returned from Crewe and Windermere respectively. A little while later, Ray was joined by Dr Ian Holden from the Metropolitan Police Forensic Science Laboratory and, as well as the train, the pair also inspected the two sets of signals tampered with by the robbers.

A large pond adjacent to Bridego Bridge was a regular haunt for the members of the Berkhampstead Angling Society and the lengthy process of interviewing all 180 members got under way to see whether anyone had noticed anything out of the ordinary during the preceding months. [12]

In the early hours of the following morning, three officers from C11, the Criminal Intelligence Department at Scotland Yard, travelled to Aylesbury to see Detective Superintendent Fewtrell and Detective Superintendent McArthur, after an informant had told them that the robbers hideaway was a farm within a twenty minute drive of Aylesbury itself. They also mentioned that the name Bobbie Welch had been given by the informant as being one of the train robbers. Enquiries in London had revealed that Welch was not at home, but his wife expected him to return in a couple of days.

The rest of their time until daybreak was spent scanning ordnance survey maps with a view to selecting which farms and smallholdings should be paid a visit that morning.

At 9:00am on Sunday 11 August some 80 policemen, drawn from both Buckinghamshire and Hertfordshire forces, received a briefing on 13 premises that were to be searched. By lunchtime, all searches had been completed without any success.

Throughout the following day, search teams combed areas west of Cheddington, again to no avail.

During the afternoon a conference took place at Hertfordshire County HQ. As a result of a suggestion made at this conference, Detective Superintendent Fewtrell issued the following to all divisions in Buckinghamshire and to the Chief Constables of Hertfordshire, Bedfordshire and Northamptonshire: 'Bearing in mind that premises might have been specifically purchased or rented for use for the immediate concealment of the stolen property and its transport, please have enquiries made of estate agents and obtain information of transactions during the past six months involving likely premises within 30 miles of Cheddington, particularly farms, derelict houses, etc. Please follow up where appropriate'. [13]

Change at the top

The investigation was not moving fast enough for Commander George Hatherill at Scotland Yard and he was becoming increasingly frustrated at the way the Buckinghamshire police were handling the enquiries. It had taken four days for Bucks police to obtain the clothes Jack Mills had been wearing at the time of the robbery for forensic examination. During that time valuable clues to the identity of some of the robbers could have been compromised or even lost forever.

And the fact that the Bucks police thirty mile search for the robber's hideaway had begun by working their way outwards from Cheddington, instead of starting from the edge of the thirty mile perimeter and working inwards, was a major miscalculation.

On Tuesday 13 August, Hatherill and Detective Chief Superintendent Ernie Millen, at that time the Head of the Flying Squad, travelled to Aylesbury for a meeting with Malcolm Fewtrell and Gerald McArthur.

The outcome of this meeting was that Scotland Yard would take control of the administration and organisation of the Aylesbury incident room, Detective Superintendent McArthur would be responsible for reports and paperwork and Detective Chief Superintendent Tommy Butler (soon to replace Millen as Head of the Flying Squad) would take overall charge of the train robbery investigation. [14]

The 51 year old Butler, known at the Yard for his professionalism and thoroughness, was a bachelor who lived with his mother in Barnes, South West London. In his autobiography, Bruce Reynolds said of him, '*We all knew Butler. He was the Flying Squad's number one 'hit man', a dedicated career policeman who knew how to get results*'. [15]

Butler, who was to be assisted by Detective Chief Inspector Peter Vibart and Detective Inspector Frank Williams, immediately established an incident room at Scotland Yard. With as many as 30 Flying Squad officers working this case, liaison officers were also set up with C11, the Yard's Intelligence Department. It was not long before Butler and his team were stretched to the full.

CHAPTER 4
The Breakthrough

One big clue

The first time Leatherslade Farm was mentioned as a possible hideaway for the robbers was late on Sunday 11 August. Whilst in an Oxfordshire club, the head of the County CID had a conversation with one of his informants who mentioned 'X's' place' at Oakley (the local name for Leatherslade) as a possible hideout due to its remoteness. [1]

The following day, the CID officer made some enquiries about 'X's' place, also known as 'Rixon's place', and felt that it could be worth pursuing. Late on Monday 12 August, he sent a message to Aylesbury stating that '*these premises were purchased a few weeks ago for a large sum of money.*'

Earlier that day, the incident room at Aylesbury had received a call from John Maris, a herdsman who was working in a field adjacent to Leatherslade Farm, who believed that the farm may have been used by the robbers.

Maris told the *Daily Mirror*: '*After I inspected the heifers, I decided to take a closer look at the farmhouse and so I climbed through a gap in the hedge. As I arrived on the track which passed between the farmhouse and the outbuildings I was struck by the scene in front of me.*

'*The windows of the house had been adorned with various covers as curtains but it was odd because they were drawn fully across the windows with only the bottom corners in the centre drawn back. Why would anyone in an isolated house on top of a hill want to black out windows in that way? I knew then that this was the hideout of the train robbers that the police were looking for. I did not hang about as I was not sure if anyone was inside. I was scared, right enough.*' [2]

However, his call was one of over 400 logged in Aylesbury that day. As no one from Buckinghamshire police had appeared, Maris rang for a second time the following day and was assured that attention would be given to it.

Based on the telephone call from John Maris, and the message received from the head of Oxfordshire County CID, two policemen, Sergeant Ronald Blackman and PC John Woolley, were sent out from the nearby Waddesdon police station. Arriving at the farm at 10:50am on Tuesday 13 August, on Sergeant Blackman's 250cc Triumph motorbike, the pair met with Maris before entering the farm.

One of the first things they discovered were two Land Rovers, both with the same registration number, BMG 757A, and what appeared to be an army lorry.

Noticing an upstairs window was slightly ajar, PC Woolley climbed in to find a bedroom containing a number of sleeping bags and blankets. Moving downstairs, he let in Sergeant Blackman through the front door. On entering the kitchen the pair found it 'chock-a-block' with provisions.

Woolley later told the BBC that: '*All over the work surfaces, in the cabinets, the larder, it was full of tinned food, packaged food, crockery and cutlery - all you would need for quite a considerably lengthy stay.*'

Spotting a trapdoor just off the kitchen area, Woolley ventured down a few steps. '*I could see the cellar was absolutely full of bulging sacks. I pulled one of those sacks over to me and saw it was a canvas mail bag - as the top flopped open I could see parcel wrappers, bank note wrappers, consignment notes, all bearing the names of high street banks. That was when it finally hit home and we knew without any doubt that this was the train robbers' hideout.*' [3]

Whilst Woolley stayed at the house, Blackman went off to telephone his superiors before returning to the farm.

It was fortunate that both Commander Hatherill and Detective Chief Superintendent Ernie Millen were in Aylesbury having their meeting with Malcolm Fewtrell and Gerald McArthur. Immediately they were informed that the hideaway had been discovered, the four set off for Leatherslade Farm.

Shortly after their arrival, it was Fewtrell who famously told the media that: '*The whole place is one big clue.*'

Keeping a low profile

After their various departures from Leatherslade Farm on Friday 9 August, most of the train robbers must have felt quite apprehensive. With all but Pop having criminal records, it was inevitable that the police would target anyone they felt might have had some involvement with the robbery. Sensibly, most of the gang decided to keep their heads down.

Bruce Reynolds knew he would be targeted by the police – the London Airport robbery had seen to that. He and John Daly drove down to Winchelsea, in East Sussex, to be reunited with their wives. Reynolds felt it would be too dangerous for him and Frances to return to their flat in Putney, so they left their young son with Mary Manson and her friend Renee and moved in with a long-time pal who lived in a big mansion block in Queensway.

Daly, his wife Barbara and daughter Lorraine booked into the Endcliffe Hotel, Cliftonville as Mr & Mrs Cox-Daly. [4]

Ronnie Biggs had told his wife Charmian that he and Pop had gone tree-felling in Wiltshire. Unfortunately, his brother had died on the eve of the robbery and his sister-in-law had been in touch with Charmian to make sure Ronnie would be at the funeral. Charmian contacted Wiltshire police who did what they could to locate Biggs – but obviously were unable to find him.

After his return home and first decent sleep for several days, Biggs and Charmian split the money into three as he had arranged for some friends to mind it for him. Biggs kept a few hundred pounds as living expenses and to pay off some bills. They also had a good night out in the West End. The following day, Biggs went to work as normal. [5]

On 10 August, the day after Jimmy White had bought the Austin Healey, London County Council received an application for a 12 month road fund licence in the name of James Patten of 36 Tetbury Court, Clapham Common. The following day, White bought a caravan from the Clovelly Caravan Site in Boxhill, Surrey for £325. Here, he gave his name as Ballard.

On 12 August witnesses saw White and his wife Sheree visit their new caravan where they were seen to unload several suitcases. The next day, shops in Reigate became suspicious of a woman paying for a number of items with dirty £1 notes. The woman and her husband had given their name as Ballard, and their address as the Clovelly Caravan Site.

When they called at the caravan, the police found it to be unoccupied. However, during a search, they did find £136 in a jacket pocket. In view of this, they decided to keep the caravan under active surveillance. [6]

Roy James and Charlie Wilson left Brian Field's house on the Saturday and James dropped Wilson back to his safe house. James then returned to Field's later in the day to collect their money.

Gordon Goody stayed at Field's house on Saturday when he was joined by his fiancée. The pair stayed the night and left on the Sunday afternoon after the Ulsterman had been to collect his share of the money. The next day Goody buried some of his money under concrete slabs in the garden of his mother's house in Putney. [7]

Buster Edwards was also collected from Field's house by a friend. His wife June and daughter Nicolette were in the car and Edwards loaded his loot into the boot before being driven back to the friend's house in Kingston-Upon-Thames.

Bob Welch, Tommy Wisbey, James Hussey and Frank Munroe were driven to Reading by Brian Field on Saturday 10 August. There they paid cash for a second hand car, a van and some suitcases. They loaded their money into the vehicles and set off for the South Coast. [8]

Welch spent that Saturday night in Pevensey Bay, East Sussex. On Sunday morning he decided to go home and during the journey to London thought he should call his wife from a telephone box. When he told her he would be home soon, she asked him to '*get some ointment for Bruno's feet as they were bad again.*'

This was a pre-arranged message to let Welch know that the police were there, probably following up the lead given to C11 by their informant. Welch did a quick drive-by of his house, saw what he thought were three Flying Squad cars parked nearby, and kept on driving. [9]

Putting their heads above the parapet

After buying the Rover 105R, and letting Jimmy White have the Wolseley, Roger Cordrey telephoned an old friend, William Boal, and asked for his help. Boal was unaware that when Cordrey had bought the Rover, he had given his name as Tomkins and his address as 23 Burnthwaite Road, Fulham – Boal's home address.

Cordrey owed Boal £650 (equivalent to over £10,000 in 2015) and told him that if he came to Oxford, he would be able to settle the debt in cash. Keen to collect what was due to him, Boal, a precision engineer by trade, arrived in Oxford at lunchtime, met up with Cordrey and the pair then went back to Cordrey's lodgings. Cordrey showed Boal his suitcases and said that he needed to find somewhere safe to store them. Whether Cordrey told Boal what was in the suitcases is unknown. If he had let on that they contained cash from the train robbery, Boal may well have headed straight home.

Boal suggested that the two men should go to Bournemouth on the south coast, where he had some friends who might be able to help. As it was getting late, Boal stayed the night at Cordrey's lodgings.

The next day, Saturday, Cordrey and Boal set off for Bournemouth, leaving the suitcases at the Oxford lodgings. The drive to Bournemouth took a couple of hours, and then another hour was spent trying to find the house where Boal's friends lived – only to find that they had moved away several years before.

Cordrey decided to stay the night in Bournemouth and rented a holiday flat above a florists shop. The owner told police that he had met a man at the property who gave his name as Thompson from Slough. Mr Thompson paid a month's rent in advance, amounting to £58.16s, in £5 and £1 notes. The owner later identified William Boal as Mr Thompson.

Cordrey then drove Boal to Winchester railway station so he could catch a train back to London. The next morning, Sunday, Cordrey drove to Oxford to collect his suitcases from his lodgings, and also collected the Boal family – William, wife Renee and their children – from Oxford station. From there, they drove to Bournemouth dropping off Renee and the children to spend an afternoon at the beach, whilst Cordrey and Boal dropped the suitcases off at the holiday flat.

The Boal family, minus William, then returned to London with Cordrey asking Renee to deliver a package to his sister Maisie at a florist's shop in Molesey – and gave her £100 for her trouble. [10]

The next day, Cordrey told Boal that he had decided to buy two cars, and to rent a couple of garages where he could hide both the money and the cars. The two men began to look for suitable cars to buy.

Their first purchase was a Ford Anglia for which Boal paid the deposit of £73.14s in cash. He told the salesman that he would return the next day to settle the balance and collect the car. He gave the garage his correct name and address in Fulham. However, as Boal couldn't drive and didn't even have a provisional licence, Cordrey had to go on the car insurance. This time, Cordrey gave his name as John Edward Thomas.

Later that day, they found a garage to rent at the home of a Miss Ruby Saunders. The deposit was paid and they walked away with the key.

One car and one garage organised, one car and one garage still to go.

Gathering evidence

Shortly after George Hatherill, Ernie Millen, Malcolm Fewtrell and Gerald McArthur arrived at Leatherslade Farm, they were joined by Brigadier John Cheney, Chief Constable of Buckinghamshire police.

A cordon was placed around the farm and it would remain under police guard for the best part of a fortnight.

The GPO connected two outside lines to the farm and an incident room was set up at Brill police station. The remainder of the day was taken up with making arrangements for the fingerprint and forensic experts to attend the scene.

The following day, Wednesday 14 August, Maurice Ray arrived early with his team of fingerprint experts, and they were soon joined by a police photographer, two chief inspectors and four staff from the Forensic Science Laboratory.

Both teams faced the daunting task of fingerprinting and examining every item in the farmhouse, going over every inch of the interior, along with the outbuildings and the surrounding grounds. This included the remains of a bonfire and the contents of the freshly dug pit.

During the three days the Fingerprint Branch were at the farm, they collected 243 photographs of scene of crime marks made up of 311 fingers and 56 bits of palm. They also took back to the Yard 1,534 bank envelopes and a number of loose items including newspapers and magazines for further examination.

Chief Inspector William Knight of C10, the department at Scotland Yard that dealt with thefts of motor vehicles, also spent a couple of hours at the farm examining the two Land Rovers and the lorry. He quickly concluded that the lorry and the older Land Rover had been bought, whilst the newer Land Rover had been stolen.

Beginning that same afternoon, in addition to the enquiries being made at the houses within the vicinity of Leatherslade Farm, a police car with a public address system toured the local villages broadcasting the following message; *'Can you help the police? Can you give us any information about the recent occupants of Leatherslade Farm or about activities at the farm in the past two weeks? If so, please call at Brill Police Station or telephone Brill 802.'* [11]

Every man for himself

Hearing the news that the police had discovered Leatherslade Farm not only stopped Charlie Wilson, Bruce Reynolds, Buster Edwards, John Daly and Roy James in their tracks, but also put the kybosh on their idea of torching the farm.

James's immediate reaction to the others was *'We're nicked.'* [12]

The five of them decided to go to a café to consider their options. Wilson was still in favour of burning the farm down that night, but no one else was interested.

Each of them, and, of course, the other gang members, now had a decision to make. They could either try to brazen it out when the police came knocking at their doors, as they surely would, or they could go on the run now.

As they left the café, they exchanged handshakes all round. After all, it might be the last time they saw each other as free men.

CHAPTER 5
The First Arrests

Roger Cordrey and William Boal

It was Wednesday 14 August, the day following the discovery of Leatherslade Farm. Whether or not Roger Cordrey was aware of the police activity at the farm isn't known, but what is known is that on this particular day Cordrey and Boal went looking for a second car and a second garage where Cordrey hoped to hide part of his share of the robbery.

This time, they bought a small Austin A35 van for £210 having knocked the owner down from £225. [1]

As before, Boal did the negotiating whilst Cordrey mooched around in the background wearing a hat and sunglasses. Far from keeping a low profile, Cordrey's behaviour was distinctly bizarre.

Boal said that the car was for his friend, pointing to Cordrey, and gave Cordrey's name as J. Gosdin from Southbourne, West Sussex.

With three vehicles now in their possession – an Anglia, a Rover and an Austin van – Cordrey's idea was to garage the latter two and use the Anglia as a runabout.

They returned to the holiday flat above the florist's shop, and loaded part of the cash into suitcases which they stored in the boot of the Rover, and then drove to the garage they had rented from Miss Saunders and parked the car inside.

All they needed now was a second garage. But this wasn't an easy find and they spent several hours searching with no luck. Eventually, Boal saw an advert in a newsagent's window and took down the address of the garage owner, a Mrs Clarke.

Unfortunately for Cordrey and Boal, Mrs Clarke was the widow of a former policeman, and she felt that something wasn't quite right when Cordrey began flashing a wad of banknotes around and offering to pay three months' rent in advance.

Whilst she gave Cordrey the key to the garage, she called the police as soon as she had shut the door on the two men.

Cordrey and Boal drove the van to the garage and parked up. As they were walking away two CID officers in plain clothes, Detective Sergeant Stanley Davies and Detective Constable Charles Case, approached them.

A struggle began between Cordrey and the two officers, with Boal joining in pretending to be a concerned citizen going to the aid of another who was being attacked by two men. Police re-enforcements soon arrived on the scene and Cordrey and Boal were both handcuffed.

Knowing the game would be up if the police searched the holiday flat, Cordrey put the door key up his backside after requesting a visit to the toilet.

At this stage, the police officers had no inkling that the pair might be connected with the mail train robbery. They had arrested Cordrey and Boal simply for acting in a suspicious manner.

When searched, Cordrey had £159.3s.3d in cash on him as well as several keys. In Boal's pockets, police discovered a further £118.10s in cash, a receipt for the purchase of the Austin A35 van, and various keys, including one with a tag on it showing the address of the garage where they had parked the Rover.

Both men were interviewed separately. However, neither gave anything away and they were returned to their cells, pending further enquiries.

At 10:30pm, Detective Sergeant Davies decided to search Mrs Clarke's garage. In the back of the A35 van was a suitcase, and in the suitcase was a green bag. When Davies opened the bag he found it bulging with £5 and £1 notes. His immediate thought was that it could be part of the money stolen from the mail train, and when it was counted back at the station the total came to £56,047.

At 11:15pm, police interviewed Boal for a second time. When asked if there were any more vehicles, Boal mentioned the Ford Anglia and said that it was parked at the Horse and Jockey hotel. An hour later, the Anglia was searched but was found to be clean.

When Cordrey was interviewed for a second time, he told detectives that the money found in the back of the van belonged to a man he had met at the Brighton races. Needless to say the police were quite sceptical of this explanation, particularly since Cordrey said he couldn't remember the man's name.

One of the keys that police had found on Boal had a tag with an address written on it in Boal's handwriting. At around 2:00am, Detective Sergeant Davies and several other officers drove to the address, opened the garage with the key and discovered the Rover 105. In the boot were several suitcases packed tight with banknotes. A count of the cash back at the police station amounted to £78,982.

An hour or so later, the police searched the flat above the florist's and found £5,060 in a briefcase, another £840 under a pillow, plus log books for the Rover and the Ford Anglia and a number of letters addressed to Boal.

The cash recovered from Cordrey and Boal totalled £141,218.1s.3d – equivalent to around £2,500,000 by today's standards.

Yet again, Cordrey was brought up from the cells, and by now he realised that there was little point in sticking to his highly improbable story of looking after cash for an unknown Brighton punter. Hoping to mitigate whatever prison sentence he might eventually receive, Cordrey admitted that the cash was from the train robbery.

When Boal was brought up for questioning for the third time, he told detectives that he was only with Cordrey due to threats made against him and his family, that he was not involved in the train robbery in any way, and that he had no idea where the cash had come from.

Detective Sergeant Davies realised that it was now time to contact the mail train robbery incident room and tell them that they were holding two suspects that they may well want to interview as soon as possible.

Early on 15 August, Detective Superintendent Fewtrell, Detective Superintendent McArthur and Detective Sergeant Pritchard arrived in Bournemouth and interviewed Cordrey and Boal. Each made a statement under caution giving their own version of how the money came to be in their possession and their activities since the day of the robbery.

Boal, understandably, continued to insist that he had nothing to do with the train robbery, after all it was the truth, and in his statement stuck to the story that Cordrey had forced him to stay in Bournemouth against his wishes.

During what turned out to be a very long day for everyone, Cordrey began to grow ever more agitated. When he realised that the key he had secreted away was now well and truly stuck up his backside refusing to budge, the police doctor was called out to attend to him and remove the troublesome item.

Later that same day, every precaution was taken to ensure that both the prisoners and the cash arrived safely at Aylesbury Police HQ, where they were logged in at 9:30pm. The money was put in a safe in Brigadier Cheney's office with instructions that those on night duty should pay the occasional visit to the office and check the safe was ok. [2]

On their arrival at Aylesbury, Roger Cordrey and William Boal were charged with conspiracy to rob and with robbery. They were also charged with three counts each of receiving stolen money. [3]

This was a really lucky break for those investigating the train robbery. They could not have expected such a result so soon after the discovery of Leatherslade Farm.

There is no doubt that Cordrey's bizarre behaviour was out of character. In his autobiography Bruce Reynolds said that '*Roger was the last person that I'd have expected to be nicked. He was so low profile and extra careful*'.

Had he kept his head down during the week following the robbery, and quietly hidden his cash away, he probably would not have been arrested. He would certainly have been questioned by the police investigating the robbery. There is no doubt about that as he had been on the radar of the Post Office Investigation Branch since 1961 in connection with the robberies on trains carried out by the South Coast Raiders. [4]

However, Maurice Ray and the Scotland Yard fingerprint team were unable to find any prints belonging to either Cordrey or Boal at Leatherslade Farm.

If the cash had been safely hidden away, there would not have been any evidence to directly link either of them to the robbery, and there was a good chance that neither would have been charged.

Cordrey and Boal, keeping it in the family

Inevitably, all addresses connected to Roger Cordrey and William Boal were subjected to a police search.

The first to receive a visit from the Flying Squad, logged at 1:05am on the morning of 15 August, was Boal's house in Fulham. On answering the door, Renee Boal was informed by police officers that her husband had been arrested in Bournemouth. She immediately took two of the officers to an upstairs bedroom and handed them £325 in five pound notes, and £5 in one pound notes.

Renee Boal was arrested and taken to Rochester Row police station for questioning. She was subsequently charged on two counts of receiving stolen property amounting to £330.

At 3:30am on the same day, police arrived at the East Molesey home of Alfred and May Pilgrim, Cordrey's brother-in-law and sister. While searching the house, police found £860 in five pound notes.

Both Alfred Pilgrim and May Pilgrim were taken to Cannon Row police station and charged on two counts of receiving stolen property amounting to £860. [5]

The three men and two women appeared at Linslade Magistrates' Court, near Cheddington, on Friday 16 August at midday. Such was the national interest in the train robbery that a large crowd had been gathering outside the Court House for some time.

Detective Superintendent Fewtrell outlined the events that had resulted in the arrest of those in the dock and, as expected, Linslade Magistrates remanded all five in custody for a week.

The three men were taken away to Bedford Prison, whilst Renee Boal and May Pilgrim were taken off to Holloway.

Mary Manson

It was also inevitable that Mary Manson would be questioned by police at some stage during their pursuit of the train robbers. After all, it was Manson who Bruce Reynolds asked Roger Cordrey to contact when Cordrey cycled into Oxford just 12 hours or so after the robbery had taken place.

It was also Manson who met Reynolds the next day in Thame, and it was Manson who later that same day accompanied Reynolds to the Chequered Flag Garage in Chiswick where he bought the Austin Healey. And it was Manson who actually paid for the car with £835 in five pound notes.

On Monday 19 August the *Daily Express* reported that police were searching for a black Austin Healey bought from a Chiswick garage on 9 August by a man and a woman who they wished to interview.

At noon on Wednesday 21 August, Mary Manson, accompanied by a solicitor's clerk, walked into Scotland Yard where she was interviewed by Detective Inspector Frank Williams of the Flying Squad.

Manson had brought with her a statement explaining her role in the purchase of the car. Williams wasn't convinced by this, particularly as the police, at that stage, believed that a woman had been at Leatherslade Farm. [6]

Manson accompanied Williams to her flat in Wimbledon where it was searched. Despite finding nothing to link her to the robbery, she was charged with receiving the sum of £835 knowing it to be stolen, and later using this to purchase an Austin Healey car.

Manson was held in custody overnight, and appeared in court the following day where she was represented by Wilfred Fordham QC. Despite his best efforts, Mary Manson was remanded to Holloway Prison.

An indication of the worldwide interest in the robbery is that the arrest of Manson, at best a very peripheral figure, was covered in the USA by the *Statesman Express* on 23 August.

Charlie Wilson

On 22 August, the initial report on the finger and palm prints found at Leatherslade Farm by Maurice Ray and his Scotland Yard fingerprint team became available to the Flying Squad.

A meeting took place at the Yard to discuss how best to use the information, with Commander Hatherill and Detective Chief Superintendent Millen keen to have photographs of those the Squad wished to interview appear on the television and in the national newspapers.

Despite opposition from Detective Chief Superintendent Tommy Butler and Detective Inspector Frank Williams, concerned that this might make the robbers go to ground, photographs of Bruce Reynolds, Charlie Wilson and Jimmy White were published later that day.

Wilson had continued to go about his everyday business after returning from Leatherslade Farm, even though his name had been mentioned by police informants as a likely train robber.

Ironically, a few hours before his picture appeared in the *London Evening Standard*, Wilson arrived at his four bedroom house in Clapham to find Detective Sergeant Nigel Read waiting for him. Two other police officers arrived within half an hour and Wilson allowed them to search his house without them presenting a search warrant. However, nothing incriminating was found.

Wilson was then taken to Cannon Row police station where he was fingerprinted, and then taken to the charge room where he was interviewed by Tommy Butler. Butler asked Wilson if he had ever been to Cheddington or Leatherslade Farm and Wilson, of course, replied that he had never been to either.

Butler then asked Wilson to confirm his movements on the morning of 8 August, and Wilson replied that he was in Spitalfields Fruit and Veg Market at 5:00am as usual. However, Butler knew that Wilson's finger and palm impressions had been found at Leatherslade Farm on the window sill of the kitchen, on a drum of Saxa salt and on a cellophane wrapping from a Johnson's travellers kit, also found in the kitchen. [7]

Wilson was cautioned by Butler, and then taken to Aylesbury police station where he was formally cautioned and charged on 23 August.

Robert Pelham

Further photographs were released to the press in time for them to appear in newspapers on Saturday 24 August. One of those photos was of Roy James.

James's fingerprints had been found at Leatherslade Farm on a blue edged glass plate, a Johnson's traveller's kit and on a page from an American magazine called *Movie Screen*. [8]

Detective Sergeant Jack Slipper of the Flying Squad had been given the job of tracing and arresting James, but Slipper knew that James would go to ground once pictures of him were published, so he had very little time in which to catch his man.

James's unquestioned ability as an amateur racing driver was well known to the police, and Slipper knew that practice sessions were being held on 22 August at Goodwood in West Sussex. Local police were dispatched to arrest James, but when they arrived, they found that he had already left.

Undeterred, Slipper then arranged for police officers to be at the Battersea garage where James kept his Brabham Ford racing car.

However, whilst he was travelling back to London, James heard on the radio that Charlie Wilson had been arrested. By the time the car towing the Brabham Ford arrived back in Battersea, the only person in the car was Robert Pelham, a mechanic working for James.

Pelham's house in Notting Hill was given a good going over by the Flying Squad and a brown paper bag was found containing £545 in £1 notes. Pelham told the officers that the money was in payment for a new engine he had supplied and fitted for James.

Pelham was taken to Scotland Yard and then told that he would be driven to Aylesbury police station where he would be formally charged with receiving money he knew to be stolen.

Up before the beak

On Saturday 24 August, the eight people arrested to date appeared at a special session of Linslade Magistrates' Court.

Roger Cordrey, William Boal and Charlie Wilson were standing in the dock accused of robbery, whilst Renee Boal, Alfred Pilgrim, May Pilgrim, Mary Manson and Robert Pelham all stood accused of receiving.

After hearing the evidence presented by the police, the magistrates remanded all eight in custody until 2 September, despite the fact that the police had informed them that they would not object to bail being admitted for the five accused of receiving.

However, when Renee Boal, Alfred Pilgrim and May Pilgrim appeared before the magistrates on 2 September, they were all granted bail.

CHAPTER 6
The Net Closes

The arrest of Charlie Wilson was a pivotal moment. If Wilson could be arrested and charged so quickly after his face appeared on the front pages of the newspapers, the others reasoned that it would not be long before they too would be receiving visits from the Flying Squad.

Brian Field and the mysterious case of the money in Dorking Woods

On Friday 16 August, John Aherne was riding to work on his motorbike with his colleague Nina Hargreaves on the pillion. According to Aherne, the bike began to overheat, so he stopped to allow it to cool down. For whatever reason, he and Mrs Hargreaves decided to take a stroll, but were stopped in their tracks when they came across three bags – a leather briefcase, a pigskin holdall and a zipped-up plastic bag.

Aherne took a quick look inside the plastic bag and found it was stuffed tight with £1 notes. In his statement to the police, Aherne said '*I immediately thought of the big train robbery.*' [1]

Aherne and Mrs Hargreaves flagged down a passing car, showed the driver the contents of the bag and asked him to contact the police immediately.

Police officers arrived fairly quickly and as Detective Inspector Basil West took custody of the three bags, a dog handler and his German Shepherd found a fourth – a suitcase also crammed with banknotes.

The bags were taken back to Dorking police station where two bank cashiers helped to count the contents. The final tally came to £100,900.

A detective constable was later given the bags so they could be checked over for fingerprints, and whilst doing this the police officer found a bill in the briefcase made out to a Herr and Frau Field, dated 2 to 16 February 1963, in respect of a room at a German hotel called Hotel Sonnenbichl.

He also found a number of fingerprints on the leather case which were photographed and subsequently examined at Scotland Yard. One of the prints was later identified as belonging to Brian Field.

The police knew that Brian Field had previously acted for Buster Edwards and Gordon Goody, and on Friday 23 August - a week after the discovery at the woods in Dorking – a warrant was issued for the search of 'Kabri', the house Field shared with his wife.

Whilst officers carried out the search, Detective Superintendent Fewtrell and Detective Sergeant Pritchard questioned the Fields. When asked about Leatherslade Farm, Field admitted that he had been there because Leonard Field had asked him to accompany him on a viewing, and that the conveyancing for the purchase had been handled by his boss John Wheater.

Fewtrell also asked to see the Field's passports. Both had entries at the beginning of February which Brian Field said was when he and Karin had taken a skiing holiday in West Germany. He also told them that they had stayed at the Hotel Sonnenbichl.

Whilst the search of the house revealed nothing of interest, the police could now link Field to both Leatherslade Farm and some of the money stolen from the mail train. However, they were not yet ready to take Brian Field into custody for questioning.

Ronnie Biggs – an inspector calls

The day following the search of Brian Field's house, Ronnie Biggs received a visit from Detective Inspector Basil Morris and Detective Sergeant Church from Reigate police station. According to Biggs, the officers were particularly interested in his friendship with Bruce Reynolds, and when asked when he had last seen Reynolds, Biggs said it was at least four years or more, when they were both in Wandsworth Prison.

Whilst he didn't have a warrant, Detective Inspector Morris asked if he could search the house. Knowing that they wouldn't find anything, Biggs said yes.

After completing the search, Morris asked Biggs to let him know should Reynolds get in touch. [2]

As they watched the police officers drive away, both Ronnie and Charmian Biggs breathed a huge sigh of relief. But how long would it be before they came back?

Bob Welch goes west

Bob Welch's criminal record was fairly clean as his only known transgressions were a spell in prison in 1958 when he was convicted of receiving stolen custard powder worth over £2000, and in 1963 when he had been fined £210 for serving and selling alcohol after hours in his club. [3]

Having spent the night of 10 August in Pevensey Bay, Welch was on his way home when he learnt that police were waiting at his house to interview him. An informant had told police that Welch might have been involved in the train robbery. When Welch failed to turn up at his house, the police left – no doubt to interview the next person on a fairly long list of suspects named by informants.

Their next visit to the Welch house was at 5:00am on 14 August, and once again only his wife was at home. Nothing untoward was discovered, although police took away a small amount of cash, a receipt issued by a hotel in Nottingham, some keys and a pair of shoes. [4]

Two days later, Welch went to Scotland Yard voluntarily as he knew the police would continue to search for him until they found him. He made a statement that he had never been to Leatherslade Farm, or anywhere in the immediate vicinity, and that he had been at home with his wife when the mail train had been robbed.

After signing his statement, Welch was told he was free to go. He briefly returned home before travelling to North Devon to stay in a rented farmhouse with friends.

Gordon Goody – a case of mistaken identity

Gordon Goody had become a police target after being found not guilty of the wages snatch at the BOAC offices at London Airport in November 1962. The fact that he had been able to arrange for vital evidence to be tampered with made it doubly galling for those in the police who had worked hard to get the case to court, and who knew for certain that Goody was guilty.

Goody was initially under suspicion as he was a known associate of some of those the police believed were involved in the train robbery, and on 16 August members of the Flying Squad searched the Putney house that Goody shared with his mother. Goody wasn't at home at the time, and the search found nothing incriminating.

At the time of the search, Goody was staying at the Windmill, a friend's pub in Blackfriars. He had stayed there during the BOAC trial and had kept some of his clothes in the room he had used 'just in case'.

Goody knew that he had nothing to fear from the fingerprint and forensic examination of Leatherslade Farm since he had meticulously kept his gloves on at all times.

However, he was so concerned that the police might try to 'fit him up' by planting evidence, that he wrote a rather bizarre letter to Detective Superintendent Oxborne at Ealing CID, a police officer who Goody felt had treated him fairly during the BOAC robbery enquiry. It read;

'*Dear Sir,*

No doubt you will be surprised to hear from me after my double trial at the Old Bailey for the London Airport robbery. At the time of writing I am not living at my home address because it seems that I am a suspect in the recent train robbery. Two Flying Squad officers recently visited my home address whilst I was out and made a search of the premises, and honestly, Mr Oxborne, I am very worried that they connect me with this crime.

The reason I write to you now is because you always treated me in a straightforward manner during the airport case. I will never forget how fair and just yourself and Mr Field were towards me. That case took nearly eight months to finish and every penny I had, and to become a suspect in this last big robbery is more than I can stand. So my intentions are to keep out of harm's way until the people concerned in the train robbery are found.

To some people this letter would seem like a sign of guilt but all I am interested in is keeping my freedom. Hoping these few lines find you and Mr Field in the best of health.

Gordon Goody'

The day after Goody sent this letter, he borrowed a car from Charles Alexander, the friend who owned the Windmill pub, and set off for Leicester to visit Maggie Perkins, a model and former Midlands beauty queen who he had met earlier in the year.

Unfortunately, the car broke down and had to be towed to the nearest garage in Cranfield, Bedfordshire. Here he gave his name as Charles Alexander and his address as the Windmill pub in Blackfriars. From Cranfield he got a lift to the Grand Hotel in Leicester where he registered as Charles Alexander.

At the hotel he bought some flowers for his dinner date from the florist in reception. The florist, in the most ironic of circumstances, alerted other staff that she had just served a train robber and the Leicester police were contacted. The name of the train robber the florist told police she had served was Bruce Reynolds! [5]

At 2:00am on Friday 23 August, police burst into Goody's hotel room. Instinctively Goody tried to bluff his way out of the situation, but he soon realised that the police knew he wasn't Charles Alexander, and so gave them his real name. He explained that a number of people he knew had been linked to the mail train robbery and that he had been staying at the Windmill until the dust had settled and all the robbers had been caught.

Goody was taken to Leicester police station, and during the morning police searched the car that had broken down, the home of Maggie Perkins and twice searched Goody's room at the Windmill pub. The second time they took away Goody's passport and a pair of shoes.

Whilst at Leicester police station Goody was interviewed twice, and then taken to Aylesbury Police HQ later that evening when he was interviewed by Tommy Butler. He told Butler that he had been in Ireland with his mother when the robbery had taken place.

At that point in time, Butler knew they didn't have enough evidence to hold Goody and so he was released early on Sunday 25 August.

Tommy Wisbey

Bookmaker Tommy Wisbey had spent time in borstal for breaking and entering when he was a teenager, and ten years later had served a four month prison sentence for receiving stolen goods. On paper, at least, he didn't appear to be a hardened criminal, although his daughter Marilyn was later to become firm friends with Frankie Fraser who was a key member of the notorious Richardson gang from South London. [6]

Wisbey was another whose name had been given to police by an informant. Aware that police had put the word out that they wanted to interview him, Wisbey went voluntarily to Scotland Yard on 20 August and made a statement that he was in a pub on the night of the robbery and that the pub landlord would corroborate this.

The police were dubious of this alibi, but had no reason to hold him. Shortly after, Wisbey went to Spain for a holiday confident that he had not left any prints at Leatherslade Farm and that he was in the clear.

CHAPTER 7
The Key to the Farm

When Bernard and Lily Rixon drove away from Leatherslade Farm on 29 July 1963, they expected legal completion, and the payment of the balance of the agreed purchase price, to take place on Tuesday 13 August.

However, completion never took place, although it is likely that had the gang still been using the farm as their post-robbery bolt hole on 13 August, the necessary funds would have been transferred to Rixon's solicitor. To have done otherwise would have drawn attention to their occupation of Leatherslade.

After the initial examination of the farm, the Flying Squad soon began looking at the documentation relating to the proposed sale, and in particular the details of the purchaser and the legal firm that was acting on his behalf.

This would inevitably lead them to Leonard Field as the proposed purchaser, to Brian Field, who had accompanied Leonard to view the farm, and to John Wheater, the solicitor who had dealt with the legal and contractual issues involved with the proposed purchase of the farm.

John Wheater

As soon as news broke that Leatherslade Farm had been discovered, John Wheater realised that it was only a matter of time before the police would pay him a visit looking for information and explanations.

To pre-empt their visit, Wheater contacted police on 14 August, the day after the discovery – after all, he reasoned, isn't that what an innocent man would do? During his interview, Wheater confirmed that Leonard Field was his client, that he was the proposed purchaser of Leatherslade Farm, and that Field's address was 150, Earls Court Road, London.

However, when Flying Squad officers went to the address, they discovered the property, a three storey Victorian House, had been divided into bedsits following its sale a few months earlier. There was no sign of Leonard Field.

When the police returned to Wheater's office the following day, he happened to mention that Field's brother had lived at 262 Green Lanes, in Stoke Newington. [1]

Wheater's file on the purchase was decidedly limited, and what was contained in the file with regard to personal information on Leonard Field was scant to say the very least.

Whilst Wheater confirmed that Field had paid the deposit on the farm, this, according to the solicitor, was in cash. The absence of a receipt in the file for the cash was not adequately explained by Wheater, and it turned out that when contracts had been exchanged, Wheater had signed on Field's behalf. Not illegal, but very unusual, and because of this the police were unable to find any trace of Field's signature.

Roll up, Roll up

On Monday 19 August, the police removed their cordon around Leatherslade Farm having done everything they needed to do and having removed what they believed to be all that the robbers had left behind.

The following day the *Daily Mirror* carried the headline '5s-A-PEEP PLAN FOR GANG FARM' publicising Bernard Rixon's idea of opening up Leatherslade Farm to the paying public, whilst the *Daily Express* had a photo of him on their front page sitting in a chair beside the fireplace at the farm. [2]

During an interview, Rixon told reporters: *'You can't blame me if I try to make every penny I can out of it.'*

In reality, visitors to Leatherslade did not get value for their money. The only items Rixon could find to put on display were a few cans of food, some used flash bulbs left lying around by the police forensic scientists and a squashed tin of yellow paint. The early novelty of being able to visit the robber's lair was to wear off very quickly.

The Mysterious Can of Yellow Paint

The paltry number of items that Bernard Rixon had on display at Leatherslade Farm was further depleted when the squashed tin of paint was reclaimed by the police on 27 August on the instructions of Dr Holden of the Forensic Science Laboratory.

Holden had been examining the items taken from William Boal's house after his arrest, and had found a small watch winder in the lining of a jacket which had minute traces of yellow paint mixed with dirt in its grooves.

Holden also found similar traces of yellow paint on both shoes that had been taken from Gordon Goody's room at the Windmill pub. He recalled that whilst he had been at Leatherslade Farm, he had noticed part of the lorry used during the robbery had been hand painted yellow, and that there had been a squashed can of yellow paint on the floor of one of the outbuildings.

On checking the long list of items retrieved from the farm by the exhibits officer, there was no mention of the paint can. An order was quickly issued to the local police, who promptly removed the paint from Bernard Rixon's display.

As soon as he received it, Holden began to make detailed tests to see whether there was any link between the paint and the watch winder and the paint and Goody's shoes. These tests would take him some time.

Cleanliness is next to godliness

The fact that items such as the three vehicles and the squashed can of yellow paint were available for forensic examination was once again all down to the failure to sanitize Leatherslade Farm before it was discovered by the police.

Describing the farm as '*one big clue*' had certainly not been an exaggeration by Detective Superintendent Fewtrell.

As Bruce Reynolds stated in his autobiography, '*It was clear to me that failing to clean up the farm was one mistake.*'

In fact it was the biggest mistake possible, and one which was to have disastrous consequences for the majority of the robbers.

CHAPTER 8
The Arrests Continue

As August gave way to September, the police could look back at the eight arrests they had already made with some satisfaction – William Boal, Roger Cordrey and Charlie Wilson had been charged with robbery and conspiracy to rob, and Renee Boal, Mary Manson, Robert Pelham, Alfred Pilgrim and May Pilgrim had all been charged with receiving.

And whilst Dr Holden was busy in the Forensic Science Laboratory, Maurice Ray and his team in the Fingerprint Department were hard at work comparing the prints taken at Leatherslade Farm with those held in the Criminal Records Office.

A number of the prints found on the Monopoly board game matched the records held for John Daly. On 30 August, Frank Williams and some of his Flying Squad colleagues visited the house in Sutton that Daly shared with his wife Barbara and daughter Lorraine. However, predictably, the house was unoccupied, although Williams was able to find Daly's passport that suggested he had gone to ground somewhere in the UK.

The Daly family had actually booked into the Endcliffe Hotel, Cliftonville as Mr & Mrs Cox-Daly a few days after the robbery. Once his photograph appeared in the newspapers Daly sent his daughter to Cornwall to stay with friends, whilst he and Barbara, pregnant with their second child, went to stay in a basement flat in Eaton Square, Belgravia. [1]

Ronnie Biggs

Prints belonging to Ronnie Biggs were also found on the Monopoly set, on a Pyrex plate and on a bottle of tomato ketchup. Having been visited by police during August, Williams felt there was a fairly good chance that Biggs had decided to front it out, rather than go to ground.

Mid-afternoon on Wednesday 4 September, Williams, accompanied by other Flying Squad officers, knocked on the front door of Biggs's home in Redhill armed with a search warrant.

Charmian Biggs opened the door and told Williams that her husband was at work. Undeterred by Biggs's absence, the police started a systematic search of the house, which was still going on when Biggs arrived home later in the day.

Despite nothing incriminating being found during the search, Williams took Biggs to Scotland Yard where he was interviewed by Tommy Butler and subsequently cautioned. From the Yard, he was then taken to Aylesbury by car, accompanied by both Butler and Williams, where he was formally charged with robbery and conspiracy to rob.

As before, Biggs was asked about Bruce Reynolds, and this time he replied *'Yes, I know Reynolds. He'll want some catching'*. [2]

Biggs appeared at Linslade Magistrates' Court the following day, and became the ninth person to be charged by police. He was remanded in custody until 10 September, and was sent to HMP Bedford. Ironically for someone whose share of the robbery was around £150,000, Biggs was granted the 1960's equivalent of Legal Aid as he had told the court that his weekly earnings were just £35 a week.

Biggs's arrest was a cause for concern amongst the other robbers still at large, fearful that this could quite quickly lead the police to Pop, the old train driver Biggs had recruited.

Not that they thought that Biggs would 'grass' anyone up, but because both he and the old boy had decided on the same alibi – that they had been felling trees in Wiltshire when the robbery had taken place.

As career criminals, the likes of Charlie Wilson, Buster Edwards, Gordon Goody and Bruce Reynolds would take being interviewed by the likes of Tommy Butler and Frank Williams in their stride. It was an occupational hazard.

However, Edwards and Goody realised that the old man would almost certainly capitulate within a matter of minutes if he was interrogated, and he could, of course, provide the police with everything they wanted to know about each member of the gang – particularly if the carrot of immunity from prosecution in exchange for his help was dangled in front of him.

Edwards and Goody decided that there was no alternative but to silence Pop permanently, before the police trail led to him. Edwards had once been with Bruce Reynolds when they had dropped Pop off at his house in Redhill, and he was confident that he could find his way there without too much trouble.

However, despite the pair driving up and down Redhill for several hours, Edwards couldn't find the house or the street he was looking for and, luckily for Pop, they eventually had to abandon the plan and return to London. [3]

James Hussey

Three days after the arrest of Ronnie Biggs, Flying Squad officers with a search warrant descended on the home of James Hussey in Dog Kennel Hill, East Dulwich just before 10:00am. Nothing was found at the house to link Hussey to the train robbery.

However, he was then taken to Scotland Yard where he was interviewed by Tommy Butler. Naturally, Hussey denied being involved in the robbery or ever having been to Leatherslade Farm. He also denied knowing any of the men that had been arrested so far, or any of those on the police wanted list whose pictures had appeared in the newspapers.

Confident that he hadn't left any finger or palm prints at the farm, Hussey agreed to his palm prints being taken.

Butler also questioned him about the Land Rovers and the lorry used in the robbery, and Hussey signed a statement to the effect that he had no knowledge of any of the vehicles.

Unfortunately for Hussey, the palm prints he so willingly gave were passed to Maurice Ray to compare with some of the yet unidentified palm prints that had been discovered at Leatherslade Farm. After a while, a match was made with a palm print found on the tailboard of the Austin lorry which had been taken to Scotland Yard on 6 September.

At 1:45pm, Butler informed Hussey that he was going to be taken to Aylesbury where he would be charged with conspiracy to rob and robbery. Realising he was now in deep trouble, Hussey asked for his solicitor to be called immediately.

Tommy Wisbey

After his voluntary visit to Scotland Yard in August, Tommy Wisbey had gone to Spain for a holiday. At that time, there was no extradition treaty between Britain and Spain, and the fact that he returned to the UK in September showed how confident Wisbey was that the police had nothing on him.

On 7 September, the same day that James Hussey was arrested, Flying Squad officers, including Frank Williams, raided Wisbey's 3rd floor flat in Camberwell at 7:00am in the morning.

However, the police found neither Wisbey nor anything incriminating. What they did find was a very tearful Renee Wisbey who told Williams that her husband had left her for another woman, and that the pair were now holidaying in Spain. [4]

Four days later, Williams was surprised to receive a telephone call from Wisbey himself. They agreed to meet at Wisbey's betting shop in Southwark, South London at 11:30am that morning. When Williams and Detective Sergeant Steven Moore arrived at the shop, Williams told Wisbey that they were going to take him to Scotland Yard where he would be questioned about the train robbery in Buckinghamshire.

When they arrived at the Yard, Wisbey had his finger and palm prints taken, and was then interviewed by Tommy Butler. Naturally, at this point, Wisbey denied ever having been to Leatherslade Farm and denied knowing any of those already charged with robbery other than James Hussey, who he said he had known for years.

Wisbey was keeping to his story that on the night of the robbery he had been in The Newington Arms Public House from 9:00pm until 11:00pm, which the landlord could confirm. At closing time, he returned to his parents' house in Camberwell, South London, where he stayed the night.

Wisbey, however, was unaware that Frank Williams had already questioned William Coupland, the pub landlord, who must have got cold feet as he said he had been out with his wife that evening and therefore Wisbey's claim couldn't be true. [5]

The final nail in the coffin for Wisbey was when his fingerprints were compared to those found at Leatherslade Farm, and proven to be identical to those discovered on an attachment to the bath.

Later that day, 11 September, Tommy Wisbey was taken to Aylesbury Police HQ where he was charged with robbery and conspiracy to rob. The following day he appeared at Linslade Magistrates' Court where he was remanded in custody. He became the eleventh person to be charged in connection with the mail train robbery, and the sixth charged with robbery and conspiracy to rob.

Leonard Field

On 9 September, Leonard Field got into his van and drove away from 262 Green Lanes on his way to Tilbury Docks. A few minutes later, he was stopped by police and told that he was to be taken to Cannon Row police station for questioning.

There, he was interviewed by Tommy Butler and Detective Chief Inspector Bradbury who told him that they knew he was the Leonard Field whose name was on the contract to purchase Leatherslade Farm from Bernard and Lily Rixon.

Field rebutted that suggestion and denied that he had visited the farm accompanied by Brian Field at the end of June. He did admit to knowing both Brian Field and John Wheater, but refused to answer any more questions without Wheater being present.

When Wheater arrived at Cannon Row, Field pleaded with him to tell the police that he hadn't been involved in the purchase of Leatherslade Farm. With the colour rapidly draining from his face, Wheater asked for a word in private with Butler.

When they were alone, Wheater told Butler that he couldn't be sure if the man in the room was the one he had been dealing with for the farm purchase, as he had only met Leonard Field once. He conceded that there was a strong resemblance to the man who paid the deposit for the farm, but he couldn't be one hundred percent certain that it was the same man.

A bemused Butler had no option other than to let Field go. However, it strengthened his determination to gather more evidence against him as quick as he possibly could.

Butler passed John Wheater's file on the purchase of the farm to Maurice Ray, and in the file Ray found a bank authority form with Field's signature on the bottom. If the fingerprint on the document matched Field's, his denial of any involvement in the purchase of Leatherslade Farm would be blown out of the water.

Early on Saturday morning, 14 September, police officers arrived at 262 Green Lanes and informed Leonard Field that he was being arrested for complicity in the mail train robbery.

Brian Field

Since the discovery of the cash in the woods at Dorking on 16 August, and the search of his house seven days later, Brian Field's name had been steadily rising up Tommy Butler's list of suspects. There were just too many strands of the investigation leading back to Brian for him to be innocent of any involvement.

Field had acted for several of the suspected robbers, including Buster Edwards and Gordon Goody, prior to the robbery. He had almost certainly accompanied Leonard Field on a viewing of Leatherslade Farm six weeks or so before the robbery. His boss, John Wheater, was the solicitor who had acted for Leonard Field in the purchase of the farm, and in a leather briefcase full of cash discovered in the Dorking woods, police had found a bill made out to a Herr and Frau Field in respect of a room at the Hotel Sonnenbichl in Germany dated 2 to 16 February 1963. Herr and Frau Field, and Mr and Mrs Brian Field were one and the same. There were just too many links to the robbery for it to be purely coincidental.

It probably came as no great surprise to Brian Field when, on Sunday 15 September, the day after Leonard Field's arrest, he found himself opening his front door to Tommy Butler and a number of other Flying Squad officers.

Butler didn't beat around the bush and immediately informed Field that he was to be arrested for his involvement in the mail train robbery of 8 August 1963.

A search of the house revealed nothing incriminating, although 22 five pound notes were found in Brian Field's wallet. One of those notes, serial number A15 901750, was close to a stolen note, A15 901857. [6]

As the serial numbers of only 1400 stolen banknotes had been recorded, the close numerical proximity of the note in Field's possession to a stolen one was considered more than just a coincidence. [7]

Once at the Yard, Field was shown both the hotel receipt and the leather briefcase. He told Butler that the case certainly wasn't his, but that the receipt was, although he said that he was very surprised to see it as he thought it was back at his house, on his desk.

Butler then had Leonard Field brought to the interview room and asked Brian Field if he was the person he had accompanied to the viewing at Leatherslade Farm. Whether Brian had spoken to John Wheater beforehand isn't known. However, his reaction to seeing Leonard was virtually identical to Wheater's – the man was very much like him, but it wasn't him.

However, Butler told both men that their fingerprints were to be taken, and then they would be driven to Aylesbury to be charged.

When Brian Field's fingerprints were subsequently checked against the prints on the leather briefcase, the Scotland Yard Fingerprint Department found a match.

On top of this, when Brian's neighbours were questioned after his arrest, police were told that on the night of Friday 9 August, there had been a procession of cars calling at Field's house. This continued throughout Saturday and into the early hours of Sunday 11 August. Field later told his neighbours that his callers were clients who had been arrested in connection with the 'Brighton horse racing gang' case which was starting the following month and that he was representing them.[8]

In his report to the Home Office in 1964, Her Majesty's Inspector of Constabulary stated that *'anyone who acquired Leatherslade Farm and remained in possession and control during the relevant period, in default of a watertight explanation, must be an accessory to the robbery. Anyone assisting with guilty knowledge must be a party to conspiracy to rob. Brian Field, on his own admission, shortly before the robbery, examined the farm with a Leonard Field whom he knew to be the relation of a convicted criminal. Upon reading about the connection of the farm with the robbery, he made no effort to contact the police with his knowledge.*[9]

The case against Brian Field and Leonard Field was becoming almost irresistible, and that against Leonard Field was further strengthened when he took part in an identification parade. Despite his efforts to change his appearance, Field was instantly picked out by Mrs Lily Rixon as the man who had viewed the farm in June. [10]

With both Brian Field and Leonard Field now in police custody, John Wheater must have feared the worst.

CHAPTER 9
The Absent Friends

The arrests of Leonard Field and Brian Field were the twelfth and thirteenth since the robbery was carried out on 8 August. However, of those thirteen, only five had been at the scene of the crime – Roger Cordrey, Charlie Wilson, Ronnie Biggs, James Hussey and Tommy Wisbey.

As at mid-September, that left Bruce Reynolds, Gordon Goody, Bob Welch, John Daly, Roy James, Buster Edwards, Jimmy White, Bill Jennings, Alf Thomas, Frank Munroe and old Pop still at large.

Buster Edwards

After being collected from Brian Field's house on Saturday 10 August, Buster Edwards had decided not to return to his home in East Twickenham, and was taken instead to a friend's house in Kingston-Upon-Thames. From there, he booked into a hotel in Richmond.

His wife June and daughter Nicolette did go back to East Twickenham for a few days and from there June arranged for them to rent a house in Old Forge Crescent in Shepperton, in the names of William and June Green.

However, on 12 September, the police released photographs of Buster and June and within 24 hours they received a telephone call from a resident in Old Forge Crescent who said that a couple resembling Mr and Mrs Edwards had recently moved into a neighbouring property.

Although the police immediately responded to this call, by the time they arrived the Greens had fled in a red Morris 1100. This was later found abandoned in Ealing.

After this, the trail went cold, even though the Edwards family moved to a house in Wraysbury, Buckinghamshire less than 10 miles from Shepperton.

Bruce Reynolds

After leaving Leatherslade Farm, Bruce Reynolds and John Daly had driven down to Winchelsea in Sussex to be reunited with their wives. Reynolds knew he would be targeted by the police and so a return to his flat in Putney was out of the question. He and his wife Frances decided to leave their young son with Mary Manson and her friend Rene and moved in with a long-time friend who lived in a big mansion block in Queensway.

However, on 22 August whilst house hunting in the Midlands with Freddie Foreman, Reynolds saw a midday newspaper which carried his name and photograph, along with photos of Charlie Wilson and Jimmy White. According to Reynolds, Frances saw a newspaper poster with the same photographs round about the same time as he did, and realised that she couldn't go back to the Queensway flat.

After the initial shock of seeing his face staring back at him, Reynolds became concerned about his share of the cash from the robbery. The garage where it was hidden had been rented out in his proper name and it wouldn't take long for the police to discover this.

On this occasion, luck was on his side and he was able to retrieve the bags of cash and stow them with a friend of Foreman's.

Over the next few days, Reynolds moved several times, each time staying with friends he knew he could trust – even though he expected the police to call on everyone he was known to fraternise with. He realised that his only chance of avoiding arrest was to keep on the move. In the meantime, Frances was staying in Canterbury.

The two of them were eventually reunited and, on 2 September, they moved to a small one bedroom flat above a cleaner's shop in Handcroft Road, Thornton Heath in Surrey.

But, how long would it be before they had to move again? [1]

Jimmy White

After buying the Austin Healey in the name John Steward on 9 August, submitting a road fund licence application in the name of James Patten on 10 August, purchasing a caravan in the name of Ballard a few days later, and then leaving the car at a London garage on 14 August, there had been no further sightings of Jimmy White.

The caravan was kept under constant surveillance by the police hoping that White would return there at some stage.

On 18 August, a man named Harry Brown was stopped by police from entering the caravan. Brown told them that a Mr Bollard, who ran a café next door to where he worked, had offered him and his family the caravan for a week's holiday. Brown was not detained and allowed to go.

It soon became apparent to the police that Steward, Patten, Bollard and Ballard were all aliases used by White. However, after searching all the addresses connected to those aliases, they were no further forward.

The police decided it was time to take a further look inside the caravan, and after removing all the interior panelling, found cash totalling £30,440. Several fingerprints were photographed which were later identified as belonging to Jimmy and his wife Sheree, but there was still no sign of White or his family.[2]

Roy James

After discovering his fingerprints at Leatherslade Farm, police had moved quickly in their pursuit of Roy James. Having received information on 22 August that he was appearing at a motor racing event at Goodwood, local police were dispatched to apprehend him, only to discover that he had already left.

The following day, police found an Austin Mini-Cooper that belonged to James and took it to Chalk Farm police garage for examination, although nothing incriminating was found in it.

By now, James was holed-up in Putney, keeping his head down at the home of a bookmaker friend where he stayed until the end of September. [3]

John Daly

John Daly was still in the basement flat in Belgravia. When Bruce Reynolds received a message that Daly wanted to see him, Reynolds was happy to make the short trip from Thornton Heath, albeit taking precautions to avoid being seen.

When the pair met up, Reynolds became concerned that Daly was being looked after by the wrong people. This concern increased further when Daly told him that he wanted his share of the money brought to him so his minders could invest it for him. However Reynolds, deciding that Daly was *a big boy, who had made his own decisions,* did what was asked of him and, via Freddie Foreman, the money was delivered. [4]

Gordon Goody

After being released from Leicester police station on 25 August, police arranged for Gordon Goody to be kept under surveillance and recorded the comings and goings at the hairdressers he owned in Wandsworth. Nothing untoward was logged. [5]

Bob Welch

Bob Welch had headed off to North Devon after making his voluntary statement at Scotland Yard in the middle of August.

However, Welch also kept on the move and booked into the Harbour Light Hotel in Mevagissey at the end of the month, stayed at the Headland Hotel in

Newquay a week later, and was then reported to be in the village of Beaford in Devon by the middle of September. [6]

Bill Jennings, Alf Thomas and Frank Munroe

According to Bruce Reynolds, Jennings had no previous convictions and kept himself to himself. No-one knew if Jennings was his real name, nor where he lived. What they did know about Jennings was that he was one hundred per cent reliable. The last report Reynolds had on him was that he was in a safe house, with female company and '*enough champagne to sink a battleship.*' [7]

Frank Munroe was reported to have visited Bob Welch whilst Welch was in the West Country.[8] Both he and Alf Thomas were in hiding, hoping to ride out the storm.

Pop

Despite the perception that Pop couldn't carry out the one job he had been hired to do, he was still given a 'drink' of £20,000. Almost certainly this was to ensure his silence, rather than for 'services rendered'.

Pop was dropped off at his house in Redhill after leaving Leatherslade Farm, and no doubt would have been worried that he too could receive a visit from the police at any time.

However, in his favour was the absence of a police record and therefore if he had been careless and left finger and palm prints whilst at the farm, the police had nothing to compare them with. It is also likely that, apart from Biggs and Reynolds, no other gang member would have known, or wished to have known, his true name and address.

In fact, the only real threat to Pop was when Buster Edwards and Gordon Goody had unsuccessfully cruised around Redhill looking for his house, allegedly with a view to silencing him permanently.

CHAPTER 10

The Tale of Goody's Two Shoes

On 29 August, Dr Ian Holden of the Forensic Science Laboratory at Scotland Yard had received the squashed tin of yellow paint that the exhibit's officer had retrieved from Leatherslade Farm two days earlier. A spectrographic analysis showed that the paint in the tin and the paint on Gordon Goody's shoes were very similar, but not quite identical.

Holden next analysed the paint from the cab of the lorry against the paint from the tin. This time there was a perfect match. However, a comparison between the paint from the cab and Goody's shoes was again similar, but not identical.

On 19 September, Holden returned to Aylesbury and took samples of yellow paint from the pedals of the Land Rovers and a comparison against these and Goody's shoes came up with an identical match. To be able to prove that Goody's shoes had been at the farm, Holden had to be able to match the paint on the soles with the paint in the tin.

The breakthrough came when Holden returned yet again to Leatherslade Farm on 28 September. On this occasion, he noticed some fine mineral deposits mixed in with the gravel which would have attached itself to the soles of Goody's shoes along with any paint he had trodden in. When Holden added these minerals to paint from the tin, he came up with a perfect match to the paint on both the shoes, and the pedals of the Land Rovers.

This was the hard evidence the police needed which meant that they could now arrest Gordon Goody.

Holden also compared the paint on the small watch winder that was found in the right hand pocket of William Boal's jacket, with the tin of paint from the farm, and came up with a perfect match. On the face of it, this also put Boal at Leatherslade Farm.

However, this begs the question as to how and why paint from the farm was discovered in the jacket pocket of someone who had not been part of the gang that robbed the train, and who had never set foot on Leatherslade Farm. As Bruce Reynolds stated in his autobiography when he learnt of the arrest of Roger Cordrey, '*Roger Cordrey and someone I'd never heard of, a man called Bill Boal, had been arrested with £141,000 in their possession.*' [1]

Perhaps all would be revealed at the forthcoming committal proceedings when the evidence against each of those arrested would be reviewed to determine if there was a case for them to answer. Where the evidence was deemed strong enough, the case would be referred to Crown Court for trial by jury.

CHAPTER 11
The Search Continues

Committal proceedings for the thirteen people so far charged in connection with the robbery were held at Linslade Magistrates' Court between 26 September and 2 December 1963. The courtroom in Linslade was nowhere near large enough to cope with both the demands of the proceedings and the huge media and public interest, so the new Aylesbury Rural District Council Chamber was altered to accommodate the hearing.

Those appearing in the dock on 26 September were Roger Cordrey, William Boal, Renee Boal, Charlie Wilson, Ronnie Biggs, James Hussey, Tommy

Wisbey, Leonard Field, Brian Field, Robert Pelham, Mary Manson, Alfred Pilgrim and May Pilgrim. By the time the proceedings were concluded, the number of those appearing in the dock had significantly increased.

Martin Harvey

On 1 October, Martin Harvey, the brother of Ronald Harvey, a known associate of Bob Welch, was visited by the police. During a routine search of his house in Dulwich, South East London, banknotes amounting to £518 were discovered. According to Harvey, he had been paid £200 to mind the cash for an unnamed member of the train robbery gang. He was arrested and taken to Scotland Yard where he made a statement under caution.

The following day, Harvey was taken to Aylesbury where he appeared at Linslade Magistrates' Court charged with receiving the £518 in banknotes knowing them to be stolen.

Harvey became the fourteenth person to be charged for offences connected to the mail train robbery. It was not long before fourteen became fifteen.

Gordon Goody

Thanks to the perseverance of Ian Holden, the police believed they now had the forensic evidence they needed to put Gordon Goody at Leatherslade Farm. His alibi, that he had been in Ireland with his mother on 8 August when the robbery had taken place, was shown to be false when police discovered that he had actually returned to the UK on 6 August.

On 3 October, Goody presented himself at Putney police station as per the conditions of his bail. He must have had a sense of foreboding when he saw that Tommy Butler and one of his assistants, Detective Chief Inspector Peter Vibart, were both waiting to interview him. Butler quickly got down to business and showed Goody a pair of size 10 brown suede shoes made by Trueform and asked him if he recognised them. Goody looked them over before confirming the shoes were his. When Butler asked if they had ever been lent to anyone else, Goody replied 'Of course not'. [1]

Butler then informed Goody that he was to be taken to Aylesbury where he would be charged with conspiracy to stop a train with intent to rob. The next day, Friday 4 October, Goody appeared at the committal proceedings, joining the fourteen men and women already sitting in the dock.

Butler and the Flying Squad were delighted to finally get the man they knew to be one of the major players in the mail train robbery. As for Goody, his concerns that the police would try to fit him up appear to have been justified. He was one hundred per cent certain that the suede shoes had been in his wardrobe gathering dust at The Windmill pub in Blackfriars all the time he had been at Leatherslade Farm.

Walter and Patricia Smith

On 10 October, acting on information received, three Flying Squad officers searched a flat in Shoreditch in the East End of London, the home of bookmaker Walter Smith and his wife Patricia.

During the search, 363 one pound notes and 65 five pound postal orders were discovered, and Mrs Smith had another 470 one pound notes hidden in the clothes she was wearing.

According to Walter Smith, he had been asked to launder the money by an unnamed man, and for doing this he was to receive a shilling for every £1 he was able to change up.

The Smiths were arrested and taken to Aylesbury where Walter Smith was charged on two counts of receiving and Patricia Smith was charged on one count. The next day, the pair appeared at Linslade Magistrates' Court where they were both granted bail.

John Wheater

A week later, on 17 October, John Denby Wheater, the 41 year old solicitor from Ashtead in Surrey, was arrested by Fraud and Flying Squad officers on two charges; conspiracy to stop a mail train with intent to rob, and 'well knowing that one Leonard Denis Field had stolen 120 mailbags, did comfort, harbour, assist and maintain him.' [2]

It would have come as no surprise to Wheater when, at 7:40am, he opened his front door to find Tommy Butler, Detective Sergeant Pritchard, and Chief Inspector Mesher of the Fraud Squad, standing on his doorstep with a warrant for his arrest and to search the premises. After all, his assistant Brian Field, and his client Leonard Field, had both been in custody for over a month, a month during which Butler and his colleagues would have been carefully compiling the evidence and the case against Wheater.

Wheater's attempt to mislead the police over a current address for Leonard Field was also to come back to haunt him when Butler informed him 'that it was alleged that he had concealed the identity of the purchaser of the farm in that he had given the address of his client as 150 Earls Court Road knowing this to be false'.

After completing the search of the family home where a number of items were taken away by the police, Wheater was then taken to his offices in Westminster which were also subjected to a thorough search.

Following this, he was taken to Scotland Yard, and then on to Aylesbury Police HQ where he was formally charged.

The next day, he appeared at Linslade Magistrates' Court where he was informed that he would be required to attend the next session of the committal proceedings. However, he was granted bail in the meantime.

Bob Welch

Bob Welch had been staying at a rented farmhouse in Beaford, North Devon since the middle of September. As well as being visited by fellow robber Frank Munroe, Welch had the company of some of his closest friends including Daniel Pembroke, Ronald Harvey (Martin Harvey's brother), John Sturm and Charles Lilley, all considered as possible suspects for one reason or another by the police. [3]

Welch was unaware that the local police had the farmhouse under surveillance, on the instructions of Scotland Yard, in the hope that someone such as Bruce Reynolds, John Daly or Buster Edwards might pay him a visit. However, as time went on, this became less and less likely.

By mid-October Welch had decided that the only option to retain his freedom was to go abroad and, with the help of Frank Munroe, he managed to obtain a passport in a false name.

With a date set for his departure, Welch decided to go up to London to see his brother for what could be the last time for a long while. [4]

Unfortunately for Welch, a police informant contacted Frank Williams and told him that Welch would be meeting his brother at London Bridge railway station at around 9:00pm on Friday 25 October. As a result there was a strong police presence at the station when Welch arrived.

As he greeted his brother, and the pair moved towards a waiting car, Williams stepped in. In his report of the arrest Williams said of Welch that '*He stood absolutely still with a look of blank astonishment on his face. He was dumbfounded and had difficulty in speaking when I told him who I was.*' [5]

Welch was taken to Scotland Yard where he was interviewed by Williams and Tommy Butler. During the questioning, Welch denied ever being at Leatherslade Farm or knowing any of the train robbers, apart from Tommy Wisbey and James Hussey.

After Welch's finger and palm prints were taken, they were compared with those found at Leatherslade Farm, and a match was made with a palm print on a half empty Pipkin beer can discovered in one of the kitchen cupboards at the farm.

The following day, Welch was taken to Aylesbury Police HQ where he was formally charged, to become the 19th person arrested with offences relating to the mail train robbery.

Of those charged, only 7 had been involved in the robbery itself, although the police believed that tally to be eight as they included William Boal amongst their number.

The farmhouse in Beaford where Welch and his friends had been staying was raided by officers from the Flying Squad and the local Devon Constabulary, but to their disappointment, no money or incriminating evidence was found despite a very thorough search.

CHAPTER 12
The Review of the Evidence

The purpose of the committal proceedings, which took place in Aylesbury between 26 September and 2 December 1963, was to review the evidence against each of those charged to ensure that it was sufficient to send them to trial by jury.

Those appearing in the dock when proceedings began were Roger Cordrey, William and Renee Boal, Charlie Wilson, Ronnie Biggs, James Hussey, Tommy Wisbey, Leonard Field, Brian Field, Robert Pelham, Alfred and May Pilgrim and Mary Manson.

After making the opening speech for the prosecution, Mr Howard Sabin told the court that police enquiries were still actively under way across the country, and as a result, it was agreed to adjourn the hearing until 4 October.

By the time proceedings resumed, Gordon Goody and Martin Harvey had joined the ranks of those sitting in the dock listening to accounts of the robbery given by train driver Jack Mills, his assistant David Whitby and GPO sorting officer Thomas Kett.

However, none of the three could identify any of the accused since the robbers had been wearing balaclavas at all times.

Ten days after appearing at the hearing, Jack Mills was presented with a certificate for bravery and a cheque for twenty-five guineas (equivalent to around £500 today) from British Railways. [1]

On 7 October, police officers from Bournemouth gave details of the arrests of Roger Cordrey and William Boal and the subsequent admission by Cordrey that the £141,218.1s.3d found in their possession had come from the train robbery.

However, Cordrey told the hearing that he had not been involved in the robbery and that he and Boal were simply minding the money for one of the actual robbers. At that stage the evidence against the pair was circumstantial since no fingerprint evidence had been produced to prove that either had been at Leatherslade Farm.

At the committal proceedings on Monday 28 October, fifteen had become nineteen with the arrival in the dock of Walter and Patricia Smith, John Wheater and Bob Welch.

Prosecution witnesses appearing that day included Bernard Rixon, the owner of Leatherslade Farm, and John Aherne, who had found the bags of cash in woods near to Dorking.

The committal proceedings were temporarily suspended so that identity parades could be set up. These took place on 20 November when none of the accused were picked out by witnesses despite Brian Field, Gordon Goody, Charlie Wilson, Bob Welch and William Boal each having to attend two parades. [2]

The last session of the committal proceedings took place on Monday 2 December and was notable for the surprise withdrawal of the charge of receiving against Mary Manson. Mr Sabin advised the chairman of the bench that the prosecution would not be proffering any other charges against her.

Although a known associate of Bruce Reynolds, Sabin told the bench that no evidence had been produced to connect her in any way to the crime. Reynolds, he said, was simply a man with whom she went to the garage (to purchase the Austin Healey) and no more, and that the prosecution could not prove that any of the money that came from her bag had come from the train robbery. [3]

That was the end of the good news, as Sabin asked that the rest of the accused be committed for trial on the basis of the charges that had been placed before the court, although Renee Boal, Alfred and May Pilgrim, Robert Pelham, Martin Harvey, Patricia and Walter Smith and John Wheater were all granted bail.

The trial was set for 13 January 1964 at the Buckinghamshire Winter Assizes at Aylesbury, despite requests from the defence that it should heard at the Old Bailey.

Compliments were then paid by the chairman of the bench to Prosecuting Counsel and to the police for the '*competent way in which the case had been presented.*' [4]

CHAPTER 13
The Early Christmas Presents

The Arrest of John Daly

Despite the trial date having been set, Flying Squad officers were still relentlessly pursuing John Daly, Roy James, Bruce Reynolds, Buster Edwards and Jimmy White.

It was now almost four months since the Travelling Post Office had been robbed and many people believed that the longer time went on, the less likely it was that the remaining gang members would be brought to justice.

However, an early Christmas present was delivered to Tommy Butler in the shape of John Daly on 3 December.

Daly and his wife Barbara had been living in the basement flat of a house in Eaton Square, Belgravia, owned by Godfrey Green, a small time thief. Whilst there, they were known as Mr and Mrs Grant and to complete the charade, John lost four stone in weight and grew a beard in an effort to alter his appearance, whilst conversely Barbara piled on the pounds as she was pregnant with the couple's second child.

As for his share of the money from the robbery, that had been sent to an apparent safe place in Cornwall by Green, along with John and Barbara's first child – a necessary separation as the police searching for Daly were on the lookout for a family of three, rather than just a man and his wife.

Frank Williams was aware that Daly was holed up somewhere in Belgravia, but on 3 December he received confirmation of the actual address from an informant.

When Butler and Williams knocked on the door of the flat, it was opened by the heavily pregnant Barbara Daly. John was siting on a settee in his pyjamas and a red dressing-gown. At first, he tried to keep up the pretence that his name was Paul Grant, but when Detective Inspector Williams reminded him that they had met before, Daly replied *'Hello Mr Williams, I'm caught.'* [1]

Butler informed Daly that he was to be taken to Scotland Yard for questioning as his fingerprints had been found at Leatherslade Farm – not strictly true as his prints had been discovered on a Monopoly board game that was found at the farm, along with those of Ronnie Biggs and Bruce Reynolds.

As expected, Daly denied ever having been at the farm, and whilst he was on route to the Yard, police officers conducted a thorough search of the flat, but found nothing of any relevance to their investigation. Later that evening Daly was taken to Aylesbury Police HQ where he was formally charged.

After her husband's arrest, Barbara Daly was collected by her brother and taken away from the flat where a large group of reporters had begun to congregate. She went to stay with Mary Manson, and three days after Christmas she gave birth to a little boy who weighed in at a very healthy nine pounds. [2]

On 4 December, a now clean shaven John Daly appeared at Linslade Magistrates' Court where he was remanded in custody pending further enquiries. When asked if he had anything to add, Daly simply replied, *'It is all lies.'*

The Windfall

Just after 6:30pm on 10 December, the Flying Squad received an anonymous phone call informing them that cash stolen during the train robbery was about to be left in a telephone box in Great Dover Street, South East London.

Even though they expected this to be just another in a long line of hoax calls, Frank Williams and Tommy Butler set off in Butler's mini. However, this time they hit the jackpot, and there in the phone box were two large sacks tied up with string, bulging with banknotes. Williams and Butler looked around to see if they could pick out anyone watching them, but it was a dark evening and no-one appeared to be particularly interested in the two policemen. With other fish to fry that evening, Williams and Butler couldn't afford to hang around for too long and got back into the mini with the sacks in the back.

When they arrived back at Scotland Yard the sacks were examined by Forensic Science technicians as well as the Fingerprint boys who took away the empty sacks and the top two and bottom two notes of each bundle of cash.

The cash was kept under guard overnight and the next morning a bank cashier was brought in to count it. His tally was £46,844 which, when added to the notes taken away for examination, brought the final cash count to £47,245.

When he left the Yard, the bank cashier took away 57 five pound notes, and when the serial numbers were checked, they were identified as being part of the consignment sent to the mail train by the Kirkcudbright and Dunoon branches of the National Commercial Bank of Scotland Limited.

Later that day, the Fingerprint Department reported that there were no prints on either the banknotes or the sacks, although the Forensic Department was able to advise that the sacks and the cash had been buried in the ground at some stage. [3]

As to who deposited the cash in the phone box, and why, has never been established and there are several theories as to the motives. The most likely is that it was a quid pro quo by one of the robbers still at large (Jimmy White or Buster Edwards), or by one of the three never identified (Bill Jennings, Alf Thomas and Frank Munroe), in return for the police closing their investigation on him. We will probably never know for sure.

The Capture of Roy James

The other fish to fry that evening for Tommy Butler and Frank Williams was Roy James, who had stayed at the Putney home of his bookmaker friend until the end of September. There he had lived as a virtual prisoner, only leaving the house on essential business. During that time, James's major concern was his share of the robbery which was being looked after by a friend of Charlie Wilson's. Once Wilson had been arrested, James became afraid that his money would disappear along with Wilson's friend.

It was only after threatening to get some serious muscle involved that James got his cash back, minus a £7,000 minder's fee. [4]

At the beginning of October, James moved into a flat at 14 Ryder's Terrace, St Johns Wood – a short walk from Lord's Cricket Ground and Regent's Park, and just three miles from the Flying Squad offices.

As with his previous hideaway, James initially lived as a recluse, hardly ever venturing outdoors.

After a while, having grown a beard to change his appearance, he took to going out for an evening walk around Regent's Park. His enforced solitude helped him to come to the decision that he would, at some stage, have to give himself up – possibly after the trial of his fellow robbers as by then he would know what length of sentence he could expect to receive. He was also missing contact with his mother and not being involved with motor racing, the other love of his life.

However, matters were taken out of his hands when, during the afternoon of 7 December, the Flying Squad received an anonymous call that James could be found at 14 Ryder's Terrace. The identity of the caller was never established, but may have been the wife of his bookmaker friend whose amorous advances James had spurned during the time he stayed with the couple at their Putney home. [5]

Following the call, Detective Sergeants Slipper and Nevill were delegated to recce Ryder's Terrace to make sure there was no way that James could slip from their grasp since he had a reputation for being a more than competent cat-burglar. The recce also included a very detailed examination of the building plans of the property, and whether there were any escape routes available to James, such as sewers and tunnels.

Whilst they were carrying out their covert activities, Slipper and Neville discovered an area of waste ground that looked as if it had been dug over recently, down to a depth of several feet, immediately beneath a flat roof. Was this a perfect landing zone for someone trying to escape from either Ryder's Terrace or the adjacent Blenheim Terrace? [6]

The arrest of Roy James was set for 8:00pm on 10 December and began when a WPC knocked on the door of number 14. Police immediately saw the curtains move as James looked out to see who was calling.

Instinct told the robber that this was the moment he had feared for the last four months. But he didn't want it to be this way. If he was going to be arrested, he wanted it to happen when he and he alone had decided that the time was right.

Sensing that James was about to do a runner, Flying Squad officers forced an entry into the flat just in time to see him disappearing through a fanlight, hanging on to a holdall.

Police gave chase across the roofs and with some 40 officers surrounding the house, James's chances of escaping were practically zero, although desperation seemed to have spurred him on.

The inevitable end came when James jumped down from the flat roof, pausing only to throw his holdall down first. Both he and the bag landed on the very patch of ground he had prepared for this eventuality. However, unfortunately for James, several detectives were also waiting for him, although even then he still tried to avoid their grasp, only to fall when he slipped on wet grass.

When the holdall was opened, police found it stuffed full of banknotes, although James denied that the bag had anything to do with him.

He was taken to Scotland Yard and questioned by Tommy Butler. When asked where he had been on 7/8 August, the night of the train robbery, he replied that nobody could remember that far back, and that he hadn't been at the farm he'd read so much about. [7]

After his interview with Butler, James was taken to Aylesbury Police HQ where he was formally charged. When searched, £131.10s was found on him, and two of the notes were identified as being amongst those stolen from the train. In addition to this, the cash in the holdall totalled £12,041 – the equivalent of around £230,000 in today's terms.

Committal Proceedings

On New Year's Eve 1963, committal proceedings for John Daly and Roy James were held at Linslade Magistrates' Court.

As with the earlier proceedings, Howard Sabin set out the case for the prosecution. Despite both Daly and James denying they had ever set foot on Leatherslade Farm, Sabin told the court that Daly's prints had been found on the Monopoly set, and James's prints had been found on a Pyrex dish and on a page of a movie magazine. Both had gone into hiding immediately after the robbery, and had also taken steps to alter their appearances. Not, argued Sabin, the actions of innocent men.

On top of that, two five pound notes found on James had been identified as belonging to the Inverness Branch of the National Commercial Bank of Scotland sent to London via the mail train.

It is fair to say that the police and the prosecution were confident of securing guilty verdicts on both men when the matter came to trial. However, in one instance, much to the surprise of everyone, including the individual concerned, they were to be disappointed.

CHAPTER 14
The Trial

As most of the UK celebrated the arrival of the New Year, nine of the men that had been party to the raid on the mail train were in prison, on remand, awaiting trial. The police count was ten, since they had no doubts that William Boal was at Bridego Bridge in the small hours of 8 August, along with fellow detainees Roger Cordrey, Charlie Wilson, Ronnie Biggs, James Hussey, Tommy Wisbey, Gordon Goody, Bob Welch, John Daly and Roy James.

Of the others, Alf Thomas and Frank Munroe had been interviewed and released without charge, whilst Bill Jennings and Pop had completely slipped beneath the police radar.

As 1963 gave way to 1964, the focus of attention for the Flying Squad was Bruce Reynolds, Buster Edwards and Jimmy White.

By now, Reynolds had left the one bedroom flat above the cleaner's shop in Thornton Heath, and had bought a cottage in Albert Mews, Kensington, which he described as '*the perfect spot, a tiny dog-leg of a street with a narrow entrance that you could easily miss. Even with an A-Z it was almost impossible to find*'. [1]

Edwards was still at 'Sunnymede', the house he was renting for £20 a week in Wraysbury, Buckinghamshire. The house backed on to the Thames which offered him an escape route should it become necessary, albeit a fairly slow one!

However, on 3 January 1964, a large yacht named Christine, registered to an Edward Anderson who police believed to be an associate of Edwards, was reported as missing after setting sail from Ramsgate in Kent. A rubber dinghy was later found tied to a buoy seven miles out of Broadstairs, also in Kent.

Reporters from the *Daily Express* subsequently tracked Anderson down to Dublin and he told them that a Dennis Bassett had hired the boat for himself and two others. On 12 February, Bassett's body was discovered on a Belgium beach, and on 1 March the *Sunday People* ran a story which quoted Anderson as saying that the yacht had been carrying two of the train robbers, one of which was Buster Edwards, together with a million pounds in cash from the robbery.

However, at the subsequent inquest, the truth of Anderson's story was questioned, and the police concluded that it was a decoy organised by Edwards to take the heat off him. [2]

As for Jimmy White, he had moved to Mansfield, whilst his wife, Sheree, had gone to stay at an army base in Aldershot with a friend whose husband had been posted overseas.

For all three, life on the run wasn't all it was cracked up to be.

The Trial Begins

The Trial proper began on 20 January 1964 with Mr Justice Edmund Davies presiding, a Welshman not exactly known for his leniency. All of the accused were handcuffed and then locked in a separate compartment in a Black Maria for the ten minute journey from the prison to the court. Just in case any of the robbers were contemplating escape, at least four police cars and a dozen or so police motorcycle riders accompanied them every day.

The morning session would begin at 10:30am with the court bailiff calling '*All rise*', as Mr Justice Davies entered the chamber. At the end of the first session, the robbers would return to prison in the Black Maria for lunch, and at around 2:00pm would return to court for the afternoon session which began at 2:30pm. This routine was repeated every day of the trial which was to last 51 days and would include the presentation of 613 exhibits and see 240 witnesses called to give evidence.

On the first morning, those travelling under police escort were joined in the dock by those who had been granted bail – Renee Boal, Martin Harvey, Robert Pelham, Arthur and May Pilgrim, Walter and Patricia Smith and John Wheater. The cases against all but Wheater were 'put down' to be heard at a later date.

Also removed from the dock that first morning was Roger Cordrey who had decided to plead guilty to conspiracy and receiving, although he continued to deny that he had taken part in the actual robbery.

This left twelve men on trial sitting in two rows of six – William Boal, Charlie Wilson, Ronnie Biggs, Tommy Wisbey, Bob Welch and James Hussey in the front row, and John Daly, Roy James, Gordon Goody, Brian Field, Leonard Field and John Wheater in the row behind. [3]

The jury was all male and drawn from the residents of Buckinghamshire with each given a file containing various documents, maps and photographs.

Inevitably, the courtroom was crowded, with all 60 seats in the public gallery filled, as were those reserved for members of the press who came from all over the world to sit beside the foremost reporters to be found in London's Fleet Street.

The Case for the Prosecution

The prosecution team was led by Arthur James QC whose opening address began on 20 January and lasted for 10 hours in total. Whilst there was no evidence to link any of the accused to the actual scene of the crime, the crux of the case for the prosecution was proving that Leatherslade Farm had been used as a hideaway in the immediate aftermath of the robbery, and then, using forensic and fingerprint evidence, being able to place nine of the accused at the farm at the appropriate time.

The prosecution case against the remaining three defendants, Brian Field, Leonard Field and John Wheater, was based on being able to connect all three to the farm through their involvement with its purchase immediately prior to the robbery.

The first prosecution witness to be called, on the third day of the trial, was Jack Mills, the driver of the train. Five and a half months had elapsed since the robbery, but the physical consequences of the ordeal he had suffered in the early hours of 8 August were there for all to see. Looking much older than his 57 years, Mills was allowed to sit rather than stand in the witness box, and there is no doubt that his appearance and frailty had a profound effect on both judge and jury.

However, as the defence would remind the court, Mills was unable to identify any of the defendants as being involved either in the robbery or in the assault on him.

Also called by the prosecution were assistant driver David Whitby and members of the Post Office sorting team who gave graphic details of the violent attack on them by members of the gang as they broke into the HVP coach.

On day five of the trial, the prosecution began by outlining the case against William Boal. When he gave evidence, Boal told the court that he had been beaten up at Bournemouth police station and that he had never said some of the statements police had attributed to him. Boal's defence counsel asked that Roger Cordrey be brought back to court to substantiate his client's submissions.

However, acting on the advice of his counsel, Cordrey refused to return to court. Were he to confirm Boal's innocence to the court, he would then be asked by the prosecution if any of the other defendants in the dock were also innocent. If he refused to answer this question, it would imply all the others were guilty, and since he would never grass on a fellow criminal, silence was his only option particularly since his counsel believed that Cordrey would forfeit the 'brownie points' he had built up with the court by being the only gang member to have pleaded guilty.

In effect, Cordrey was between a rock and a hard place.

Sadly for Boal, despite knowing that he was at no stage involved in the planning and execution of the robbery, none of the other train robbers spoke up on his behalf either. In their eyes, it was every man for himself.

The prosecution case against Boal was further strengthened on day thirteen of the trial (5 February) when Dr Ian Holden presented his evidence. Speaking first about the small watch winder found in Boal's jacket pocket, Holden told the court that the yellow paint found on this was identical in composition to the yellow paint found at Leatherslade Farm.

As for the yellow paint found on the shoes belonging to Gordon Goody, Holden told the court that the odds of the paint not originating from that found at Leatherslade were a million to one against, adding that '*this is why I said it was highly improbable you would get it from anywhere else.*'

However, in his interview to the *Observer* newspaper in 2014, Gordon Goody claimed that the shoes in question '*weren't the shoes I'd worn for the train. I wore desert boots. They took my brown suede shoes and they appeared at court, complete with yellow paint. The judge knew I'd been fitted up.*' [4]

If public interest in the trial had diminished a little as the trial formalities dominated proceedings, an event the following day, day fourteen, put the trial back onto the front pages of all British newspapers.

Whilst giving evidence for the prosecution, Detective Inspector Basil Morris of Surrey Police, stationed at Reigate, told the court that when interviewing Ronnie Biggs at his home on 24 August 1963, he asked Biggs if he knew any of the gang who the police wished to interview in connection with the mail train robbery.

Morris said Biggs had replied, '*I know Reynolds, I met him when we were doing time together.*' [5]

In order to be seen to have received a fair trial, it is imperative that a jury is unaware if an accused has a criminal record. In quoting Biggs as saying that he had met Bruce Reynolds whilst they were both in Wandsworth Prison, Detective Inspector Morris had inadvertently let it slip that Biggs had at least one previous conviction to his name, a conviction serious enough to have landed him in jail.

As a result of this error, the jury was instructed to leave and Biggs's counsel, Wilfred Fordham QC, after briefly discussing the matter with his client, asked the judge to discharge Biggs without a verdict, pending a trial in front of a new jury. The judge had no option other than to grant the application and Biggs left the court to be taken back to Aylesbury jail to await a date when a new trial would take place.

In his autobiography *Odd Man Out*, Biggs revealed that '*I nursed a hope that my lawyers could arrange for the venue of my trial to be changed – perhaps to the Old Bailey – where friends could possibly 'get at' someone on the jury to hold out for a not guilty verdict.*'

Unfortunately for Biggs, he learnt that his new trial was to take place on 8 April in the same court, in front of the same judge, but with a completely new jury.

The case for the prosecution came to an end on Tuesday 11 February, the seventeenth day of the trial, and the jury were not in court for the next couple of days whilst the various defence counsels made submissions on behalf of their clients that there was no case to answer. All but one submission was rejected by Mr Justice Davies, the one exception being that presented by Mr Walter Raeburn QC on behalf of John Daly.

The only evidence of Daly's involvement in the robbery tendered by the police were the fingerprints found on the Monopoly set used by the gang whilst they were at Leatherslade Farm. Mr Raeburn argued that there was no evidence when these prints were left – they could easily have been left during an innocent game of Monopoly played some considerable time prior to the robbery.

After considering the matter overnight, the following morning, Friday 14 February and day twenty of the trial, Mr Justice Davies recalled the jury and instructed them to acquit Daly.

John Daly left the court a free man and was driven back to Aylesbury prison to collect his belongings from the cell where he had spent the last 79 days. From there he was reunited with his wife Barbara and the couple's two children, the youngest having been born whilst Daly had been on remand.

The Case for the Defence

As well as the acquittal of John Daly, Friday 14 February 1964, also marked the beginning of the case for the defence. The closing speeches were not concluded until Saturday 14 March, the fortieth day of the trial.

The defence counsel for William Boal, Mr W.A. Sime QC, was aware that his client would get no support from any of the train robbers. Even Roger Cordrey, who had enticed Boal to assist him in the days following the robbery, said absolutely nothing in defence of his so-called friend.

When Boal was called to the witness box by Mr Sime he told the court that on the day of the robbery he had received a National Insurance cheque amounting to £8.16s.6d to cover the time when he could not work due to suffering from an attack of dysentery. He had taken the cheque, which was dated 7 August 1963, to his local post office the following day. [6]

Understandably given the circumstances, Boal continued to protest his innocence, even to the point of claiming that he knew nothing about the £141,218.1s.3d that the police found in his and Cordrey's possession when they were arrested. Almost certainly the jury found his claims of innocence difficult to swallow.

The prosecution cases against James Hussey, Tommy Wisbey and Bob Welch were based on their fingerprints being found at Leatherslade Farm. Hussey's palm print had been found on the tailboard of the Austin lorry, Wisbey's was found on a chrome bath rail and Welch's on a half empty Pipkin can of beer.

The defence case was based on trying to prove to the jury how the prints of the three men could have been left at the farm, without any of them having been involved in the robbery. The story that they came up with involved Hussey being asked to accompany a friend called Ronnie Darke on a delivery of fruit and veg to Oxfordshire on Saturday 10 August – two days after the robbery. The lorry containing the food was to be left at the destination point and Hussey, following the lorry in his car, would then give Darke a lift back to London.

Hussey informed the court that he told Darke that he couldn't do the job, but had suggested that Wisbey and Welch might like to do the trip in his place. Before the three men left, Hussey said that he had reached into the back of the lorry to take an apple, and so this must have been how his palm print came to be on the tailboard.

When Darke, Welch and Wisbey arrived at the property in Oxfordshire they found it to be a farm, but didn't see anything to suggest that they were at the hideaway used by the train robbers. Before doing the return journey to London by car, Wisbey said that he used the bathroom, which was how his palm print ended up on the bath rail.

When it came to his turn, Welch explained that, as a former licensee, he had picked up the Pipkin beer simply because he had never seen one before.

When Ronnie Darke was eventually called to appear as a defence witness, he corroborated the story and even gave Hussey an alibi for the day of the robbery telling the court that Hussey had been at his house that day. However, Darke was not the most convincing of witnesses and the jury almost certainly found the whole story a bit too far-fetched.

On Wednesday 19 February, day twenty three of the trial, counsel for Roy James called several witnesses to give evidence in support of his client. One of those was a London black cab driver called Derek Brown who told the court that he had picked James up from the Bagatelle Club in London at 2:30am on 8 August, took him back to his flat and stayed there drinking tea with James until 4:00am. Taken at face value, this appeared to provide James with a strong alibi – he couldn't have been in two places at once.

However, when cross-examined by counsel for the prosecution, Brown admitted that he had visited James on seventeen occasions whilst he had been on remand at Aylesbury Prison, giving him ample opportunity to perfect his story. More crucially, James decided not to go into the witness box, and therefore no explanation was given as to how his fingerprints had been found at Leatherslade Farm on a blue edged glass plate, a Johnson's traveller's kit, and on a page from an American magazine called *Movie Screen*.

The following day, it was the turn of Mr Sebag Shaw QC to offer the defence on behalf of his client, Gordon Goody. Mr Shaw explained that Goody had gone to ground in the immediate aftermath of the train robbery, not because he was guilty of any involvement, but because he was being hounded by the press.

Mr Shaw also pointed out that no fingerprint evidence had been proffered by the prosecution linking Goody to Leatherslade Farm, that none of the stolen money had been found in his possession and that he had not been picked out at two identity parades. In fact, as he told the jury, the prosecution case had been built solely on the paint found on a pair of shoes owned by Goody, which Goody was adamant had been in his wardrobe for several months, gathering dust back at The Windmill pub in Blackfriars, until they were removed by police on Friday 23 August – over a fortnight after the train robbery had been committed.

When asked by Mr Shaw whether he could account for how the paint got onto the soles of his shoes, Goody said he couldn't. However, throughout his defence, the jury was left in no doubt that Goody believed the paint was applied to his shoes whilst they were in police custody.

Although the defence also called upon expert witnesses, the best they could do was to say that the paint on the shoes could have come from the paint found at Leatherslade Farm, rather than it definitely hadn't. And, when the prosecution recalled Dr Holden, he refuted any suggestion that the shoes might have been tampered with whilst they were within his care.

Charlie Wilson, like Roy James before him, also decided against going into the witness box. Instead, he opted for his legal right to say nothing, nor offer an explanation in response to statements made by the prosecution that his finger and palm impressions were found at Leatherslade Farm on a window sill in the kitchen, on a drum of Saxa salt and on a cellophane wrapping from a Johnson's traveller's kit, also found in the kitchen.

Known in the USA as 'taking the fifth amendment', it is inevitable that some members of the jury took Wilson's non-appearance in the witness box as an indication of guilt. Indeed, when sentencing Wilson, Mr Justice Davies told him that '*No-one has said less than you throughout this long trial. Indeed, I doubt if you have spoken a half a dozen words. Certainly no repentance has been expressed by you.*' [7]

On 24th February, the 26th day of the trial, Lewis Hawser QC began his defence of Brian Field. When in the witness box, Field accepted that two of the four bags containing banknotes from the robbery, that were found in woods near Dorking on 16 August, did in fact belong to him.

However, he told the court that he had lost both bags some weeks before the train robbery when they had disappeared from the offices of James & Wheater. A secretary working at the law firm corroborated Field's story.

Field also accepted that he had lied to Tommy Butler on the day he was arrested when, having been brought face to face with Leonard Field, he told Butler that Leonard looked like the man who accompanied him on the viewing of Leatherslade Farm, but that it wasn't actually him. His explanation for this lie was that, at that time, he was tired, confused and anxious not to be embroiled in something he was innocent of.

Field also told the court that Leonard Field had come to see him armed with Estate Agents details of Leatherslade Farm and told him that he was interested in buying it and wanted to view it before making up his mind – hence the reason why Brian had agreed to accompany him to the farm on the day they both met Mrs Rixon.

Brian Field said that it was after this visit that he had passed Leonard over to John Wheater since conveyancing was Wheater's main occupation. [8]

The remainder of Mr Hawser's defence of Brian Field was a procession of people paying testament to his client's good character.

The penultimate defence heard by the jury was that of Leonard Field which began on Friday 28 February. Field was represented by Michael Argyle QC who wasted no time in getting his client into the witness box, where he remained for the rest of the day.

The trial resumed on Monday 2 March (1964 being a leap year) with Leonard Field once again in the witness box. However, rather than continuing along the lines of what he had told the jury three days earlier, Leonard Field now admitted that he had lied to them about certain matters when giving his evidence, and therefore he was guilty of committing perjury. In doing so, he almost certainly destroyed any remaining credibility with the jurors.

According to Leonard, he had originally been told by Brian Field that Leatherslade Farm was to be used to hide stolen cigarettes, and that he would be given £12,000 in return for allowing his name to be used as the purchaser on the contract of sale.

However, after sitting in court for more than thirty days, he realised that, if found guilty as charged, he was facing more than just a 'slap on the wrist', and also realised he would get no help whatsoever from either Brian Field or John Wheater who, he said, had lured him into 'fronting' the purchase of the train robbers hideaway.

Leonard Field now told the court that Brian Field had informed him on 9 August, the day following the robbery, that Leatherslade Farm had been used by the train robbers and that he and John Wheater would make sure that he was not implicated in any way. He now claimed that Brian also told him to keep away from the law firm's offices and that he would get a considerable sum of money if he did what he was told.

Throughout the time he was giving evidence, Field continued to insist that he had had absolutely nothing to do with planning the robbery, nor the actual robbery itself, and that his only mistake was to trust Brian Field and John Wheater.

When Brian Field was recalled to the witness box, he of course denied every aspect of Leonard's new testimony.

The final defence that this particular jury heard was that conducted by Graham Stanwick QC on 3 March 1964 on behalf of John Wheater. Mr Stanwick began proceedings by calling character witnesses, including Paul Bryan, his former commanding officer and now a Member of Parliament and Vice Chairman of the Conservative Party, and Brigadier Geoffrey Barrett, director of Army Legal Services. [9]

The court was informed that Wheater was mentioned in despatches whilst in action with the Royal West Kent Regiment and that he was later awarded an MBE for services in the field.

Whilst Wheater had acquitted himself well during his time in the army, the picture painted by his defence team was of a civilian life far less noteworthy, and that he was in fact totally unsuited to a legal career. Wheater himself admitted in court that many of his clients probably suffered as a result of his carelessness, and members of his staff went on to paint a picture of a chaotic and untidy office, due in no small measure to their employer's poor administrative abilities and forgetfulness.

The Summing Up

The closing speeches on behalf of each of the accused by their counsels began on Tuesday 10 March and lasted until Saturday 14 March. Mr Justice Davies began his summing up on the following Monday, although this was delayed when one of the jury informed the court that he had been approached by someone unknown to him who had offered him money if he could persuade his fellow jurors to pronounce not guilty verdicts when the time came.

Despite this, the judge, anxious to avoid a retrial, issued a warning to all twelve jurors, advising them that '*We are going to get a verdict in this case.*'

Resuming his summing up, even though Mr Justice Davies had told the jury that he would not be reviewing each item of evidence that had been presented during the trial, his speech still lasted six days and extended to over 250,000 words. [10]

On Friday 20 March, having informed the jurors that their homes and families would receive round the clock police protection whilst they were sequestered, he announced that his summing up would be concluded by the following Monday.

True to his word, just after 3:30pm on Monday 23 March, the jury decamped by coach to the Grange Youth Club in Aylesbury to deliberate and, hopefully, reach a verdict.

Whilst the jury was *incommunicado*, Mr Justice Davies agreed that four separate trials would start on 8 April for Martin Harvey, Robert Pelham, Renee Boal, Arthur Pilgrim, May Pilgrim, Walter Smith and Patricia Smith, all of whom were accused of receiving money from the train robbery.

As it happened, these trials didn't start until 16 April, after the conclusion of the re-trial of Ronnie Biggs.

At 8:15pm on Wednesday 25 March, the jury reached their verdicts on each of the accused. Mr Justice Davies was informed and the court was convened at 10:30am the following day for those verdicts to be delivered.

CHAPTER 15
The Verdicts and the Trial of Ronald Biggs

'*M*embers of the jury, are you agreed on your verdicts?'
'*We are*' replied the foreman of the jury, who then delivered the unanimous verdicts on the ten accused standing in the dock facing him:

.

- William Boal – guilty of conspiracy to rob and robbery
- Charlie Wilson - guilty of conspiracy to rob and robbery
- James Hussey - guilty of conspiracy to rob and robbery
- Tommy Wisbey - guilty of conspiracy to rob and robbery
- Leonard Field – guilty of conspiracy to rob and conspiracy to obstruct justice
- Brian Field - guilty of conspiracy to rob and conspiracy to obstruct justice
- Gordon Goody - guilty of conspiracy to rob and robbery
- John Wheater – guilty of conspiracy to obstruct justice
- Bob Welch - guilty of conspiracy to rob and robbery

- Roy James - guilty of conspiracy to rob and robbery

As they left the dock to be taken back to the Hospital wing of Aylesbury Prison to await sentencing, Mr Justice Davies informed them that sentencing would not take place until the conclusion of the trial of Ronnie Biggs which was scheduled to start on 8 April.

That trial, in front of a new jury, was to last just 5 days.

Biggs's defence was based on an alibi provided by Norman Bickers, an old cell-mate. So the story went, Bickers had been invited to take part in a 'bit of business' at a place called Leatherslade Farm and Biggs tagged along as he needed £500 towards the purchase of the house he and his wife Charmian were renting in Redhill.

However, when the pair got to the farm, they found it deserted, but noticed what looked like military vehicles parked up in one of the outbuildings. At this point, according to Biggs, they got cold feet and decided to head back to London. As they were hungry, they decided to make themselves a quick meal from the mountain of food they discovered in the kitchen – hence how Biggs's fingerprints came to be found on a Pyrex plate and on a bottle of tomato ketchup.

Biggs said he also found a Monopoly set in one of the rooms, and not having played the game for years, decided to open it and have a look inside – leaving his fingerprints behind in the process.

In his autobiography, Biggs admits that this story was pretty pathetic.[1] However, to make matters worse, when Bickers was called to give evidence on Biggs's behalf, he had mysteriously disappeared. Even a private detective was unable to find him.

Despite his counsel's best efforts to convince the jury that his client was totally innocent of any wrongdoing, they didn't need too much time to come to the unanimous decision that Biggs was guilty of conspiracy to rob and robbery.

The guilty ten had become eleven.

CHAPTER 16
The Sentencing

On Thursday 16 April 1964, the eleven convicted men were joined by Roger Cordrey, who had pleaded guilty, and then taken by Black Maria to the holding cells in the basement of Buckinghamshire's Crown Courthouse to await sentencing.

It took Mr Justice Edmund Davies, cloaked in his crimson gown, just 32 quiet minutes to pass sentences totalling over 300 years.

The first to learn his fate was Roger Cordrey.

Reading from his prepared notes, Mr Justice Davies spoke directly to Cordrey. '*You are the first to be sentenced out of certainly eleven greedy men whom hope of gain allured. You and your co-accused have been convicted of complicity in one way or another in a crime which in its impudence and enormity is the first of its kind in this country. I propose to do all in my power to ensure it will also be the last of its kind.*

'*To deal with this case leniently would be a positively evil thing.*

'*When arrested, you immediately gave information to the police which enabled them to put their hands on nearly £80,000 and the remainder was eventually recovered. Furthermore, at the outset of this trial you confessed your guilt and I feel I should give recognition to that fact.*'

Roger Cordrey was sentenced to 20 years for conspiracy to rob, 20 years for receiving £56,037, 20 years for receiving £79,120 and 20 years for receiving £5,060 with all four sentences to run concurrently. He was found not guilty of robbery.

As the sentence was delivered, there were gasps of astonishment from the packed courtroom. If Cordrey received a 20 year sentence after having pleaded guilty, what sentences could the others expect?

Cordrey was taken down to a cell away from the other prisoners, and his place in the dock was taken by William Boal, who, at that stage, had no idea of the sentence handed out to his erstwhile friend.

Wasting no time at all, Mr Justice Davies told Boal, '*You, substantially the eldest of the accused, have been convicted of conspiracy to rob a mail train and of armed robbery. You have expressed no repentance for your wrongdoing. Instead you continue to assert your innocence but you beg for mercy. I propose to extend to you some measure of mercy. I do this on account of your age and because having seen and heard you I cannot believe that you were one of the originators of the conspiracy or that you played a very dynamic part in it or the robbery itself. Your participation in any degree, nevertheless, remains a matter of extreme gravity.*'

William Boal was sentenced to 21 years for conspiracy to rob, and 24 years for robbery, with both sentences to run concurrently.

One can only guess how Boal must have felt as he was led away from the dock. Twenty four years in prison for a man whose only crime, as Ronald Biggs put it in his autobiography, '*had been to give Roger* (Cordrey) *a lift and help him hide the money.*' [1]

Boal was replaced by Charlie Wilson to whom Mr Justice Davies said, '*No one has said less than you throughout this long trial. Indeed, I doubt if you have spoken half a dozen words. Certainly no word of repentance has been expressed by you. If you or any of the other accused still to be dealt with, had assisted justice, that would have told strongly in your favour.*

'*The consequence of this outrageous crime is that the vast booty of something like £2,500,000 still remains entirely unrecovered. It would be an affront to the public if any one of you should be at liberty in anything like the near future to enjoy those ill-gotten gains.'*

Charlie Wilson was sentenced to 25 years for conspiracy to rob and to 30 years for robbery with both sentences to run concurrently. He was taken down to join Roger Cordrey and William Boal.

The procession continued with Ronnie Biggs the fourth to face the Judge who told him that *'Yesterday you were convicted on both the first and second counts of this indictment. Your learned counsel has urged that you had no special talent and you were plainly not an originator of the conspiracy. Those submissions I bear in mind. I do not know when you entered the conspiracy or what part you played. What I do know is that you are a specious and facile liar and you have this week perjured yourself time and again.'*

Biggs was sentenced to 25 years for conspiracy to rob and to 30 years for robbery, with both sentences to run concurrently.

To say that Biggs was less than impressed with his sentence, and the Judge that delivered it, is an understatement. *'The old boy's totally off his rocker, I thought to myself. Only spies get locked away for thirty years. With remission for good behaviour, I calculated, it meant that I was looking to do at least twenty years in the nick. Twice the amount of bird you might get for bumping somebody off, for Christ's sake.'* was how he described it in his autobiography. [2]

It was then the turn of the remaining members of the South Coast Raiders to learn their fate – Tommy Wisbey, Bob Welch and James Hussey.

Mr Justice Davies told Wisbey that *'In your case, again, I have no evidence on which I can measure the degree or quality of your participation in the vast criminal enterprise which has given rise to this trial. Your counsel has urged you are plainly not a dominant character and the part you played was subsidiary and was perhaps connected with transport matters. You yourself have thrown no light on that or any other topic. You have not thought to mollify the court by any repentance.'*

The Judges' comments to Welch were in a similar vein. *'You have been convicted on the first and second counts of this indictment. Your counsel has urged on me that there is no evidence of any sudden flow of money into your pockets or when you joined the conspiracy or what you actually did. Those and all other matters and your antecedents I have sought faithfully to bear in mind.'*

And James Hussey found that his previous criminal record did him no favours as Mr Justice Davies informed him that *'You have previously been convicted of grave crimes including two involving violence. On the other hand, I accept that as a son you are warm hearted. It is obvious you have qualities of personality and intelligence which you have put to very good stead in this case.'*

All three were sentenced to 25 years for conspiracy to rob and to 30 years for robbery, with both sentences to run concurrently.

The eighth member to be sentenced was Roy James.

He was told by Justice Davies that '*You are the only one out of all the accused in respect of whom it has been proved you actually received a substantial part of the stolen money. You still had £12,000 in your possession, and I have no doubt the original sum far exceeded that figure. Your record in the past is a bad one. Corrective training seems to have done you little or no good; yet you have the ability of a kind which would have assured you an honest livelihood of substantial proportion, for in a very short space of time you had what your counsel described as a brilliant and meteoric success as a racing driver.*

'*I strongly suspect it was your known talent as a driver which enabled you to play an important part in the preparation of this grave crime. It may be that you have never personally resorted to physical violence. You have told me you went to Leatherslade Farm knowing you were doing wrong, that you became involved, but not in the robbery, and then ran away. I don't find it possible to differentiate your case from most of the accused.*'

It came as no surprise to James when he too was sentenced to 25 years for conspiracy to rob and to 30 years for robbery, with both sentences to run concurrently.

Gordon Goody was the 9th in the dock, and the 8th of those that were actually at Bridego Bridge on 8 August 1963. Before confirming the length of the sentence to be imposed, Mr Justice Davies told Goody that '*In some respects you present one of the saddest problems in this trial. For you have manifest gifts of personality and intelligence which could have carried you far had they been directed honestly. I have not seen you in this court for three months without noticing signs that you are a man capable of inspiring the admiration of your fellow accused. You have become a dangerous menace to society.*

'*The Crown has said they don't consider this criminal enterprise was the product of any mastermind. I don't know that I necessarily agree with the Crown in that respect and I strongly suspect you played a major role both in the conspiracy and the robbery. Suspicion, however, is not good enough for me anymore than it would be for a jury. It would, therefore, be quite wrong for me to impose any heavier sentence on you than on the other accused, and I will not do so. You will go to prison for concurrent terms of 25 years on the first count* (conspiracy to rob) *and 30 years on the second* (robbery).'

In 2014, in an interview with the *Observer* newspaper, Goody suggested that during the course of the trial, the Judge had developed a begrudging admiration of him. '*The Judge knew I'd been fitted up. But I had the worst record of them all. He said I was the saddest case in front of him, and said my powers of leadership would have won me medals in a war. Then he pulled a 30 stretch.* [3]

The final three to be sentenced were Brian Field, Leonard Field and John Wheater.

To Brian Field, Mr Justice Davies said '*Your strength of personality and superior intelligence enabled you, I strongly suspect, to obtain a position of dominance in relation to your employer John Wheater. I entertain no serious doubts that you are in no small measure responsible for the disastrous position in which this wretched man now finds himself.*

'You are one of the very few convicted persons in this trial of whom it can be said with any degree of certainty what it was you were able to contribute to the furtherance of crime. Whether it was a product of your mind or of Leonard Field or of some entirely different person that originated the idea of acquiring the possession of Leatherslade Farm with the subterfuge that it was wanted for purely honest means, I have no way of knowing.

'Whether it was simply a remarkable coincidence that two of the bags found in the Dorking Woods were yours or whether they might have been evidence of your duplicity, I have no means of knowing, but I accept the jury's verdict. That you played an essential role in the major conspiracy is clear. Out of that there naturally flowed the later conspiracy to obstruct justice.'

Brian Field was sentenced to 25 years for conspiracy to rob and 5 years for conspiracy to obstruct justice with both sentences to run concurrently.

His namesake Leonard Field replaced Brian in the dock, and the words of Mr Justice Davies quickly made it apparent that he too was facing a lengthy custodial sentence. *'Not only have you perjured yourself repeatedly in this trial to save your own skin, but on your own showing at one stage you perjured yourself in an endeavour to ruin the accused, Brian Field.*

'How and when you entered the major conspiracy I do not know. Whether you joined it at the instigation of another, again I do not know, but an overt act committed by you in pursuance of that conspiracy is established beyond doubt and very important it was.

'I cannot agree with your learned Counsel that your part in acquiring possession of Leatherslade Farm may properly be described as a small contribution to the criminal enterprise. On the contrary it was a vital contribution. Once having joined the major conspiracy, the lesser conspiracy to obstruct justice was a natural outcome.

'I can see no valid grounds for differentiating your case from Brian Field. You will accordingly be sentenced to concurrent terms of 25 years on the first count (conspiracy to rob) *and 5 years on the twelfth count* (conspiracy to obstruct justice).

And then there was just one more to be sentenced and that was John Denby Wheater, owner of the legal practice James & Wheater. It was perhaps fitting that Wheater was the twelfth and final person to stand before Mr Justice Davies to learn what the future held for him. Whatever the outcome, Wheater knew that he would never practice law again, the Law Society would see to that.

Judge Davies summed up the contradiction that was John Wheater in his opening remarks. *'Your case is in many respects the saddest and most difficult of all. You have served your country gallantly in war, and faithfully in peace. There is no evidence that you contributed to your present disastrous position by* *profligate living of any kind. Indeed your standards seem to have been distinctly lower than your managing clerk (*Brian Field)*. Your conviction on count 12 (*conspiracy to obstruct justice*) establishes, as I interpret the verdict that sometime after the robbery the criminal purpose became clear to you as indeed it must have done. You could then have given the police vital information. A decent citizen would have volunteered to do that thing whatever his strictly legal obligations might be. Instead of assisting justice you were obstructing it and that at a time when speed was of vital concern to the forces of law and order.*

'Why you participated in it, I don't know. You have not told me, and your learned Counsel has been able merely to hazard a guess. Whether or not all the facts, if known, would speak in your favour or to your prejudice, I have no means of telling and must not speculate. But I am disposed to accept the view that you allowed yourself to be overborne in some manner by your more able and masterful managing clerk. Such conduct on the part of any citizen is gravely blameworthy. Criminality is grave when operated by an officer of the Supreme Court. That fact must weigh heavily against you.'

Wheater was sentenced to 3 years in prison for conspiracy to obstruct justice.

The day's proceedings did not end there for Mr Justice Davies as there were still charges of receiving outstanding on Renee Boal, Martin Harvey, Robert Pelham, Alfred and May Pilgrim and Walter and Patricia Smith.

Renee Boal, Alfred Pilgrim and May Pilgrim all pleaded not guilty to receiving and elected to stand trial together. With no evidence offered by the Prosecution, Mr Justice Davies directed the jury to return not guilty verdicts and the three were discharged.

Robert Pelham, the car mechanic who worked for Roy James, pleaded guilty to receiving £545 in £1 notes which the police had found in a brown paper bag when searching Pelham's house in Notting Hill. Pelham was adamant that the money was in payment for a new engine he had supplied and fitted for James.

After hearing Pelham's plea, Mr Justice Davies told him, *'I am disposed to think that no public good will be served by sending you, a man with no previous convictions of any kind, to prison, despite the gravity of this offence.'* Pelham was granted a conditional discharge and, much to his relief, he walked out of court a free man.

Next, it was the turn of husband and wife Walter and Patricia Smith to face the music. When police searched the Shoreditch home of Turf Accountant Walter Smith on 10 October 1963, his wife Patricia had been found with 470 one pound notes hidden in her clothes. A further £688 was found in the flat and in total Walter was charged with receiving sums totalling £2,000.

According to Walter, he had been asked to launder the money by an unnamed man, for which he was to receive a shilling for every £1 laundered.

Walter Smith pleaded guilty and Patricia Smith pleaded not guilty.

In a surprising turn of events, Mr Justice Davies discharged Patricia. However Walter was remanded in custody and subsequently sentenced to 3 years for receiving £1,000 and 3 years for receiving a further £1,000 – both sentences to run concurrently.

Finally, Martin Harvey, who had pleaded guilty to receiving £518 from an unnamed member of the train robbery gang, was sentenced to 12 months in prison.

And so a trial that had lasted 51 working days, with evidence from 264 witnesses, came to an end. In addition there were 2,350 witness statements and over 1,700 exhibits. The words spoken in court filled in excess of 30,000 foolscap pages and the cost of the trial was estimated to be just under £40,000, equivalent to around £650,000 by today's standards.

The reaction to such draconian prison sentences delivered by Mr Justice Davies had much of the country in an uproar. To many, the long sentences seemed disproportionate to the crime. To others, the train robbers simply got their just desserts.

The *Daily Sketch* on Friday 17 April 1964, the day following the sentencing, carried the headlines '**30 YEARS - ALL BRITAIN ARGUES IS THIS TOO HARSH?**' And *Sketch* reporters wrote '*Thirty years. Too Severe? Or fair enough? The argument raged all over Britain last night after 30 year sentences were passed on seven men in the Great Train Robbery.*

Some people thought the robbers asked for what they got. Others compared the 30 year sentences to those passed in murder cases and cases of sexual offences against children.' [4]

To Bruce Reynolds, watching the news on the television with wife Frances at their Kensington bolt hole, the 30 year sentences were at least twice what he thought his friends and fellow robbers would actually get at the hands of the British judiciary, and it was then that he realised that he could no longer remain in hiding in the UK. [5]

CHAPTER 17
The Appeals

After sentencing, the convicted robbers were sent off to different prisons around the country, no doubt in a state of shock given the length of the sentences. Even with full remission, those serving 30 years would not be released until 1984 at the very earliest. With nothing to lose, appeals were lodged by the counsel's for each of the twelve, and these were scheduled to begin on 6 July 1964.

Before the appeals were heard, Bruce Reynolds, having obtained a false passport in the name of Keith Clemens Miller, left England on 4 June in a private aeroplane bound for Ostend. After a night in Ostend, Reynolds boarded a flight for Mexico via Toronto and arrived in Mexico City at 7:00pm on 6 June. Frances Reynolds and their son Nick eventually joined Bruce in Mexico at the end of July, having travelled under the names Angela and Kevin Green.

Buster Edwards also realised that a long sentence faced him if caught and he too started exploring the possibility of quitting the UK. However, June Edwards faced a real dilemma. Going abroad was the last thing she wanted, but she couldn't contemplate a life without her husband. As far as Buster was concerned, the outcome of the forthcoming appeals would be the deciding factor. If the sentences were reduced significantly, he would seriously consider giving himself up to Detective Inspector Frank Williams – Williams and Edwards had carried on a dialogue through intermediaries since the robbery, with the policeman trying to broker a deal whereby Edwards would surrender to him in return for a lighter sentence. [1]

Like Reynolds and Edwards, Jimmy White was stunned at the 30 year prison sentences. By now, he had been reunited with his wife Sheree and their young baby, and the three were living at Crown Edge Farm on the outskirts of Glossop in Derbyshire, bought with the help of two of his friends, Henry Isaacs and Alfred Place. However, in June 1964, Isaacs was sent to prison for fraud and White feared that it was only a matter of time before a forensic examination of his friend's business dealings would lead the police to Crown Edge Farm.

Once again, the Whites went on the run.

Despite the satisfaction of seeing the majority of the train robbers now behind bars, Tommy Butler had absolutely no intention of resting on his laurels. His sole aim in life now became the arrests of Reynolds, Edwards and White – and woe betide anyone who got in his way.

The Appeals, heard in front of Mr Justice Fenton Atkinson, Mr Justice Lawton and Mr Justice Widgery, began on Monday 6 July 1964. Mr Justice Atkinson gave the appellants little cause for optimism when he stated early on that *'Last year's £2,500,000 raid was warfare against society and an act of organised banditry touching new depths of lawlessness. In our judgement severe deterrent sentences are necessary to protect the community against these men for a long time.'*

The first batch of appeals on behalf of Ronnie Biggs, Gordon Goody, Roy James, James Hussey, Bob Welch, Charlie Wilson and Tommy Wisbey, were dismissed. Leave to appeal to the House of Lords was also refused to all seven.

On Thursday 9 July, it was the turn of Brian Field and to everyone's surprise, not least of all Field himself, his appeal against the conviction for conspiracy to rob was allowed. This left only the conviction of conspiracy to obstruct justice, but the appeal against this was dismissed. However, this still represented a real result for Field. When he returned the following week for sentencing, Field walked into court with a 25 year sentence around his neck, and then floated out of court with just a 5 year sentence to serve. With full remission, he could look forward to being released within three years.

And the good luck extended to Leonard Field as his appeal against his conviction for conspiracy to rob was also allowed. The rationale behind that decision was that '*No facts had been established that he knew of the intention to stop and rob the train.*'

As with Brian Field, Leonard's appeal against his conviction for conspiracy to obstruct justice was dismissed, but he too walked out of court with a prison sentence reduced from 25 years to just 5 years.

However, there was no such good fortune for John Wheater whose appeal against his conviction for conspiracy to obstruct justice was dismissed.

The final appeals were those submitted on behalf of Roger Cordrey and William Boal.

William Boal had been charged with conspiracy to rob, robbery and three charges of receiving. His appeal against the conviction for robbery was allowed when the counsel for the Crown, Mr Arthur James QC, admitted that the prosecution was now '*unhappy about Boal's case*' since the scientific evidence at the trial had turned out to be inconclusive.

However, his appeal against the conviction for conspiracy to rob was dismissed, and whilst his overall prison sentence was reduced from 24 years to 14 years, it still represented a gross injustice. Had justice prevailed, Boal should have been sentenced to no more than 3 years on the three counts of receiving. With full remission, he would have served just 2 years leaving him a free man to enjoy the remaining years of his life.

If Boal was guilty of anything, it was of naivety in allowing himself to be manipulated by his so called 'friend' Roger Cordrey.

Having pleaded guilty to conspiracy to rob and three counts of receiving, Roger Cordrey was appealing against the length of his prison sentence (20 years) and not his conviction. His appeal was allowed and his sentence reduced to 14 years, the same as William Boal.

It is difficult not to feel compassion for William Boal and his family. Whilst Cordrey was fully involved in the planning and execution of the robbery, Boal had not become involved until several days after the robbery had taken place. That both men should end up serving identical sentences was desperately unfair.

CHAPTER 18
The Great Escaper

Just over a month after his appeal was dismissed, Charlie Wilson escaped from Winson Green Prison in Birmingham. At the time of his escape, at around 3:00am on the morning of 12 August 1964, Wilson had served just seventeen weeks of his thirty year sentence.

Whilst most prisoners shared a cell with two others, Wilson had a cell all to himself. Being on maximum security, his cell light was kept on at all times, and a warder would check on him at regular intervals through a spyhole in the door.

The gang of three men involved in 'springing' Wilson from the prison were believed to have taken a ladder from an adjacent builder's yard which they then used to climb over the perimeter walls from a nearby mental hospital.

Once into the main yard, they opened several doors with duplicate keys, which suggested that they had had inside help when planning their audacious raid. On their way to Wilson's cell block, they came across 50 year old prison officer William Nichols who they knocked unconscious before tying him up and gagging him. With the way clear they opened the door to Wilson's cell, gave him a balaclava, a black sweater, dark trousers and plimsolls to change into, and then retraced their steps – locking every door behind them.

They were in and out within the space of just a few minutes.

Prison Officer Nichols was freed at around 3:20am, but a call to the local police wasn't made until almost 4:00am as Nichols and his colleagues believed Wilson and the three intruders were still in the building as all the doors were still locked. [1]

By the time the police arrived, Wilson had been free for almost an hour and was well away from the prison by then.

News of Wilson's escape reached Bruce Reynolds in Mexico and he was delighted that his old friend had put one over on both the police and the UK Establishment. *'Nice one, Chas! Charlie's success filled me with pride. We'd finessed the Establishment yet again; they had thought it was all over, the dust had settled, but now the storm was raging again. The Press took it up, hounding the Home Secretary, the prison authorities and the police. They wanted blood. How could a notorious criminal serving what amounted to a double life sentence for robbery escape from saturation security in a maximum-security prison?'* [2]

Henry Brooke, the Home Secretary at the time, was on an official trip to the Channel Islands, but returned to London immediately he received news of the escape and ordered an inquiry to begin at once. In the meantime, prisons holding the rest of the train robbers were ordered to double up on their security arrangements, roadblocks were set up on motorways, and airfields and ports all over the UK were put under surveillance.

Later in the day, the secretary of the Prison Officer's Association told a news conference that security arrangements should have been enough to meet all normal requirements. *'But'* he added, *'today's happenings are abnormal. It seems likely that somehow or other a master key has been obtained which allowed these people to effect a simple entry to the prison after scaling the wall.'*

Less than impressed with this explanation was Tommy Butler. As well as tracking down Bruce Reynolds, Buster Edwards and Jimmy White, he now had Charlie Wilson to add back to the list once again.

There are several theories as to the identity and motives of the three men who were responsible for Wilson's escape from Winson Green. Of these, one has Wilson effectively being kidnapped by them in return for a share of the mail train money – the vast majority of which has never been recovered.

The News of the World newspaper ran a story that the three men were ex-Special Forces who had trained at a high walled castle in France to replicate the obstacles they would face when they did the job for real.

This story also had a converted petrol tanker waiting outside the prison with Wilson climbing inside and then the hatches being battened down. [3]

However, according to Bruce Reynolds, who knew him better than most, Wilson had been planning an escape for some time and his three rescuers were all old and reliable friends. The main man was indeed a Special Forces veteran, who had been a member of the BOAC robbery gang in November 1962. As Reynolds put it, 'He was truly one of our own.'

His two accomplices were also ex-military. [4]

There is also speculation as to where Wilson went immediately after his escape. The most likely scenario is that as a Londoner, having been born in Battersea, he headed back to a safe house in Knightsbridge, despite the fact that he had become Britain's 'most wanted', and that all of his known associates and old haunts would be trawled by Tommy Butler and the Flying Squad.

With his wife and family being watched closer than anyone else, there was obviously no chance of Charlie trying to contact them.

Having left Crown Edge Farm following Henry Isaacs's imprisonment for fraud, Jimmy White was on the run again with wife Sheree and their young son. However, with the help of Joanna Isaacs, Henry's wife, the Whites were able to find some stability in their lives when they moved into Pett Bottom Farm, a farmhouse Joanna rented on their behalf near Folkestone, Kent.

Much to Tommy Butler's frustration, once the media attention on Charlie Wilson's escape had quietened down, the trail which he had hoped would lead him to Bruce Reynolds, Buster Edwards, Jimmy White and Charlie Wilson, was growing progressively colder. Little did Butler know at the time, but during 1965 that number would increase from four to five.

CHAPTER 19
The Second Great Escaper

Jack Mills was undoubtedly a very brave man who had put himself at risk in an attempt to stop the train robbers taking control of his engine on 8 August 1963.

In January 1965, for this act of bravery, Mills received a payment of £250 from Anthony Wedgwood Benn, the Postmaster General, equivalent to around £4,400 today (2015). A month later, Mills received another £250, this time donated by the clearing banks. I think it fair to say that these awards were fairly derisory for a man who was never the same again after the physical injury and the psychological trauma he had suffered at the hands of the robbers.

Once the appeals for the principal members of the train robbery gang had been dismissed in July 1964, and the thirty year prison sentences remained unaltered, Buster Edwards knew that his only option was to follow Bruce Reynolds to sunnier climes. In February 1965, Edwards sent a message to Reynolds, via a mutual friend, to sound him out as to whether it was ok for Buster, June and their daughter Nicolette to join Bruce, Frances and Nick Reynolds in Mexico City.

Only a handful of people knew Reynolds was in Mexico, and there was always the risk that word would get around that not one, but two of the remaining train robbers were together in the same place, even though, at that time, there was no extradition treaty between Mexico and the UK.

However, on balance, Reynolds felt that the risks were well worth taking for his old friend, and the message went back to Buster that he and the family would be more than welcome. A month or so later, Jack and Pauline Ryan, along with their daughter Kate, arrived in Mexico City.

Around the same time, Charlie Wilson, after the best part of 8 months lying low at his safe house in Knightsbridge, acquired a passport in the name of Ronald Alloway, and crossed the channel on the Dover to Calais ferry. At Calais he was picked up by a friend who drove him to the South of France.

Later on in 1965, Wilson, still using the same alias, surfaced in the French-speaking town of Rigaud, which is about 50 miles outside of Montreal in Canada. Six months or so later, he was joined in Rigaud by his wife Pat and their three daughters. Pat had sold the family home in Clapham and had gone off the police radar, having left no forwarding address!

Unbeknown to Tommy Butler, at that time three of the four he was hunting were now out of the country.

The Dorking Wood Mystery is Solved

However, earlier in 1965, Butler had been able to tie up one loose end when, acting on a tip-off, he and Detective Sergeant Nevill visited Reginald Field, Brian Field's father, at Mr Field's home in Whitton, Middlesex.

According to Mr Field, in August 1963 he had found '*a holdall, an embossed leather case, a brief case and a round leathery sort of hat box*' in his garage. Inside these he had found bundles of cash which he realised must have come from the train robbery.

His statement continued, '*I had no idea how they came to be in my garage. I decided that the best thing to do was to get rid of it as soon as possible. As I had no car I had to give the matter a lot of thought because there was too much to carry. Eventually, I thought of Gordon Neal who lives in Blanford Avenue and who had grown up with my son. I told him that I had found some money in my garage which I felt sure had come from the train robbery, and asked if I could borrow his car to go and get rid of it. Gordon volunteered to drive the car for me. I put the money in the car and we drove out to Dorking where I threw the money out of the car and we continued our journey and came home. I feel sure that I dumped the money at about 11:00pm on the night before it was found at a place I know to be Leaf Hill, Dorking.*

'*I want to get this off my chest as it has been playing on my mind for a long time and it has been making me ill. Now I have told you about it, I wish to God I had done so before.*'

Gordon Neal corroborated Reginald Field's statement.

In his report, Tommy Butler made the point that the money found was less than the total share received by Brian Field and that someone removed part of the cash before the rest was dumped in Dorking Wood. Butler's report continued '*Although there is no evidence to prove it, there are firm grounds for believing that Brian Field accompanied his father and Neal to Dorking. His presence would have probably been insisted on by both.*' [1]

Neither Reginald Field nor Gordon Neal ever faced prosecution.

By summer 1965, the Great Train Robbery was considered a bit 'old hat', having been replaced in the public and media interest by the activities of two violent London gangs – the Krays from East London and the Richardsons from South London. However, all that was to change on 8 July.

Biggs goes over the Wall

Whilst in Wandsworth Prison, Ronnie Biggs had been befriended by Paul Seabourne, a prisoner who was coming to the end of a four year sentence. Biggs, at this time, was getting tired of the extra security measures that had been put in place on all the train robbers following Charlie Wilson's escape from Winson Green Prison, and felt that going over the wall was now his only option, if it could be arranged by someone on the outside.

After Seabourne's release, Biggs arranged for him to be given £10,000, part of which he spent on an old removal lorry. Seabourne cut away the top of the roof and built a scaffold tower inside which could be raised to reach the top of a 20 foot prison wall. He also got hold of an axe, a rope ladder and two shotguns, and hired some extra muscle, each paid £2,500. [2]

The escape was set for Wednesday 7 July. The plan needed Biggs to be in the exercise yard at 3:00pm, but unfortunately a heavy shower just beforehand meant that exercise that afternoon had to be taken indoors rather than outside.

Although the escape team was already in place outside the prison wall, they hadn't drawn any attention to themselves so it was just a matter of postponing everything for 24 hours.

Fortunately the sun was shining the following afternoon, and the converted lorry, painted a bright scarlet, and a green Ford Zephyr, parked up in a private road outside the prison wall just before 3:00pm.

A couple of minutes later, one of the prison officers supervising the exercise saw a head covered by a stocking suddenly appear at the top of the wall. Before he had time to react, there was a shout, two ladders were unfurled and a second figure appeared at the top pointing a shotgun at the exercise yard.

As well as Biggs, three others made for the ladders and as prison officers tried to stop them they were blocked off and wrestled to the ground by several prisoners who were being paid to cover the backs of the escapees.

Watching things unfold from her bungalow was Mrs Winifred Williams, the wife of a prison officer. '*I got to the door and saw the red van backing and the Zephyr following it. I saw a man get out of the van. He had a silk scarf over his head and tied on top; it looked like a coconut. I thought 'He's springing someone.' There was a platform on top of the van and something was going over the wall from it. It must have been the ladder. The man was quite stockily built, with blue overalls on.*

'*Then I looked at the Zephyr. A man came out with a silk stocking over his head, with a scarf and a peaked cap. I noticed he had a rifle. I thought 'This is where I go in'. I went in quickly and shut the door and bolted it, because there was nothing I could do to help.*

'*After I calmed down, I looked through the bedroom and saw two prisoners coming over the wall. I only saw two. They were dressed in blue overalls and striped shirts: prison uniform. I took the number of the Zephyr down and handed it in....I didn't know whether to dive under the bed when it happened. I am still petrified. This was so well organized.*' [3]

The green Ford Zephyr was later found abandoned a mile away from Wandsworth Common railway station whilst the red removal lorry was left at the scene. When the local police arrived, they found overalls and a loaded shotgun inside.

Four prisoners escaped that afternoon; Biggs, Robert Anderson (serving 12 years for conspiracy to rob a sub-postmaster), Eric Flower (12 years for armed robbery) and Patrick Doyle (4 years for conspiracy to rob).

Of the prisoners left behind in the exercise yard, five were later found guilty of helping Biggs to escape, and had their sentences increased.

Immediately after the escape, Biggs, Paul Seabourne and Eric Flower were taken to a first floor flat in a semi-detached house in Dulwich. According to Biggs, later on in the day he was moved to a flat in Bermondsey, where he stayed for a week or so, and from there he went to a '*spacious apartment in Camberwell.*' [4]

Later that day, the Home Secretary, Sir Frank Soskice, visited Wandsworth Prison accompanied by the police officer leading the investigation into the escape, Detective Chief Superintendent Lewis, who told reporters '*It was engineered without a doubt, with collusion inside the prison.*'

A few days later, police arrested Paul Seabourne who was subsequently sentenced to 4 and a half years for the part he played in helping Biggs escape.

Inevitably, with two train robbers now having escaped, the security arrangements at the prisons holding the remaining robbers were considerably beefed up once again.

In Leicester Prison, Tommy Wisbey got on to the roof to protest about being confined to his cell for 23 hours a day. '*That's when Dad lost some of his remission and he got bread and water for his trouble*', wrote his daughter, Marilyn Wisbey. [5]

Tommy Wisbey was subsequently moved to the high security block at Durham Prison, where he was joined by Gordon Goody and Roy James.

Around about the time Biggs was going over the wall at Wandsworth, Jimmy White and his family were on the move once again, leaving Pett Bottom Farm for a flat at Claverly Mansions in Littlestone-on-Sea, on the South coast of Kent.

Two months after his escape, Ronnie Biggs also moved on again, this time to a house in Bognor Regis on the Sussex coast. However, his stay in Bognor was a short one, and in October he was taken to Antwerp by boat, and then driven to Paris. Four days after Christmas Day, he took a plane from Orly to Sydney via Zurich, using a passport in the name of Terence Furminger. It would be 35 years before Ronnie Biggs would set foot on British soil again.

CHAPTER 20
The First to be Released

John Wheater was the first of those sentenced in April 1964 to be released from prison. He regained his liberty on 11 February 1966 having completed two of the three year sentence he had received for conspiracy to obstruct justice. He was, of course, unable to return to his former profession since whilst he had been in prison, the Law Society's disciplinary process had banned him from ever again practicing law in the UK.

Shortly after his release, Wheater wrote two articles that appeared in the *Daily Telegraph*. Whilst there was little in these that could be called a revelation, Wheater did confirm that there were still several members of the gang at large who had never been publicly named nor apprehended by the police.

He also wrote that there was a link between the gang and an insider in the Post Office Security Department, who had made contact with one of the gang via a relative acting as an intermediary.

Forty eight years later, this was verified by Gordon Goody in the interview he gave to the *Observer* newspaper in September 2014. At the first meeting Goody and Buster Edwards had with Patrick McKenna, the Ulsterman, Goody had asked him for the source of his information about the Travelling Post Offices. He and Edwards were reassured when McKenna told them it was from a relative (either a brother or a step-brother) who worked for the Post Office. It later transpired that the Belfast born McKenna also worked for the Post Office.

After getting this off his chest, John Wheater is believed to have moved to Harrogate in Yorkshire where he ran the family laundry business. He died in 1985 aged 64.

CHAPTER 21
The End of the Road

The Arrest of Jimmy White

By April 1966, Jimmy and Sheree White, together with their young son Stephen, had been living in Littlestone-On-Sea for around 9 months. Here they had changed their names to Bob and Claire Lane and were living a fairly normal family life. However, always at the back of their minds, they knew that they were living on borrowed time. By now, just £3,000 of White's share of the robbery was left (equivalent to around £50,000 in 2015).

During his time on the run, the Flying Squad had received a large number of reported sightings of White, all of which turned out to be red herrings. However, at the beginning of April, the Squad had several calls suggesting a man answering White's description was living in Littlestone.

On 21 April, Detective Sergeants Slipper and Hyams made the short journey to the Kent coast to Claverly Mansions, and knocked on the door of Flat 4. It was the knock Jimmy White had dreaded for over two and a half years, but in a strange way it was something of a relief after all that time constantly looking over his shoulder, fearing someone may have recognised him.

After his arrest, White was taken to Hammersmith police station where he was interviewed by Tommy Butler who told him he was to be taken to Aylesbury, where he was subsequently charged with robbery and conspiracy to rob.

The following day he appeared before Linslade Magistrates and was remanded in custody.

Committal proceedings took place on 6 May and the trial of Jimmy White began on 16 June. After initially pleading not guilty to both charges, White had a change of heart after learning that the prosecution had fingerprint evidence that placed him both at Leatherslade Farm, and at the caravan in Boxhill where the police had found over £30,000 hidden away.

Whilst he continued with his plea of not guilty to the conspiracy charge, he decided to plead guilty to robbery. The prosecution accepted both pleas and White was sentenced to 18 years imprisonment – significantly less than the 30 years the majority of the robbers had received at their trials two years earlier.

Edwards faces the Music

Buster and June Edwards, together with their daughter Nicolette, had been in Mexico for some time when they heard the news that Jimmy White had been caught.

But when Buster learnt that White had received a much lighter sentence than other members of the gang, he began to mull over the possibility of doing a deal with the police to pave the way for a return to the UK.

The Edwards family had never really settled in Mexico and June, who had never been abroad before, was uncomfortable in their new surroundings and was desperately missing her friends and family, especially her mother. She was also concerned that daughter Nicolette was missing out on a UK education. On top of that, Buster's money was beginning to run out.

Before moving to Mexico, Edwards had had dialogue with Frank Williams via a third party, and a tentative agreement had been reached whereby Edwards would receive a lighter sentence if he gave himself up and, at the same time, returned a significant amount of the money he had received from the robbery.

The length of the sentences dished out to those convicted in March 1964, and the dismissal of their subsequent appeals, put the kybosh on any deal as far as Edwards was concerned at that time.

The difference with striking a deal this time around was that Edwards no longer had any money to bargain with. Despite this, he was still willing to take a chance that just his offer to surrender would be a strong bargaining point. This begged the question as to how badly did the police, and Tommy Butler in particular, want him behind bars?

Dialogue was reopened through the same third party as before, and encouraging noises were coming back to him from the UK, although no guarantees were given.

On Friday 16 September 1966, Buster, June and Nicolette bade their farewells to the Reynolds family and boarded the plane that would take them back to the London they had all missed so much.

At 1:00am on the following Monday, Frank Williams received a telephone call to say that Buster Edwards was ready and willing to give himself up. Williams rang his boss, Tommy Butler, who told him that this was probably just another in the long line of hoax calls they had had over the last three years. [1]

However, at the agreed time and place, Frank Williams found Buster Edwards waiting for him. After being cautioned by Williams, Edwards passed the Flying Squad man a statement which he had written earlier that read; '*For a long time now I've been going to give myself up. I was definitely going to come in, in a few weeks' time but now I'm glad that I've made it now.*

'*I didn't do the train robbery like people say I did. That's why I'm writing this because I want a fair deal.*

'*I didn't go up the farm until after the robbery had happened. My job was to clean it down and burn the rubbish. I did do a bit of this and you can call it panic if you like, but something happened at the farm and I got the wind up. This was because the job was so big that I could hardly believe it.*

'*Some money was left in the kitchen for me and I was to get more afterwards. I never did get it.*

'*Although people think I had a lot more, the truth is I didn't get very much. I have nothing left now, that's one of the reasons I've given myself up.*' [2]

Edwards was then taken to Scotland Yard where he was interviewed by both Williams and Tommy Butler who cautioned him once again. Later that day he was taken to Aylesbury police station where he was formally charged.

The committal proceedings were again held at Linslade Magistrates' Court, and as before, the press were present in large numbers. *The Daily Telegraph* informed its readers that '*since his arrest, Edwards had denied he took part in the robbery of the mail train. Superintendent Williams agreed...that Edwards had asserted he did not go to Leatherslade Farm...until after the robbery. He also agreed there was no other direct evidence connecting Edwards with the attack on the train.*' [3]

The trial of Ronald 'Buster' Edwards was held on 8 and 9 December 1966 at Nottingham Assizes before Mr Justice Milmo. Counsel for the Defence, Mr Bernard Caulfield QC, told the jury that they shouldn't think of Edwards as a master criminal and that his role, which was to clean up Leatherslade Farm after the robbers had left, was purely peripheral.

However, when the prosecution called train driver Jack Mills to take the witness stand, it would have been impossible for the jury not to have had feelings of deep sympathy for the man called to give evidence. Looking pale and unwell, the 61 year old Mills told the court that he had always enjoyed good health up to the time of the robbery, but that he had felt 'pretty awful' since then.

As well as the testimony from Jack Mills, the prosecution produced evidence to show that Edwards had left his prints on one of the Land Rovers found at Leatherslade Farm, and also on a bank wrapper that came from the High Value Package coach.

It didn't take long for the jury to return a verdict of guilty on both counts and on sentencing Edwards to 12 years for conspiracy to rob and 15 years for robbery, with the sentences to run concurrently, Mr Justice Milmo told him,

'You have been convicted on overwhelming evidence of a crime which shocked every person in this country....You played for high stakes and punishment must, in the public interest, be severe.

' I deal with you on the footing that you were in on this at a very early stage indeed, but nevertheless that you were not one of the leading planners, or a leader in the matter at all. I deal with it on the footing that you were in the hierarchy, if that is the proper word to use, somewhere below (Jimmy) *White.'*

15 years was longer than the 5 years Edwards had been hoping for, but was still 3 years less than Jimmy White had drawn and half of what the others had received. With full remission, he could be out in 9 years.

With Edwards and White now safely behind bars, only three names remained on Tommy Butler's list – Charlie Wilson, Ronnie Biggs and Bruce Reynolds.

CHAPTER 22
The Change of Scenery

The length of Buster Edwards's sentence shut the door on any thoughts Bruce Reynolds may have had about a return to the UK. As far as he was concerned, a deal where he would still get a fifteen year stretch was most definitely not a deal.

However, as well as missing Buster and June, Bruce and Frances Reynolds were struggling to make ends meet in Mexico. With no income to speak of to supplement his share of the robbery, he was rapidly running out of money. As a result, not long after Buster began his prison sentence, Bruce and Frances decided to up sticks, quit Mexico and head for Canada and Charlie Wilson.

They made the journey in their Cadillac and crossed the border to Canada the day before Christmas Eve, with Bruce presenting a passport in the name of Keith Miller, and Frances presenting hers and Nick's, which were still in the names of Angela and Kevin Green.

They were very impressed with Canada and the lifestyle that Charlie, Pat and their three daughters had adopted in Rigaud, and decided they would like to stay in the country. However, they thought it prudent not to settle in the same area as the Wilson's, so looked to put down some roots in and around Vancouver.

'After years of craving adventure, and living for the moment, I wanted to settle down and lead a normal life. I wanted a home, a job, Nick in school and a few quid in the bank' was how Reynolds put it in his autobiography. [1]

One problem though, was that their passports were in different names, so Reynolds got in touch with the person who had provided the first set of forged passports, and asked for a new set, this time to be in the names of George, Pauline and Kevin Firth. Having flown to Brussels to pick up their new identities, Reynolds wasted no time in lodging applications to live in Canada permanently.

However, weeks went by and nothing was heard, and Bruce and Frances were getting more and more agitated, particularly since they knew of other couples having their applications approved within a couple of weeks of submission.

In the end, tired and frustrated at the lack of progress with their application, and fearing there was more to it than just 'red tape', the Reynolds were soon on the move again. After saying their good-byes to Charlie and Pat Wilson, they caught a flight to the South of France.

In April 1967, Brian Field was released from prison, three and a half years after he had been arrested. Field was very lucky – in his case, the punishment certainly did not fit the crime.

After all, it was Field who had started the ball rolling when he introduced the robbers to Patrick McKenna, the Ulsterman, and at the very least, he should have served a lengthy term for conspiracy to rob since his appeal against that charge should never have been allowed.

Karin Field had returned to her native Germany shortly after the conclusion of her husband's trial. Whilst in prison, Brian divorced his wife after learning that she was expecting a child fathered by Wolfgang Lohde, a German journalist.

On release, Field changed his name to Brian Carlton and managed to slip off the radar to start a completely new life away from the journalists and the various criminals he had mixed with during his time as a solicitor's clerk.

However, the public would be reminded of the name Brian Field, and the part he played in the Great Train Robbery, one last time, under tragic circumstances, in 1979.

Leonard Field was released from prison in May 1967 and, like Brian Field, also went to ground.

Little is known about him other than he married his wife Pauline in 1976, and is thought to have died in 2005.

In July 1967 a new Criminal Justice Act was passed which was to have a major impact on the train robbers and, in particular, those that had received the 30 year prison sentences.

In order to reduce the ever increasing prison population, a parole system was introduced for convicts who had completed 12 months or one third of their sentence. Recommendations for parole were to be made by an independent review body. This reduced sentences in cases where further rehabilitation was thought to be ineffectual.

For the likes of Gordon Goody, Bob Welch, James Hussey, Tommy Wisbey and Roy James, this Act could potentially knock up to ten years off their sentences if the new Parole Boards deemed that keeping them in prison would not serve any further purpose and where it was felt that the prisoner could be safely released back into the community.

CHAPTER 23
The Sweet Smell of Success

Butler gets his man

Tommy Butler had been due to retire in 1967 on his 55th birthday. However, such was his obsession with catching the remaining train robbers still at large, that he managed to persuade Sir Joseph Simpson, the Commissioner of the Metropolitan Police, to defer his retirement so he could continue his pursuit of Charlie Wilson, Bruce Reynolds and Ronnie Biggs.

Frank Williams had been lined up to replace Butler as Head of the Flying Squad, but the deferment of Butler's retirement frustrated Williams to the point that he decided he couldn't wait any longer for Butler to go, and so he transferred over to Scotland Yard's Murder Squad.

This was probably the right move by Williams. There was a feeling amongst the hierarchy at Scotland Yard that Buster Edwards had got away with an unduly light sentence which was due, in no small measure, to the evidence Williams had given in his favour. Because of this, it was now highly unlikely that he would ever succeed Butler.

One major obstacle in the way of Butler's efforts to capture Wilson, Reynolds and Biggs was the fact that all three were, at the beginning of 1968, living abroad – Wilson was in Canada, Reynolds was in the South of France and Biggs was in Australia.

Keeping tabs on known associates of the three was standard procedure and in the case of Wilson, was eventually to pay dividends. Butler and the Flying Squad had been keeping a watch on one particular business partner for several months and he was eventually followed to Montreal. At this point, Butler requested that the Royal Canadian Mounted Police take over surveillance of the man.

When he arrived at Rigaud, the Mounties photographed him with Charlie Wilson and his family. They decided not to make an immediate arrest since they hoped that Bruce Reynolds might put in appearance at some stage. [1]

Eventually, it was decided to move in and arrest Wilson, and that privilege was given to Butler who flew over from London.

At precisely 8:00am on Thursday 25 January 1968, Wilson was on the point of taking his three daughters to school in his Pontiac Saloon when there was a knock on the door. The moment Charlie Wilson had been dreading had arrived. On his doorstep was Tommy Butler, backed up by a rather large number of Mounties. Game over!

After extradition formalities were completed, Butler flew back to London with Wilson handcuffed to his right wrist. On arrival at Heathrow, Wilson was taken to the high security wing at Parkhurst on the Isle of Wight, already home to fellow train robbers Gordon Goody, Roy James, Tommy Wisbey, James Hussey and Roger Cordrey.

Two down, one to go

The Great Train Robbery was back in the news with the arrest of Charlie Wilson, and Tommy Butler, reinvigorated by the satisfaction of putting Wilson back behind bars, was now pulling out all the stops to locate and arrest Bruce Reynolds and Ronnie Biggs, before he was made to retire by his bosses at the Yard. He knew he was on borrowed time so he needed to strike lucky as soon as possible.

Scotland Yard continued to receive tip-offs as to where Reynolds was now hiding, including one that suggested he was in the South of France – which, of course, he was. The Reynolds family were renting a small bungalow on the seafront in Sainte-Maxime, just a few miles from Saint-Tropez.

Photographs of Bruce and Frances, which had been taken whilst they were in Mexico, had been found at Charlie Wilson's house in Canada, so the Flying Squad had fairly up to date likenesses of both.

By now, with his cash rapidly diminishing, Reynolds decided the only option was for them to return to London to try to recover money that was owed to him, and, if possible, earn some more.

Ironically, the first month back in the capital saw them renting their old place in Albert Mews, Kensington, after which they moved to Newdigate, a small village between Dorking and Horsham.

Bruce's efforts to find work drew a blank. With Tommy Butler and the Flying Squad hot on his trail he had become a bit of a liability and other criminals felt it judicious to give him a wide berth.

Realising that if he stayed in the South of England it was only a matter of time before he had his collar felt, Bruce and Frances rented a house in Torquay. Having left their bungalow in the French Riviera, they had now taken up residence in the town known as the English Riviera.

However, on Friday 8 November 1968, just after 6:00am, the inevitable happened – there was a knock on the door, and a knock that early in the morning could only mean one thing.

Yet Bruce, still in bed, shouted out for son Nick, now almost seven years old, to answer the door.

The next thing he heard was the sound of voices and of feet pounding up the stairs. '*The bedroom door burst open and a dozen policemen piled through, diving on the bed and pinning me down.*' was how Reynolds described it in his autobiography. [2]

There, standing in the doorway, was Tommy Butler, the man who had been pursuing him for over 5 years. Butler had finally got his man.

After tearful hugs, kisses and goodbyes to Frances and Nick, Bruce Reynolds was driven from Torquay to Aylesbury where he was charged with conspiracy to rob and robbery.

This time, there was no deal on the table like the one that Buster Edwards had struck with Frank Williams, although Tommy Butler agreed that if Reynolds pleaded guilty to both charges, there would be no charges brought against Frances or anyone else that had helped him to evade arrest for the past 5 years. It was an offer Bruce couldn't refuse – no child should be brought up with both parents in jail.

The trial of Bruce Reynolds took place on 14 January 1969 in the old courthouse in Aylesbury's Market Square with Mr Justice Thompson presiding. With Reynolds having pleaded guilty to the charges of conspiracy to rob with robbery, it was left to his counsel, Cyril Salmon QC, to plead mitigation. But, in reality, the dice were loaded against Reynolds. There was ample evidence to link him to the robbery including fingerprints on the monopoly set and a bottle of ketchup found at Leatherslade Farm, and when Tommy Butler was asked by the prosecution what position Reynolds occupied in the hierarchy of the gang, he replied '*somewhere near the top.*'

Prior to sentencing Reynolds, Mr Justice Thompson told him; '*The fact that you avoided arrest for five years and, presumably, during that time were able to enjoy the fruits of your crime, does not, in my view, constitute any reason for passing upon you any less sentence now than you would have received then, even though it is no doubt true that your enjoyment of those fruits were associated with the fear of ultimate arrest.*

'*Bruce Richard Reynolds, I sentence you to twenty five years' imprisonment.*'

Shortly after sentence was pronounced, Reynolds was taken to the maximum security wing at HMP Durham. As he left the court, Tommy Butler was asked by a reporter '*Does this mean that this is the end as far as the train robbery is concerned?*' To which Butler replied '*No, I've got to catch Biggs first.*' [3]

CHAPTER 24
The End of the Beginning

But the final act of putting the handcuffs on Ronnie Biggs was not to happen in Tommy Butler's time as Head of the Flying Squad.

After arriving in Sydney at the end of 1965, Biggs had moved on to Adelaide three months later, and in the process changed his surname from Furminger to King. He was joined by wife Charmian and their two children in June 1966. Their third son, Farley, was born on 21 April 1967.

Soon after, Biggs received an anonymous letter warning him that the police were aware he was living in Adelaide. This prompted the Biggs family to move again, making the 450 mile car journey to Melbourne, where they changed their names once more – becoming Terry and Sharon Cook. [1]

For a time, Ronnie and Charmian lived a fairly normal family life. However, in March 1969, a few weeks after Bruce Reynolds began his 25 year prison sentence, the Australian magazine *Woman's Weekly* published an interview with Frances Reynolds, accompanied by several pictures, one of which featured Ronnie.

Despite the risk that the picture might be seen by people who knew him, Ronnie and Charmian decided to stay put – after all, only someone with something to hide would do a runner.

However, 6 months later, during a visit to the Melbourne Police Headquarters, a Reuter's correspondent happened to see a memo suggesting that Ronnie Biggs and his family could be residing somewhere in Melbourne, and, within hours, pictures of Biggs were appearing on the Channel 9 news.

Charmian drove Ronnie to a motel early the next morning, but on her way home she was stopped by armed police, arrested and charged with illegal entry into Australia. However, thanks to her lawyer, Charmian's bail application was successful – having three dependent children the determining factor.

In the meantime, her husband went into hiding, staying with a friend of a friend.

At the beginning of January 1969, Detective Chief Superintendent Thomas Marius Joseph Butler MBE was compulsorily retired after 34 years as a London copper.

True to form, Butler declined the opportunity of a farewell celebration to mark his many achievements, preferring instead to simply shake the hand of the Commissioner of the Metropolitan Police, Sir John Waldron, and then make a quiet exit.

As one newspaper put it, '*The British Underworld received a heartening piece of news today. Scotland Yard's top crook catcher retired*'. [2]

With every known member of the gang who were present at Bridego Bridge on 8 August 1963 now behind bars, with the exception of Ronnie Biggs, most people at that time considered that this was the end of the Great Train Robbery story.

However, to paraphrase Sir Winston Churchill, '*This was not the end. It was not even the beginning of the end. But it was, perhaps, the end of the beginning*'. There were, in fact, plenty of twists and turns still to come.

CHAPTER 25
The 1970's

On the 4th February 1970, Jack Mills passed away, aged 64. He had been suffering from chronic lymphocytic leukaemia, although the actual cause of death was given as '*Leukaemia with complications due to bronchial pneumonia*' by the West Cheshire Coroner.

The following day, on the other side of the globe, Ronnie Biggs, using the doctored passport of his friend Michael Haynes, boarded the RHMS Ellinis in Melbourne as one of 1,668 single class passengers. Eighteen days later, he disembarked at Panama where, a few days later, he caught a plane to Caracas.

On 11 March 1970 Biggs arrived at his final destination, Rio de Janeiro in Brazil, with little money and little knowledge of Portuguese, the official language of Brazil. Quite a disadvantage considering Portuguese is spoken by 99% of the population.

On 8 May 1970, Tommy Butler passed away after a short illness battling cancer. Butler, a bachelor who lived with his elderly mother, was just 57 years old when he died. The police force had been his life and he would have died a happy man had he achieved his ambition of recapturing Ronnie Biggs and putting him back behind bars.

Whilst his retirement and departure from Scotland Yard was a very low key affair, his passing certainly wasn't. A memorial service at St Margaret's Westminster was packed out with friends and former colleagues there to pay their respects. [1]

A third train robbery related death occurred on 8 June 1970 when the very unfortunate William Boal died after suffering from a brain tumour. He was just 56 years old.

Quite simply, Boal should not have been in prison at the time of his illness. Whilst his sentence had been reduced to 14 years on appeal, he was guilty only of handling stolen money, and had justice prevailed, he should have received a sentence measured more in months than in years.

Every member of the gang knew that Boal played no part in the planning or execution of the robbery, yet not one spoke up on his behalf until many years after his death. Sadly, this is understandable to a certain extent. Anyone saying categorically that Boal wasn't at the robbery was admitting their own guilt, otherwise how else would they know Boal was innocent?

On 2 January 1971, Nicholas Biggs, the 10 year old eldest son of Ronald and Charmian Biggs, was killed in a car accident at Kilsyth, 20 miles east of Melbourne. Charmian had been driving at the time when her car was hit by another vehicle that went straight across a junction despite Charmian having the right of way.

Charmian's letter telling her husband of their son's death took over a month to reach Biggs in Rio de Janeiro.

Roger Cordrey, the man primarily responsible for the injustice that befell William Boal, was released from prison in April 1971.

Cordrey's wife had left him for another man a few days before the robbery, taking their children with her, so after his release from prison he hadn't an immediate family to go home to.

For a time he went to work in his sister's florist shop to satisfy the Parole Board and demonstrate that he had permanent full time employment. But as soon as there was no chance of his being returned to prison, Cordrey moved down to the West Country.

In November 1971, Tommy Wisbey's 16 year old daughter Lorraine was critically injured in a car accident. Tommy was allowed to travel from Parkhurst, on the Isle of Wight, to see Lorraine, but sadly she died a couple of days after her father's visit.

However, Wisbey was prevented from attending his daughter's funeral when Home Secretary Reginald Maudling refused to give his consent, even though the prison authorities had no objection to Tommy being allowed out on compassionate grounds.

On 6 January 1972, shortly after finishing his shift with British Railways, David Whitby, fireman and assistant train driver to Jack Mills, sadly suffered a fatal heart attack just minutes after returning home. He was just 34 years old.

His sister, Nancy Barkley, said that David had never properly recovered from the trauma of the robbery.

The whereabouts of Ronald Biggs, who was still using the name Michael Haynes, remained unknown until he was tricked into providing an interview with the *Daily Express*. The newspaper gave his location to the police and on 1 February 1974, during one of his interview sessions with the Express reporter in a hotel room in Copacabana, Detective Chief Superintendent Jack Slipper, together with Detective Inspector Peter Jones, burst into the room.

From there they went first to Biggs's flat, to collect some warm clothes suitable for the British winter, and then to the Federal police station in Rio.

However, as luck would have it, Biggs had learnt that morning that his girlfriend, Raimunda de Castro, was expecting his baby, and because of this the Brazilian government, furious that a foreign police force was operating clandestinely on its soil, turned down Britain's request that Biggs be extradited. Jack Slipper had no option other than to return home empty handed and was somewhat cruelly dubbed 'Slip-up of the Yard' by the British press.

Six and a half months later, on 16 August 1974, Michael Fernand Nascimento de Castro Biggs was born.

In 1975, a cluster of train robbers were released from prison with Jimmy White and Buster Edwards the first two, both released in April.

White, with his wife Sheree and son Stephen, now 12 years old, went to live on the Sussex Coast where he found employment as a roofing contractor, using the alias James Patten.

Now no longer the bread-winner, Buster Edwards soon found himself back in prison later that same year when, in August, he was sentenced to 6 months for stealing £65 worth of clothes from Harrods department store in Knightsbridge. However, when he came out of prison for the second time, he acquired a pitch outside Waterloo station selling flowers.

That same month, Roy James was released on parole having served 12 years of his mammoth 30 year sentence – 8 years earlier than he had envisaged, thanks to the 1967 Criminal Justice Act. The thought that he might be able to resurrect his motor racing career had kept him going during those dark years in prison.

However, what had been left of his share of the train robbery money when he had been arrested had long since gone, having been spent by the person James had entrusted it to whilst he was inside. And by now, old friends such as Mickey Ball, the second getaway driver for the BOAC robbery, had disappeared off the radar.

If fortune and finance were not on his side, neither was fate.

Many in the driving fraternity had felt James had been dealt a raw deal and that the thirty year sentence he received was far too long for the role he played in the robbery. A second chance for James came when he was offered the opportunity to have a test drive in a Ford Atlantic at Silverstone at the end of the 1975 motor racing season.

As David Mills, later to become manager of five time Le Mans winner Derek Bell, recalled, '*It was really too powerful for him. Like all racing drivers, he thought he would be even better in a faster car, but after all those years in prison....*' [2]

James, now 40 years old, caught a wheel on the grass, lost control and hit a crash barrier full on, breaking his leg.

There would be no more chances for Roy James, and he had to accept the fact that he would never be the driver he once was, reluctantly returning to his former occupation as a silversmith.

The next train robber to enjoy freedom was James Hussey who was released on 17 November 1975. Hussey then married his long-time girlfriend Gill a few weeks later on Christmas Eve. The couple subsequently opened up a restaurant in Soho called 'Chaplin's' with Gill as licensee since Hussey's criminal record preventing him from holding a license.

On 23 December 1975, the day before Hussey's wedding, Gordon Goody was released from HMP Parkhurst. He immediately went back to live with his mother who had had a stroke while he was in prison, and was now suffering from cancer.

After she passed away, Goody decided to move to Mojácar in southern Spain. In 2014, Goody told the *Observer* newspaper why he had decided to quit Britain at that time; '*I knew if I stayed in England with my pals I'm going to go at it. So I thought 'no' and here I am.*' [3]

Goody had been more fortunate than most of the other members of the gang. Some of the money from the robbery had been invested, as had the proceeds from earlier crimes, and £20,000 that had been put into property in South West London had increased in value fivefold.

Tommy Wisbey was released from prison in February 1976, four months before his long standing friend Bob Welch. Wisbey had entrusted his share of the money to one of his brothers, and as a result his family lived a comfortable life whilst he was in jail.

Whilst he had been in prison, his wife Renee and daughter Marilyn had taken on the tenancy of a pub in Remington Street, Islington. Six months after Tommy's release, the brewery that owned the pub told the Wisbeys that they were not selling enough beer. However, the brewery was willing to let them buy the freehold and Tommy Wisbey managed to get a bank to lend him £28,000 to complete the purchase. [4] Slightly ironic given that Wisbey had taken far more than that from the bank 12 and a half years earlier!

Then it all went wrong shortly after, as Marilyn Wisbey put it; '*Dad got banged up on remand for 15 months over about forty grand's worth of travellers' cheques.*' [5]

However, he was later released when the trial judge acknowledged that he had played just a minor role in the crime. He had already served more time on remand then he would have been sentenced to if found guilty.

Bob Welch came out of Wormwood Scrubs on 14 June 1976 and went to live with Jean Steel and their son in New Cross, South East London. The nightclub that he owned at the Elephant and Castle prior to going to prison was long gone, and instead he became a second hand car dealer as well as continuing to enjoy gambling, a lifelong passion.

Whilst in prison Welch had undergone a knee operation on a cartilage which, unfortunately, had not gone at all well, causing him constant pain, and leaving him dependent on crutches to get around.

Following the birth of Ronnie Biggs's son Michael in 1974, Charmian Biggs had agreed to divorce her husband, although this wasn't finalised until 1976.

In July 1976, Bruce Reynolds was moved from Parkhurst on the Isle of Wight, to HMP Maidstone as he was no longer considered a Category A prisoner. Despite his first application to be released on parole being declined, Reynolds was offered day release in April 1978, before finally being released on parole two months later. He had served less than 10 years of his 25 year sentence.

Initially he found work difficult to come by, but eventually began working for Frank Munroe, one of the three robbers who were never prosecuted by the police. Munroe had gone 'legit' and was running a waste paper collection and scrap metal business. Sadly, working for Munroe didn't turn out to be a long term arrangement for Reynolds, though the pair parted on good terms.

On 18 December 1978, Charlie Wilson, the last of the train robbers still in prison, was released from HMP Pentonville in Islington, North London, having spent most of his sentence in Parkhurst.

Wilson and his wife Pat would eventually move to Marbella in Spain, but not before he and Roy James became involved in an attempt to import gold without paying excise duty in 1983.

In April 1979, an attempt was made to kidnap Ronnie Biggs when a small team of mercenaries, led by John Miller, posed as members of a second unit filming 'Moonraker', the latest James Bond film. Offering Biggs a cameo role in the film as bait, their intention was to lure him onto a yacht for the proposed scene, sail it into international waters and then on to a Commonwealth country from where Biggs could be extradited.

However, their scheme failed when a reporter who had heard rumours about a possible kidnapping, telephoned Biggs's home thinking he had already been taken, and so was able to forewarn him.

The following month, May 1979, Brian Field (who had changed his name to Brian Carlton after being released from prison) was driving on the M4 motorway in his Porsche on-route to Wales when a Mercedes driving on the eastbound carriageway hit the central reservation, flipped over and landed on top of the Porsche, instantly killing Field and Sian, his third wife.

It was several weeks after the accident before the true identity of Mr Carlton, was revealed. When the news broke of his previous involvement with the Great Train Robbery almost 16 years earlier, it came as a complete and utter surprise to the friends and family of Mr and Mrs Brian Carlton.

Three months later, Brenda Field, Brian Field's first wife, passed away aged just 45. [6]

CHAPTER 26
The 1980's

In March 1981 there was a second attempt to kidnap Ronnie Biggs, carried out by members of a security firm headed by John Miller, who had been involved in the first attempt a couple of years earlier.

Biggs was taken from a bar in Rio de Janeiro and bundled into a waiting van where he was tied up and gagged. From there, he was taken by plane to a waiting yacht bound for Barbados.

However, luck was again on Biggs's side when the boat suffered mechanical problems, and the stranded kidnappers, along with their captive, were rescued by Barbados coastguards and taken into custody.

The kidnappers were subsequently released and took the yacht on to Antigua before flying back to the UK, whilst Biggs was held in a Bajan jail as representatives from Brazil and Britain argued as to which country he should be returned.

After 40 days in Barbados, judges from the Barbados High Court decided that Biggs should be allowed to return to Rio.

In 1983, Bruce Reynolds was arrested and charged with dealing in amphetamines, a charge he strenuously denied. However, the jury found him guilty and he was sentenced to three years in prison.

Initially sent to Wandsworth, he was fairly quickly transferred to Spring Hill in Aylesbury, a Category 'D' open prison, and in March 1985 his application for parole was granted.

In 1984, the engine driven by Jack Mills on the night of the robbery was withdrawn from service and subsequently dismantled and cut up for scrap. [1]

On 10 February 1984, Roy James, by now 48 years old, married Anthea Wadlow, the 18 year old daughter of bank manager David Wadlow, at the Croydon Register Office. Mr Wadlow was 3 years younger than his new son-in-law.

That same year, James and Charlie Wilson were accused of a VAT fraud involving Krugerrands, gold coins minted in South Africa. Their trial had run for 45 days when the judge accepted submissions that he had allowed inadmissible evidence to be given, and so ordered a retrial. In that retrial, James was acquitted and after the jury failed to agree on a verdict for Charlie Wilson, Wilson came to a financial agreement with HMRC to avoid a second retrial.

The following year, Wilson spent four months in jail awaiting trial for the alleged armed robbery of a security van. He was freed amid allegations of police corruption.

John Wheater died in 1985 aged 64. No longer able to practice as a solicitor, it is believed that when he was released from prison in 1966, Wheater had moved to Harrogate in Yorkshire where he ran the family laundry business.

In 1967, Stanley Baker had produced and starred in the film 'Robbery', a fictionalized version of The Great Train Robbery, although the 25 minute train robbery scene was taken entirely from court evidence recorded at the 1964 trials.

Twenty one years later, in 1988, the film 'Buster' was released to coincide with the 25th anniversary of the robbery. This film was loosely based on the part Buster Edwards played in the Great Train Robbery and his relationship with his wife June. Singer/songwriter Phil Collins played the title role, with Julie Walters cast as June. The part of Bruce Reynolds was played by the versatile Larry Lamb.

In his autobiography, Bruce Reynolds wrote that '*The actual robbery scenes were done very well. I went up to watch the filming near the Railway Museum in York. For the scenery shots, they had found a place that looked a lot like*

Bridego Bridge, and after some paint and bits of cardboard were added it looked virtually identical. When the film was finally released, I was very disappointed.' [2]

On 5 August 1989, Tommy Wisbey (then aged 59) and James Hussey (aged 56) were back in prison after pleading guilty to drug-trafficking charges.

When sentencing the pair, Mr Justice Sanders told them *'You are both old enough and experienced enough to know exactly what you were doing and your motive was greed in each case, regardless of the welfare of your fellow citizens.'*

Judge Sanders ordered that £47,389 found by police at two separate addresses should be confiscated.

Wisbey and Hussey had been seen in a park exchanging bags of cocaine with a street value of £583,000. Wisbey was sentenced to 10 years for supplying one kilo of cocaine to Hussey, and a further 10 years for possessing cocaine with intent to supply. He was also given three months imprisonment for possessing cannabis. All three sentences were to run concurrently.

Hussey was sentenced to 7 years imprisonment after pleading guilty to possessing a kilo of cocaine with intent to supply. [3]

CHAPTER 27
The 1990's

Charlie Wilson was shot dead at his home in Marbella on 23 April 1990. Wilson and wife Pat had moved to Spain in 1984, shortly after he and Roy James had appeared in court accused of a VAT fraud involving South African Krugerrands. The Spanish and British police, and British Customs and Excise were all convinced that Wilson was involved in drug smuggling. [1]

Charlie Wilson was buried in Streatham cemetery on 10 May 1990. His funeral was attended by fellow train robbers Bruce Reynolds, Buster Edwards, Roy James, Jimmy White and Bob Welch.

Unfortunately for Roy James, his marriage to Anthea Wadlow did not last. James was granted custody of the couple's two children, although he had to make a substantial financial settlement to his estranged wife, believed to be in the region of £150,000. However, James couldn't honour this settlement, and inevitably the non-payment was the cause of friction between him and his father in law, David Wadlow.

In May 1993, matters boiled over between the pair. When Wadlow and Anthea brought the children back to James's Surrey home after a day out, an argument broke out. This quickly escalated and came to a head when James pulled out a pistol, hit Anthea with it, and then shot her father three times, leaving him permanently disabled.

Realising what he had done, James called the police and offered no resistance when they arrived.

At the Old Bailey on Thursday 3 February 1994, Roy James was sentenced to six years imprisonment for shooting David Wadlow and wounding Anthea James. The jury found him not guilty of attempting to murder Mr Wadlow, and also cleared him of wounding Mrs James with intent to cause her grievous bodily harm.

In his defence, James had told the court that he was depressed at the time of the incident due to financial and personal problems.

On Tuesday 29 November 1994, some thirty one years after the Great Train Robbery, Ronald 'Buster' Edwards was found by his brother Terence, hanging from a steel girder inside his lock-up near Waterloo Station, shortly after midday. He was 63 years old.

According to witnesses, Edwards was at his flower stall as usual that day, but many said he looked ill and depressed. He asked a friend to mind his stall for a few minutes, but was never to return.

A worker on the Jubilee underground line, Graeme Bradley, was possibly the last person to see Edwards alive. He said; *'When I saw him he looked very poorly, very ill looking. I asked him what he was doing for Christmas and he didn't seem to know. A couple of hours later, one of the lads came into the office and said he was dead.'* [2]

An open verdict was recorded by the Southwark Coroner's Court on 9 February 1995, as Edwards had been suffering from acute depression and had had a serious drink problem. He was drinking a bottle of vodka a day at the time of his death and had made two previous suicide attempts. [3]

During his spell in prison, Roy James developed heart problems, and in 1996, whilst still inside, he underwent a triple by-pass operation. However, this by no means cured the problem and, with his health failing, he was released from prison in 1997. Sadly, on 21 August 1997, he passed away with heart failure given as the cause of his death.

Stunned when he heard the news, Bruce Reynolds wrote: *'I couldn't believe it. He had been the youngest and fittest of us all.'* [4]

As the decade wore on, Ronnie Biggs's health deteriorated and he suffered a stroke in March 1998 and then two more during September 1999. The third stroke, the most serious of the three, left Biggs without the power of speech, and he began to contemplate a return to the UK.

He realised that time was not on his side, but one thing he knew for certain was that he wanted to die on British soil. He wanted to go home.

CHAPTER 28
The Year 2000 to 2015

On 7 May 2001, Ronald Biggs finally returned to the UK when a private plane provided by the *Sun* newspaper touched down at RAF Northolt, in the London Borough of Hillingdon, at 8:47am.

Accompanying him were his son Michael, together with his old friend Bruce Reynolds and Bruce's son Nick.

It had been to Reynolds that Biggs had written: '*I am a sick man. My last wish is to walk into a Margate pub as an Englishman and buy a pint of bitter. I hope I live long enough to be able to do that.*' [1]

Having been on the run for a total of 13,068 days, Biggs was arrested immediately he stepped off the plane by Detective Chief Superintendent John Coles. Accompanying DCS Coles were around 60 police officers, seven police vans and at least three police cars.

After being charged, Biggs was taken to the Hospital Wing of HMP Belmarsh in Thamesmead, South East London, home to over 900 Category A prisoners, via Chiswick police station and the West London Courthouse.

In theory, Biggs had still to serve 28 years of his original 30 year sentence, and his return to the UK sparked a massive debate as to how British authorities should treat him.

Friends of the train robber said they hoped he would be treated with compassion in view of his poor heath, whereas Shadow Home Secretary and Maidstone MP Ann Widdecombe called for a 'hard-headed' attitude, saying he should spend the rest of his life behind bars.

Six months after his arrival at Belmarsh, Biggs petitioned for his early release on compassionate grounds. This was rejected as was a second attempt in 2005 following more ill-health.

That same year saw the passing of two of the police officers that had been involved in the hunt for the train robbers back in the 1960's - Malcolm Fewtrell and Jack Slipper. Slipper died on 24 August 2005 aged 81, having been diagnosed with cancer four years earlier, whilst Fewtrell passed away on 26 November 2005 at the grand old age of 96.

Also believed to have passed away in 2005 was Leonard Field who would have been 74 years old at the time of his death.

In July 2007, Ronnie Biggs was transferred to HMP Norwich having spent over 6 years in Belmarsh, and in April 2009 submitted a parole application, stating: '*I am an old man and often wonder if I truly deserve the extent of my punishment. I have accepted it and only want freedom to die with my family and not in jail.*'

'I hope Mr Straw decides to allow me to do that. I have been in jail for a long time and I want to die a free man. I am sorry for what happened. It has not been an easy ride over the years. Even in Brazil I was a prisoner of my own making. There is no honour to being known as a Great Train Robber. My life has been wasted.' [2]

Unfortunately for Biggs, the Justice Secretary, Jack Straw, declined his application, despite the Parole Board recommending that Biggs be released. Straw gave his reasons stating that *'Mr Biggs chose to serve only one year of a 30 year sentence before he took the personal decision to commit another offence and escape from prison, avoiding capture by travelling abroad for 35 years whilst outrageously courting the media.*

'Had he complied with his sentence, he would have been a free man many years ago. I am refusing the Parole Board's recommendation for parole. Biggs chose not to obey the law and respect the punishments given to him – the legal system in this country deserves more respect than this.'

Jack Straw's decision received wide-ranging criticism. Even Ann Widdecombe had a change of heart, saying Biggs should be released as *'The prisons are bursting at the seams.'*

However, at the end of July 2009, the High Court granted Biggs's lawyer permission to launch a judicial review of Straw's decision, and a week later, the Justice Secretary announced that he would free Biggs on compassionate grounds. Ronnie Biggs became a free man on 7 August 2009.

On 30 December 2010, Frances Reynolds, wife of Bruce, passed away. Frances was in her mid-sixties at the time of her death and, during the last 25 years of their married life, she and Bruce had enjoyed a happy and peaceful life, growing old together.

On 12 November 2012, James Hussey died in St Christopher's Hospice in Sydenham, South London. He was 79 years old. Hussey made a deathbed statement hours before he passed away stating that it was he who had struck train driver Jack Mills during the robbery, and that he had 'bottled it up' for almost fifty years.

A friend said that Hussey had always feared another prosecution, but he didn't want to take the secret to the grave. However, doubt was thrown on his confession when John Mills, the 72 year old son of Jack Mills, told reporters that his father had revealed who had hit him, and that it definitely wasn't James Hussey.

So why would Hussey take the blame for something he may not have done? It has been suggested that Hussey was paying a debt of so-called 'criminal honour' so as to keep suspicion from another gang member, perhaps one of the three who were never prosecuted. [3]

But with the majority of the known robbers either dead or in their twilight years, this theory would seem unlikely.

November 2012 claimed another train robber when Jimmy White passed away still using the alias James Patten, which he had originally used to cover his tracks in the immediate aftermath of the robbery.

On 28 February 2013, Bruce Reynolds passed away in his sleep at his home in Croydon. He was 81.

In 2008, Reynolds had written in the *Guardian* about the aspirations of being a thief: '*We all have our benchmarks, and for us the benchmark was the Brinks robbery in 1950 which was the largest robbery in the United States at that time. We wanted to do something as spectacular as that. We wanted to draw our line in the sand. I was quite young at the time and I liked the challenge. I wanted to move in those circles. It's insanity, of course, and we knew that we would be in the frame as soon as the robbery happened, but it's the same madness, I suppose, that drives people to bivouac on the north face of the Eiger.*'

Talking about the Securitas Robbery in 2006 in the same article Reynolds went on to write: '*Their other problem was that their robbery, like ours, was too big. You throw down the gauntlet to society and obviously society has to respond. The police are given carte blanche. We always wondered that, if what we had stolen had been smaller – say £875,000 – whether there would have been such pressure to catch and punish us. We knew there would be a hubbub but we didn't know that it would be so lengthy. Normally, there is a lot of publicity for a couple of weeks and then it dies down. With us, it went on for months – and is still going on after 40 years.*' [4]

Around 200 people attended the funeral of Bruce Reynolds which was held at St. Bartholomew the Great, Smithfield, in the City of London. Amongst the mourners were Ronnie Biggs and Bob Welch. Reynolds's brother-in-law, John Daly, was too unwell to attend.

Nick Reynolds said of his father: '*He was a romantic, a true adventurer, a journeyman who chose a lunatic path, and paid the price.*'

John Daly, the only member of the train robbery gang to be acquitted, died on 10 April 2013, just six weeks after the death of Bruce Reynolds. His funeral took place at the Catholic Church in St. Stephen's Hill, Launceston, near the home where he had lived for almost 40 years.

The fiftieth anniversary of The Great Train Robbery on 8 August 2013 was marked by Nick Reynolds when he buried the ashes of his parents, Bruce and Frances, close to the tomb of Karl Marx in Highgate Cemetery.

The ceremony was attended by Ronnie Biggs and the sons of train robbers Roger Cordrey and Jimmy White. The three other surviving members of the gang, Gordon Goody, Bob Welch and Tommy Wisbey, were said to be too ill to attend.

A day earlier, some of the police officers who pursued the train robbers were honoured in a ceremony in Oxfordshire attended by Sara Thornton, the Chief Constable of Thames Valley, who said: '*What struck me is that the focus as always is on the offenders who committed the notorious crime. I wanted to balance that by recognising police officers and staff from 50 years ago who played a very important role in making sure these men were brought to justice.'*

In all, eighteen retired Buckinghamshire Constabulary investigators and backroom staff were reunited at Eynsham Hall in Witney, Oxfordshire.

On 18 December 2013, Ronnie Biggs passed away at Barnet General Hospital, close to the Carlton Court Care Home in East Barnet, where he had spent the last years of his life. He was 84 years old. Friends who were present at the hospital said his final request was for a cup of tea.

His funeral took place on 3 January 2014 at the Golders Green Crematorium in North London with more than 200 people present. As the coffin went down the aisle, draped in a Union flag and a Brazilian flag, together with a hat and red-and-white Charlton Athletic scarf, mourners clapped and reached out to touch it. [5]

On 3 March 2014, the *Daily Mirror* reported that Nick Reynolds had taken the last handful of his parent's ashes and had scattered them at the Valley of the Kings in Egypt.

By now 83 years old, and residing in Spain, Gordon Goody, for reasons known only to himself, decided to reveal the identity of the man previously known only as the Ulsterman, in an interview with the *Observer* which appeared in the newspaper on Sunday 28 September 2014. This revelation, coming as it did over 51 years after the robbery, stunned many people, not least the family of Patrick McKenna, the man named by Goody, who had no inkling that the former post office worker, who died in 1992, had any connection whatsoever to the robbery.

According to Goody, McKenna loaded his share of the cash into the back of a grey Austin 10 saloon a few days after the robbery, yet not a penny of this ever found its way to his family. Where it did eventually end up is a complete mystery, so thanks to Goody, as one question is answered another takes its place.

At the end of his interview, Goody told the *Observer* reporter that he was writing a book about the robbery explaining that: *'I suppose it is time to put a few things straight.'* [6]

How to Rob a Train written by Douglas Gordon Goody, was released on 10 November 2014.

On 2 December 2014, in a ceremony held at Crewe station, a locomotive was named after Jack Mills, and a plaque unveiled to recognise the courage and bravery of both Mr Mills and his co-driver David Whitby.

The name plate on the train was unveiled by Crewe and Nantwich MP Edward Timpson who said he was proud to mark the bravery and courage of both men. *'Little did Jack and David know on that fateful night what lay in store for them. It was a traumatic event which clearly affected them for the rest of their lives.'* said Mr Timpson. *'That's why it's so important we remember their part in what has become a very-well known story in the lifetime of this country.'*

Pop music impresario and railway enthusiast Pete Waterman, who had been due to unveil the plaque himself, asked David Whitby's sister to do it, saying; *'Why don't you pull the curtain? It's more important.'* [7]

On 11 December 2014, Charmian, the first wife of Ronnie Biggs, died in Epworth Eastern, a private hospital in Box Hill, Melbourne, Australia. She was 75 years old and left behind two sons and four grandchildren.

Charmian had taken the name Brent in later years, having changed her surname by deed poll. [8]

THE VICTIMS

CHAPTER 29
The Workers on the Train

Jack Mills

Jack Mills was born on 1 September 1905 in Crewe, Cheshire. At the time of the Great Train Robbery, Mills was 23 days short of his 58th birthday, and whilst it is indisputable that he sustained a serious head injury in the early hours of 8 August 1963, other aspects of the assault on Mills remain unclear.

The identity of his assailant is shrouded in mystery. At the time of his death in a London hospice in 2012, James Hussey confessed to being the guilty party. However, speaking shortly after the demise of Hussey, John Mills, the son of Jack Mills, informed reporters that his father had told him the name of the robber who had hit him – and it wasn't Hussey.

Yet Mills had never picked anyone out at the various identity parades he had attended, and as far as it is known, the robbers all wore balaclavas for the duration of the robbery.

At various times, Buster Edwards and Ronnie Biggs have been named as having struck Mills. Whilst Edwards had proved himself to be capable of a similar act of violence during the BOAC robbery, it is unlikely that, on this occasion, it was down to him as at the time of the assault he was most probably some distance from the driver's cabin, taking care of assistant driver David Whitby.

It is also unlikely that Biggs was involved in storming the cabin, since his one and only designated task was to act as minder to Pop, the engine driver brought in to move the train the short distance from Sears Crossing to Bridego Bridge.

Other possibilities include Alf Thomas and Frank Munroe, neither of whom ever stood trial for participating in the robbery. But the likelihood is that the identity of the person responsible will forever remain unknown and continue to be the subject of conjecture and speculation.

The weapon used on the assault of Jack Mills has been variously described as an iron bar, a pick axe handle and a cosh. Mills himself described it as '*a large staff wrapped in white cloth. It was about 2 feet long.*' [1]

Whilst the wounds suffered by Mills required 14 stitches and were to keep him in the Royal Bucks Hospital in Aylesbury for over 48 hours, the worst of his injuries were caused when he hit his head on the train's curved steel dashboard as he fell.

A combination of the physical injuries and psychological trauma suffered during the robbery meant that it was some nine months after the robbery before Mills was considered fit enough to return to work on light duties.

18 months later, he was diagnosed as suffering from shingles. In the majority of cases, shingles occurs for no apparent reason. However, occasionally, a period of stress seems to trigger the virus. Mills was forced to endure another 12 months of sick leave but returned to work again in January 1967 before finally retiring from British Railways later that year.

In retirement, his health continued to be poor and he was diagnosed as suffering from chronic lymphocytic leukaemia (CLL). People that have had a severe episode of shingles have a slightly higher chance of developing CLL, although it is equally possible that the shingles was actually an early symptom of the illness rather than a cause.

Jack Mills died of bronchial pneumonia on 5 February 1970 aged 64. The West Cheshire Coroner's verdict was that '*Leukaemia with complications due to bronchial pneumonia was the cause of Jack Mills' death. I am aware that Mr Mills sustained a head injury during the course of the train robbery in 1963. In my opinion, there is nothing to connect the incident with the cause of death.*'

There is no doubt that Jack Mills was a brave man who put himself on the line for his employers, British Railways. His reward from his employers was a one-off payment of £250, equivalent to around £4,400 today (2015). A derisory figure when compared to the huge pay-outs these days to people suffering even minor injuries at work.

When Charmian Biggs sold the story of her life on the run with husband Ronnie to the *Daily Mirror* newspaper for a reported £65,000, there was public outrage, given the size of the British Railway award to Jack Mills. In response, in October 1969, the *Daily Mail* launched an appeal on his behalf which raised £34,000. Mills and his wife Florence used part of the money (£5,000) to buy a centrally-heated bungalow in Crewe. Tragically, Mills died shortly after they had moved in.

Just as the train robbers had to live with the consequences of their actions on that fateful August day, so did Jack Mills, every single day for the remaining six and a half years of his life. There must have been so many times when he wished he had simply put his hands up, done what he was told to do and let the robbers just get on with it. However, like many brave men, he reacted to the situation without thought – and paid a very heavy price for his courage.

Speaking to reporters in 2012, John Mills said of his father, who was fit and healthy until the robbery, '*He just went downhill. He aged ten years in no time. He looked pained after the robbery. Everyone was shocked.*' [2]

'*He got shingles, what the doctor said was delayed shock coming out. His right hand shook, it never stopped until the day he died, and he started to sway. From that day he went downhill. He was not my dad of old.*' [3]

David Whitby

Accompanying Jack Mills on the Crewe to London part of the Travelling Post Office journey was fireman/assistant driver David Whitby, who was just 25 years old at the time, and, like Mills, also hailed from Crewe. Whitby had been working on the railways for over 10 years and lived barely a ten minute walk from Crewe station.

When Mills brought the train to a halt at the red light at Sears Crossing, Whitby climbed down from the driver's cabin so he could make a call to the nearest signal box from the trackside telephone. Despite finding the wires had been cut, Whitby wasn't unduly concerned and when he saw a figure in overalls standing between the second and third coaches, he naturally assumed that this was a British Railways maintenance worker there to sort out the problem.

However, as he got to within touching distance, the man in the overalls (Buster Edwards), who had his back to Whitby since he wasn't wearing anything to cover his face, turned quickly around and pushed Whitby down the embankment where he was grabbed by two men wearing balaclavas and carrying coshes. There, Whitby was told in no uncertain terms that he would be a dead man if he struggled or called out for help. One can only imagine the terror that Whitby would have felt at that precise moment in time.

Within a few minutes, Whitby was led back to the driver's cabin where he was handcuffed to a bloodied Jack Mills. If he had any doubts whether the robbers would carry out their threats of violence, the sight of Mills quickly dispelled them.

At this point, both men would have been unaware that the robbers had brought along someone who they were led to believe would be able to drive the train to Bridego Bridge. However, when it became apparent that Pop was struggling to get the train moving, they quickly uncuffed Mills and put him back in the driver's seat.

Once he had stopped the train at the markers at Bridego, Mills and Whitby were handcuffed together again, taken to lay face down at the embankment and told to keep their eyes shut.

However Whitby, taking a chance, was able to catch sight of what he thought was a three or five ton army lorry.

Once the mail bags had been loaded onto the lorry, Mills and Whitby were taken to the HVP coach, where they were again told to lay face down, this time alongside the five post office workers. It was not long before the robbers left the scene and the relief in the HVP coach when they had gone must have been almost tangible.

By 5:00am, Whitby and Mills had arrived at the Royal Bucks Hospital still handcuffed together, and round about the same time a police constable was despatched from Aylesbury Police HQ with a key.

Being handcuffed to Jack Mills must have had a considerable effect on David Whitby. With no signs of any visible injury to Whitby himself, understandably the focus of everyone's attention would have been on Mills – both at the scene of the crime and subsequently at the hospital. It must have been a relief for both men when the handcuffs were eventually removed.

It is quite likely that, at some stage, Whitby would have had feelings of guilt that his older companion had been subjected to a violent attack. He would have been asking himself whether he too should have stood up to the robbers when he had been initially restrained. Had he done so, almost certainly he would have suffered injuries from the coshes of his captors, and this would have achieved nothing to change the events of 8 August. He did the right thing in remaining passive.

Yet, there would have been constant reminders in the immediate aftermath of the robbery with all the newspapers carrying photos of Mr Mills with his forehead wrapped in bandages.

The term Post Traumatic Stress Disorder (PTSD) wasn't officially recognised as a mental health condition until 1980 even though cases were first diagnosed as early as the First World War when it was known as 'shell shock'.

PTSD is known to affect 1 in 3 people involved in a traumatic experience, and symptoms may not become apparent until weeks, months or even years after the event. It is well documented that PTSD can be triggered by any situation that invokes feelings of helplessness or intense fear. It is likely that both Jack Mills and David Whitby suffered from a form of PTSD after the robbery, and in both cases, probably for the remaining years of their lives.

In 2015, those suffering from PTSD would be treated with a combination of psychotherapy and medication. 50 years earlier, a common treatment for those suffering from depression, anxiety and stress caused by a traumatic event was to tell them to 'buck their ideas up.'

I have no doubt that Jack Mills and David Whitby were treated by their friends and relatives with compassion, support, patience and understanding. However, they almost certainly would not have received the psychotherapy and medication their conditions required.

On 6 January 1972, having finished his shift with British Railways, David Whitby returned home, where he died shortly afterwards, having suffered a heart attack. He was just 34 years old.

His sister, Nancy Barkley, told the *Chester Chronicle* on the 50th anniversary of the Great Train Robbery that David never recovered from the trauma of the robbery and that he feared for his life during the attack on the train. '*My brother never got married; he never had the chance of having children. He never had the chance of seeing his niece and nephew growing up. My brother was 25 and he had led a very sheltered life. He was never the same after the robbery. He was so quiet – never the same. Personally, I think this* (the robbery) *contributed to it. When he went back to work the first time and they went through the spot where it happened, the driver with him let him drive the train. He said there was no way he was going to stop. He said he went through there at about 90 miles an hour.*'[4]

Frank Dewhurst, Thomas Kett, Leslie Penn, John O'Connor and Joseph Ware

The attack on the HVP coach took the five men inside completely by surprise. It began with a shout of '*get the guns*' from someone outside and was quickly followed by windows being broken by iron bars and doors being smashed in with axes. During the brief but ferocious attack, 49 year old Londoner and Postman Higher Grade Frank Dewhurst was struck 5 or 6 times, Assistant Post Office Inspector Thomas Kett was struck on the arm and the head, and Postman Higher Grade Leslie Penn was struck twice across the shoulders.

Together with their colleagues John O'Connor and Joseph Ware, the five men were then ordered to lay face down with their eyes closed. One minute the five men had going about their routine business sorting the mail, sixty seconds or so later they were the victims of a violent attack, the like of which none of them had ever experienced before. From that moment on, all five would be remembered by friends and family, and a fair number of the general public, as having been on the receiving end of one of the most audacious crimes in British history.

Whilst the mail bags were being loaded onto the robber's lorry, the post office workers were under the constant threat of further violence, and the relief when the robbers finally drove away from the train must have been enormous even though the parting shot from one of them had been; '*No one should move for a half an hour as we are leaving someone behind to make sure you do as you are told.*'

After 15 minutes or so, Frank Dewhurst ventured outside, and seeing that the immediate vicinity was deserted, he sent two of his colleagues off to find a telephone to report the incident.

Once the police had arrived on the scene, all five were taken to Aylesbury Police HQ where they gave detailed statements before being allowed to go home.

Inevitably there was no immediate closure for any of them. There were the constant reminders on radio, television and in the newspapers. There was the build up to the trial and the anxiety knowing they would be called as witnesses for the prosecution. And then the trial itself where they would be giving evidence against the accused, all of whom would be sitting just a few yards away from the witness stand.

Frank Dewhurst in particular was in the limelight since the charge against each of the accused was that '*On the eighth day of August 1963, in the County of Buckinghamshire, being armed with offensive weapons or being together with other persons robbed Frank Dewhurst of 120 mailbags.*' [5]

It is quite likely that some of the five, particularly those that were physically assaulted, would have suffered from PTSD or from general stress related symptoms such as flashbacks, insomnia, panic attacks and depression. They would have been supported by their family and friends and their local GP's, but, as with Jack Mills and David Whitby, they would not have had the same quality of care as is available to victims of serious crime in the 21st century.

Subsequently, Frank Dewhurst was promoted to Assistant Inspector, but sadly he died of a heart attack on 30 December 1965, aged just 51. Whether this was a consequence of the robbery is not known. However, of the five in the HPV coach, he was the only one not to live through to old age.

However, with life expectancy for a UK male around 75 years during the period 1965-1972, three premature deaths out of a sample of 7 is disproportionally high with Jack Mills, David Whitby and Frank Dewhurst dying aged 64, 34 and 51 respectively.

At the beginning of the 1970's there were, on average, 164,000 male deaths annually attributed to cardiovascular disease. Of these, just 0.6% were in the age range 0-35 (David Whitby was 34 when he passed away) and 7.7% in the age range 45-54 (Frank Dewhurst died aged 51).

These statistics are almost certainly due to a freak spike given that the sample numbers are so low (two out of six). However, one can't help thinking that a contributory factor to their premature demise from heart related conditions may well have been the stress and trauma caused by the robbery.

CHAPTER 30
The Robbers and their Families

William Boal

William Boal, born in Durham in 1914, came to London in his teens and trained as an engineer. Shortly after the end of the Second World War, he became friends with Roger Cordrey and ended up lodging with Cordrey and his mother. However, this friendship was one he would later come to regret for the remaining years of his life.

In 1948 Boal was arrested for buying stolen clothing and as a result received an 18 months prison sentence. When he came out of prison, he lost touch with

Cordrey, and in 1952 married London born Renee Richbell. By the time of the train robbery, the couple had three children; two boys, David and Anthony and a girl, Deborah.

Boal became reacquainted with Cordrey towards the end of the 1950's and by now had his own engineering workshop in East Sheen, South West London. Cordrey had a gambling habit and Boal would often lend him money to cover his debts to local bookmakers. At the time of the train robbery, Cordrey was in debt to Boal to the tune of £650 – equivalent to almost £11,700 in 2015.

The day after the robbery Cordrey rang Boal and told him that if he came to Oxford he would be able to settle his debt. Given the amount of money he was owed, it is easy to understand why Boal didn't hesitate to do as Cordrey asked.

Cordrey and Boal were arrested in Bournemouth on 14 August and the following day the pair were taken to Aylesbury where they were charged with conspiracy to rob and with robbery.

They were also charged with three counts each of receiving stolen money. Boal continued to profess his innocence, saying that he had been coerced into helping Cordrey against his will.

Following a search of Boal's house in Fulham, Renee Boal was also arrested and taken to Rochester Row police station for questioning where she was subsequently charged on two counts of receiving stolen property amounting to £330.

In truth, William Boal, like his wife, should only have been charged with receiving. The fact that he was innocent of any involvement in the planning and execution of the robbery has been well documented. As Bruce Reynolds wrote in his autobiography *'Roger Cordrey and someone I'd never heard of, a man called Bill Boal, had been arrested with £141,000 in their possession.'*

And in his autobiography 'Odd Man Out', Ronnie Biggs said of Boal: *'whose only crime had been to give Roger a lift and help him hide the money.'* [1]

The Scotland Yard fingerprint team were unable to find any prints belonging to either Cordrey or Boal at Leatherslade Farm. Cordrey had worn gloves at all times whilst at the farm, and Boal's prints weren't found simply because he had never gone anywhere near the place.

However, it is easy to understand the charges that were brought against Boal at the time. The arrest of Cordrey and Boal was the first breakthrough the police had had, even though a week had already elapsed since the robbery. It is also fair to say that the behaviour of both men was fairly bizarre and, after all, they had been caught in possession of over £141,000 of stolen money.

The amount of publicity attracted by the robbery was immense. It was dominating all domestic media and attracting international attention as well. The police were under significant pressure from the Home Secretary downwards and it was therefore hugely important that they were seen to be making early and significant progress with the arrest of those involved.

Had they not been able to progress the case against Boal, then the lack of any evidence placing him at the farm would have meant a downgrading of the charges against him to 'receiving stolen property' only.

The police were obviously concerned about this and the damage that it could do to their credibility, and there is no doubt that they pulled out all the stops to get the convictions they needed. As far as the police were concerned, Boal and Cordrey were both guilty – end of story.

Whilst examining items taken from Boal's house after his arrest, Dr Ian Holden of the Forensic Science Laboratory had found a small watch winder in the lining of a jacket which had minute traces of yellow paint mixed with dirt in its grooves.

There must have been huge sighs of relief at Scotland Yard when Holden informed them that the paint on the watch winder was a perfect match to a tin of paint found at Leatherslade Farm. As far as the police were concerned, this irrefutably put Boal at the farm.

However, this begs the question as to how the watch winder, and the yellow paint in the grooves, came to be in the lining of a coat worn by someone who had never set foot on the farm?

There are three possible explanations. Firstly, one of the robbers planted the winder in Boal's pocket. Secondly, Dr Holden's analysis of the paint and winder was flawed and he made a genuine error. Thirdly, the winder was slipped into Boal's pocket whilst both the jacket and the paint can were in police possession.

Roger Cordrey was the only train robber who Boal came into contact with until the first day of the trial on 8 January 1964. Cordrey had access to the tin of yellow paint whilst he was at Leatherslade Farm, and could have acquired a watch winder. So he had the means, but did he have the motive? Boal and Cordrey had known each other for 15 years or more, and the first person Cordrey turned to for help with stashing away his share of the money was William Boal. He had already implicated Boal with the robbery by association and would have been aware of the consequences for Boal if they were apprehended together by the police. So what possible motive could Cordrey have had for planting the winder in the lining of Boal's jacket?

The likelihood of Dr Holden making a mistake when analysing the paint on both the winder, and on the shoes taken from Gordon Goody's room at the Windmill pub, is negligible.

We are therefore left with the hypothesis, admittedly unproven, that the winder was doctored with the yellow paint and put into Boal's jacket whilst it was in police possession.

Did a similar fate befall Goody's shoes? After all, Goody had been the beneficiary of evidence tampering when the hat he was wearing during the BOAC robbery was switched to one several sizes larger by a helpful copper in return for a £200 'bung'.

Could this be an act of revenge against Goody, and viewed by some as poetic justice? And was it a case of the boot (or shoe) being on the other foot?

Planting or tampering with evidence was the only sure-fired way to secure Boal's conviction as a train robber, and so, on 20 January 1964, William Boal found himself on trial at the District Council Chambers in Aylesbury for conspiracy to rob, robbery and three counts of receiving.

As noted earlier, neither Roger Cordrey nor any of the eight robbers in the dock alongside Boal, spoke up on his behalf. Had they done so, and told the court that they knew Boal to be innocent, it would have confirmed their own guilt.

Almost inevitably, on Thursday 26 March, William Gerald Boal was found guilty and sentenced to 21 years in prison for conspiracy to rob and 24 years for robbery. Sentenced and incarcerated for crimes he didn't commit.

In his autobiography, Bruce Reynolds wrote of Boal; '*Bill Boal was an innocent man. The Establishment sent him to prison.....If the train driver Jack Mills was the victim of our crime, then Bill Boal was a victim of the judicial process. And while we, the Great Train Robbers, accepted responsibility for injuring Jack Mills, I have yet to hear of anyone accepting responsibility for what was done to Bill Boal.*' [2]

Boal subsequently lodged an appeal against both the sentence and the conviction and this was heard in July 1964.

His appeal against the conviction for robbery was allowed. However, his appeal against the conviction for conspiracy to rob was dismissed, and whilst his overall prison sentence was reduced from 24 years to 14 years, this still represented a gross miscarriage of justice. Had justice prevailed, Boal should have been sentenced to no more than a couple of years on the three counts of receiving, leaving him a free man to enjoy the remaining years of his life.

Sadly, William Boal died from a brain tumour on 8 June 1970 after having been admitted to hospital on 29 May. Right up to the end he was, understandably, still protesting his innocence.

However, that is not the end of the William Boal story.

In July 2013, 50 years after the robbery, Boal's son Anthony told the *Sunday People*; '*We plan to use publicity that will be generated by the 50th anniversary to highlight the injustice suffered by my father and hope to convince the Appeal Court to reverse a conviction that condemned him to a life of suffering in prison*'

The family's cause was supported by the sons of robbers Bruce Reynolds and Roger Cordrey who both told the Boal's that their respective fathers had always insisted that William had absolutely nothing to do with the robbery.

Nick Reynolds told the *Sunday People*; '*Everyone knew the truth – Bill was stitched up by the police and the courts. His only crime was in knowing Cordrey....Bill never played any part in it and the rest of the guys were completely stunned when he was convicted. The first they ever knew of Bill was when he was standing in the dock.'*

The Boal family told the newspaper that they hoped other relatives of the train robbers would also come forward to help their campaign and that the conviction of William had left his wife and children 'shattered'.

Boal's son David said that his father's conviction virtually destroyed his life and those of his mother Renee, his brother Anthony and his sister Debbie.

Forty five years after his death, it is time that William Boal's conviction for conspiring to rob the Glasgow to London mail train was at long last quashed. It would at least give some form of closure to his family and allow history to acknowledge that, on this occasion, British justice had simply got it wrong.

'Pop' – The Robbers' train driver

On the face of it, a member of the train robbery gang who was never named nor prosecuted is hardly 'victim' material. With no previous convictions, even if the police had found his fingerprints at Leatherslade Farm, they had nothing to compare them with.

However, it is obvious that Pop was out of his depth, and when he agreed to act as a stand-in engine driver, he hadn't appreciated what he was letting himself in for. Ronnie Biggs and Bruce Reynolds in their respective autobiographies both give the impression that the old boy thought that he was going on a 'Jolly Boy's Outing.'

According to Biggs, after they arrived at Leatherslade Farm, Pop *'found a deckchair and relaxed in the sun, puffing away at his pipe and blending in with the pastoral surroundings. He might have been in his own back yard.'* [3]

In the hours leading up to the robbery, as members of the gang swapped jokes and anecdotes, Pop told Biggs *'I like your friends. They're such a jolly crowd.'* [4]

However, any thoughts that he might have had that he was involved in a bit of harmless fun were quickly dispelled when he was summoned to the engine to get the train moving. As he got into the driver's cabin he caught sight of Jack Mills bleeding profusely from a head wound.

As he sat in the driver's seat the reality of what he had got himself into hit him like a sledge hammer. Far from being a 'jolly crowd', he saw the ruthless side of the train robbers, who now expected him to get the train moving as soon as he sat down in front of the controls.

Unfortunately for Pop, the brakes were locked and the vacuum pressure was at zero, so he was unable to get the train moving. After a few seconds of inactivity whilst Pop fumbled with the controls, the robber's impatience led to calls for Jack Mills to be brought back to the driver's cab and Pop's contribution to the robbery came to an abrupt end. Biggs was told to take Pop to one of the Land Rovers and keep an eye on him.

By the time the gang got back to the Farm, Pop was genuinely concerned that his failure to move the train would mean some form of retribution, particularly from those who had given him such a hard time when he couldn't get the train moving – even though this really hadn't been his fault.

Concern rapidly turned to fear when he saw a hole being dug in the garden, and he told Biggs that they were digging a grave to bury him in.

Thankfully for Pop, the hole was just an attempt to hide empty mail bags, but it wasn't until Bruce Reynolds told him as much that he was able to relax a bit. [5]

How much cash he was given for his time with the robbers is debatable. According to Biggs, Pop was given £40,000, although there are other suggestions that he received just half of this – although £20,000 was still a very tidy sum back in 1963. Another possibility is that Pop's conscience may have got the better of him, and that he refused to accept any money when it was offered.

However, there is also a school of thought that Biggs may not have passed any of the money on to Pop and instead kept it for himself. [6]

When the gang decided to quit Leatherslade Farm, Pop and John Daly hitched a ride home with Mary Manson.

Almost certainly, Pop would have told his wife what he had really been up to whilst he had been away from home, and when the news broke that Ronnie Biggs had been caught and arrested, Pop must have feared that he would be the next one to receive a visit from the police. One advantage of not having received any money was that there would be no immediate evidence linking him to Leatherslade Farm.

If he did receive the money Biggs said he gave him, it is more than likely that Pop would have disposed of it, along with the clothes he had worn whilst at the farm, either soon after returning home or on hearing the news of Biggs's arrest.

Pop would also have been extremely worried about his own safety, not just from the police, but also from the robbers themselves. And he had every right to be so.

He had been a rank amateur alongside the rest of the gang, all of whom had previous form and were career criminals. If anyone was likely to grass to the police, the gang would have put a fair chunk of their money on that person being Pop. Certainly that was true as far as Buster Edwards and Gordon Goody were concerned as the pair would spend a fruitless afternoon driving around Redhill looking for Pop's house allegedly with the intention of silencing him permanently. Thankfully for Pop, they were unable to find it. [7]

In his book *The Train Robbers, Their Story*, Piers Paul Read stated that he met Pop (or Stan Agate as he called him) and his wife a dozen or so years after the robbery, still living in the same house. Read got the impression that Pop was '*somewhat senile*' and wrote that he got an angry reaction from Pop's wife whenever he mentioned the name Ronnie Biggs. [8]

In 'The Robbers' Tale' written by Peta Fordham, Fordham describes Pop as a 'corrupted railwayman' who was 'just a weak, hard-up man.' [9]

If he was 'corrupted', it was almost certainly because he had been misled by Biggs who had given the old man the impression that he and the rest of the gang were gentlemen thieves, latter-day Raffles come Robin Hoods.

Biggs also wrote that he was pleased that 'he (Pop) never had his collar felt by Old Bill...and it is nice to think that at least he....got to enjoy the spoils of that night's work.' [10]

However, the fact that Pop and his wife were still in the same house without any obvious signs of wealth when Read met them, suggests that the old boy had little or no spoils to enjoy or spend.

When all is said and done, it would seem that Pop was a fairly weak and easily led individual who, until he met Biggs, had always kept on the right side of the law. However, with retirement on the horizon, his combined Railway Pension and Old Aged Pension was probably not enough to enable him and his wife to live out their old age in relative comfort. Indeed, his combined pension income may well have been much less than the salary he earned from British Railways.

When Biggs presented him with an opportunity to be free from financial worry in his retirement, he probably found this a temptation and an offer too good to refuse.

Pop was a non-violent man and told Biggs that he wouldn't hurt or kill anyone for money. [11]

Therefore there is no doubt that the sight of Jack Mills bleeding and bandaged made him fearful of the robbers who had demonstrated just how ruthless they could be. Could that ruthlessness be extended to getting rid of him, making sure that he wouldn't be around to confess all if arrested by the police?

Despite being safely returned home after the robbers decided to quit Leatherslade Farm early, his fear of them and the police never went away, and it would have resurfaced every time the robbery made the headlines. And this it did with some regularity.

It could be argued that Pop didn't deserve to enjoy his freedom during the latter years of his life, and that all his worries were self-inflicted. However, the same cannot be said of his wife who, perhaps, was the real victim of her husband's foolishness and naivety.

The Three Wives of Brian Field

There is no doubt that Brian Field played a major and pivotal role in the planning of the Great Train Robbery. Without his input as facilitator the robbery would never have taken place.

It is therefore a gross travesty of justice that he should spend less than four years in prison whilst others such as William Boal served far longer sentences.

Field was just 28 years old at the time of the train robbery and had served in Korea with the Royal Army Service Corps. When his time came to leave the army, he left as a 'man of very good character' and went to work for solicitors in Bethnal Green. A year later, in 1960, he joined James and Wheater, having first come across John Wheater during their time in the army.

Field's first wife Brenda, whom he married in 1958, also worked for John Wheater, although the pair divorced in 1961. The following year, Field married his second wife, a German woman named Karin.

It was whilst working for Wheater that he met Buster Edwards and Gordon Goody. Field was not averse to passing the occasional titbit of information to the pair about the contents of the country homes of some of his more wealthy clients.

The Fields lived in a very nice country house themselves, which they named 'Kabri', and it is more than likely that the purchase of 'Kabri' was in part funded by the gratitude of Edwards, Goody and any others who were the recipients of the odd nugget from Field.

It was Brian Field who put Goody in touch with the Ulsterman who, according to Field, had detailed knowledge on the movement by rail of large sums of cash across the country. The true identity of the Ulsterman remained a mystery for over 50 years until Goody revealed him to be post office employee Patrick McKenna in an interview with the *Observer* newspaper published on 28 September 2014.

In the article, Goody said of McKenna that he was '*absolutely essential to the robbery. It simply would not have happened without him. The information that he provided was spot-on.*' [12]

Field was arrested on 15 September 1963 and was charged with conspiracy to rob, robbery, receiving and conspiracy to obstruct justice.

A month after his arrest, the Home Office gave permission for Field to be taken home to see his wife. Karin Field had been four months pregnant when her husband had been arrested, and just a month later she had given birth to a baby girl who was sixteen weeks premature. The medical view was that the stress of her husband's arrest, combined with the constant travelling to and fro whilst he was on remand, had brought about the birth. When he arrived home however, Field found his wife in the bedroom without their daughter who had been rushed to a hospital in Reading in a critical condition.

Sadly, the little girl, who they had named Jacqueline, was too weak to survive and was buried on 16 October 1963 at a church close to the Field's Oxfordshire home. Field was given permission by the Home Office to attend the funeral of the daughter he never got to see. [13]

On 26 March 1964, Brian Field was found guilty of conspiracy to rob and guilty of conspiracy to obstruct justice, and was sentenced to 25 years imprisonment.

Amazingly, given the various parts he played in the planning and execution of the robbery, his appeal against the charge of conspiracy to rob was allowed, and whilst his appeal against the charge of conspiracy to obstruct justice was dismissed, his overall sentence was reduced from 25 years to just 5 years.

Despite the fact that Field could be out of prison as early as 1967, Karin Field returned to Germany, the country of her birth, shortly after the trial ended. There she met investigative journalist Wolfgang Lohde who had achieved fame 6 years earlier when he uncovered a secret Nazi operation to hide stolen art treasures in Lake Toplitz.

By April the following year (1965), Karin Field was expecting Lohde's child and, when he found out, Brian immediately began divorce proceedings from his prison cell.

After his release in April 1967, Brian Field slipped off the radar in an effort to start a completely new life away from the public, the journalists and the various criminals he had mixed with during his time as a solicitor's clerk. Some of the latter would almost certainly have made contact with him, hoping to find out if he knew where any of the cash from the robbery was stashed. To this day, over £2,000,000 is still unaccounted for.

Field was certainly very successful in rebuilding his life. Fairly soon after his release he changed his name to Brian Carlton and became a successful sales manager for the Children's Book Centre in Kensington, often travelling abroad running book exhibitions in schools.

He got married for a third time, and bought Spring Cottage, an idyllic 'chocolate box' property in one of the most sought after parts of Cornwall, in the heart of the Lizard Peninsula. Life must have seemed far removed from what it had become in the 1960's. We can only speculate if he ever revealed any details of his past to his wife Sian.

Shortly after selling Spring Cottage in 1979, Field was driving on the M4 motorway in his Porsche, on-route to his in-laws house in Wales, when a Mercedes driving on the east bound carriageway hit the central reservation, flipped over and landed on top of the Porsche, killing Field and Sian instantly.

The occupants of the Mercedes, a man, his wife and their two children, were also killed. The accident made the headlines since the woman who died in the Mercedes was the 28 year old pregnant daughter of Raymond Bessone, otherwise known as the celebrity hairdresser Mr Teasy Weasy. It was also reported that her husband, who was driving at the time, had been drinking.

Several weeks later the true identity of the Porsche driver was revealed. Discovering that his real name was Brian Field, and that he had been so heavily involved in such an infamous crime as the Great Train Robbery, must have come as a complete surprise and shock to both family and friends who had only ever known him as Brian Carlton.

Brian Arthur Field was just 44 years old when he died. His life, which was tragically cut short, was certainly very eventful. His military service did him credit, and after being released from prison in 1967, it appears that he rebuilt his life as Brian Carlton, the successful and respected sales manager.

Perhaps he appreciated his good luck and the second chance that fate and the appeal judges had handed him. So much so that on his release he resolved never to set foot inside a prison again.

But ultimately, his past had a profound effect on the lives of those close to him, and in particular, each of his three wives.

Brenda, his first wife, who he divorced in 1961, sadly passed away in 1979, the same year as Brian. She was just 45 years old.

Had Brian Field kept his nose clean and not succumbed to the temptations put his way after joining James and Wheater, the daughter he lost with his second wife Karin may have gone the full term and survived, as their marriage may also have done.

Then, he would almost certainly never have met Sian, the woman who was to become his third wife, and she and Brian would not have been travelling along the M4 on the day they both lost their lives.

Nicholas, Christopher and Farley Biggs

Charmian Powell was 17 years old when she first met husband-to-be Ronnie Biggs in October 1957. Biggs was 28 at the time.

The pair married on 20 February 1960 and their first child, a boy they named Nicholas, was born five months later in Redhill County Hospital in Surrey.

A self-employed carpenter, Biggs kept out of trouble for the best part of three years, forming a partnership with the bricklayer husband of one of Charmian's old school friends.

However, the arrival of their second child, another boy who they named Christopher, left Ronnie and Charmian somewhat strapped for cash. [14]

Hoping to borrow some money to tide him over, Biggs made his life-changing telephone call to his old friend Bruce Reynolds and a week or so later, Reynolds drove down to Redhill with his wife Frances and their son Nick.

The outcome was Reynolds agreeing that Biggs could join the train robbery team in return for Ronnie recruiting Pop as a back-up train driver. The rest, as they say, is history.

Biggs was subsequently arrested on 4 September 1963, was found guilty of robbery and conspiracy to rob on 14 April 1964, and sentenced to 30 years imprisonment the following day.

After his appeal against both convictions was dismissed, Biggs was transferred from Brixton to HMP Wandsworth.

On 8 July 1965 Biggs and three other prisoners escaped from Wandsworth. According to Biggs, the whole escape plan cost him '*£55,000....roughly a third of what I had netted from the robbery.*' [15]

If this is true, it would suggest Biggs walked away with around £165,000 - £20,000 more than each of the other robbers. This discrepancy may well have been the £20,000 'drink' that was supposedly given to Pop, which Biggs might have pocketed.

Alternatively, realising what he had got himself into, Pop may have given the money to Biggs telling him he didn't want anything to do with it. We will probably never know precisely what happened.

Biggs eventually found his way to Sydney, Australia, on 30 December 1965 using the alias Terry Furminger.

Six months later, with Biggs now living in Adelaide, he was joined by Charmian and their two children. Charmian had brought with her what was left of his share of the cash from the robbery, around £7,000 – equivalent to over £100,000 today.

On 21 April 1967 their third child, Farley Paul Biggs, was born. By now, Mr and Mrs Furminger had changed their names to Terry and Sharon King. However, soon after the birth of Farley, Biggs received an anonymous letter tipping him off that the police were aware that a Terry King living in Adelaide bore a striking resemblance to the British fugitive Ronnie Biggs. Off they went again, Adelaide was swapped for Melbourne, and Mr and Mrs Terry King became Terry and Sharon Cook.

For the next couple of years, Mr and Mrs Cook were able to lead a fairly normal life, but all that changed on the evening of 16 October 1969, when a picture of Biggs was broadcast on Australian television.

Very early the next morning, Charmian drove Biggs to a motel on the outskirts of Melbourne, but on her return journey a large number of police, some of them armed, descended on her. Charmian was arrested and the boys were put into care, although she was released a few days later and reunited with her children.

Charmian later told the *Daily Express* that '*I got a few hundred yards down my street when all hell broke loose and police cars came from everywhere, and my car was pulled up and they dragged me out of it, and they were waving guns and I was arrested. When I heard that the children had been taken away, I was weeping uncontrollably. It was awful.*'

The report of her arrest became global news and Charmian agreed to sell her story to the Packer Organisation for which she received $25,000 after tax. Most of that went on buying a house for her and the children.

In his autobiography Biggs wrote that Charmian was able to get $2,000 to him just before he sailed on the SS Ellinis to Panama, which left Melbourne on 5 February 1970. [16]

It was another four years before they set eyes on each other again.

However, on 2 January 1971, a tragedy occurred that would unite husband and wife in grief, even though they were over 8,000 miles apart. Their eldest son Nicholas, aged 10, was killed in a car accident at Kilsyth, 20 miles east of Melbourne.

In an interview given to Australian broadcaster ABC in 2001, Charmian Biggs described the accident and the aftermath; *'Nicky was right where the car struck us on the passenger side and he was badly injured. And the ambulance took quite a while to get there and even when it came and even though we had a police escort, it was involved in a collision on the way to the hospital and Nicky was dead on arrival. So that changed everything again.*

I had to write and tell him (Biggs) what had happened. He didn't know about it. He thought of giving himself up, but I had said to him in the letter not to do that because it wouldn't change anything, wouldn't bring Nicky back.

The authorities here must have thought he would turn up at the funeral. The funeral was something of a fiasco in as much as it was overrun with police and media and even to the point where all the floral tributes had had all their cards removed so I didn't know who'd sent flowers or anything. I didn't know who to thank. I just felt like a zombie.'

The news of the accident, in which their youngest son Farley also suffered some bad cuts, didn't reach Biggs, who by now was in Rio de Janeiro, until over a month later when the letter from Charmian arrived.

On reading this devastating news, Biggs wrote in his autobiography that he almost turned himself in at the British Consulate, but after downing a couple of large brandies he came to the conclusion that giving up his freedom in favour of a return to the UK, and the resumption of his long term prison sentence, was not what his son would have wanted. [17]

To help with the grieving process, Charmian Biggs decided to enrol at the University of Melbourne. She did so well in her first year that she won a Commonwealth Scholarship which would pay for her tuition fees.

Charmian eventually graduated from Melbourne University with an honours degree in Pure English and went on to have a successful career in public service and as a writer and editor in a publishing company.

Speaking to the media in 2012 at the launch of a five part ITV television drama called 'Mrs Biggs', Charmian said that she had no regrets about going on the run with husband Ronnie: *'I would do it all again. My only regret is something I could do nothing about, and that is the death of my son. There have been some fantastic times as well as very sad ones, but that's life. You have to have the lows to appreciate the highs.'*

When asked about her two other sons, Christopher and Farley, Charmian said that they had had little to do with their father and that *'He abandoned them. They felt abandoned.'*

Understandably, both sons, who are now middle aged, have done their best to maintain anonymity due to their father's notoriety, and, to their credit, both have been able to enjoy established professional careers.

When reflecting on his life Ronnie Biggs said; '*If you want to ask me if I have any regrets about being one of the train robbers, I will answer NO! I will go further: I am proud to have been one of them.*' [18]

However, Biggs did acknowledge that many did suffer as a result of the robbery; '*The people who paid the heaviest price for the Great Train Robbery are the families. And that is the families of all the people involved with the Great Train Robbery. The Robbers' families, the families of Old Bill, the families of the rail men and the post office workers, and even the families of the people that have helped us over the years. All have paid a price, one way or another, for our collective involvement in the robbery - a very heavy price, in the case of my family. For that I do have my regrets, but it still has been a life well worth living*'. [19]

With both Charmian and Ronnie Biggs stating that they had no regrets at the way their lives unfolded, it is difficult to have sympathy for either, despite the agonies both must have gone through at the death of their first child.

Charmian in particular received 'hate' mail, blaming her for the death of her son.

But the real victims here were Nicholas whose life was tragically curtailed at the tender age of 10, and the couple's two other children, Christopher and Farley, who were brought up without a father's influence, although some might say that it was a good thing in this instance.

Understandably, the two boys repaid their father's absence through their childhood years by having nothing to do with him as they moved into adulthood, and there must have been countless times when Ronnie Biggs deeply regretted not being part of his children's lives.

However, the lives of all the Biggs family would have turned out completely different had Ronnie not made that initial telephone call to Bruce Reynolds with the sole purpose of borrowing money from his old friend. The irony here is that before going off to Leatherslade Farm, he actually won £500 on the horses – the same amount he had hoped to borrow from Reynolds.

That £500 would have been enough to solve his short term debts, but by then he had managed to become part of the train robbery gang and the opportunity to earn some really big money was just too irresistible for Biggs.

The Family of Patrick McKenna

The Great Train Robbery added to the list of its victims some 50 years after it took place.

In an interview with the *Observer* newspaper in September 2014, timed to coincide with the release of a documentary film called *The Great British Train*

Robbery: A Tale of Two Thieves, 84 year old Gordon Goody, now living in Spain, claimed that the mysterious character previously known only as the Ulsterman was in fact Belfast-born post office worker Patrick McKenna. McKenna was living in Islington in North London at the time of the robbery. [20]

Goody told the *Observer* that he and Buster Edwards had been introduced to the Ulsterman by a third party (solicitor's clerk Brian Field) and that he met the Ulsterman on four occasions in total.

One of these meetings took place in Kensington Park, and Goody claims that he discovered the Ulsterman's true identity when he picked up a glasses case with the name Patrick McKenna inside, after it had fallen from the man's jacket pocket. At the time, McKenna had gone off to buy some ice creams.

It was at the first meeting that the Ulsterman told Goody and Edwards about the trains known as Travelling Post Offices and specifically the train that ran overnight from Glasgow Central Station to London Euston. When Goody asked about the source of this information the Ulsterman told them that it was from a relative (brother or step-brother) who worked for the Post Office. Whether the source of the information was a relative, or McKenna himself, will never be known. What is known though, is that the information given to Goody and Edwards was absolutely spot on.

In the *Observer* article, Goody reveals that after the robbery, the Ulsterman collected his share of the money, which had been packed into a couple of holdalls and a mail bag, from Brian Field's house, then put it into the boot of a grey Austin 10 car, before driving off.

Goody's revelations obviously came as a shock to Patrick McKenna's family who now live in Manchester. They describe the Patrick McKenna they knew as a *'quiet post office employee, very straight-laced and honest.'*

McKenna died of a heart attack in 1992 aged 72 and his grandson Mark told newspaper reporters; *'When I was young I remember going shopping with him at Asda. Me and my mum lived with my grandparents, so he was like my dad. He was one of those who would sit there at the end of the month comparing till receipts to his bank statement.*

'When mum was younger they struggled with money. She was walking around with holes in her shoes. Every time he bought a car it had to be on hire purchase. It's obviously quite a shock that he could have been involved in something like this.

'My reaction was 'What, my grandad? Mum doesn't believe it at all. If he did get this kind of money, none of us saw any of it. I am still finding it all very hard to believe because of the kind of person that he was. The documentary makers insist it can't be anyone else, however.'

So if Patrick McKenna was the Ulsterman who stuffed bags of cash into the boot of his car, where did that money go? It seems that it was never spent on his family.

According to Simon Howley, the producer of the documentary 'The Great British Train Robbery: A Tale of Two Thieves,' McKenna was *a quiet church-going man who lived a simple life, continuing in the post office until his retirement. McKenna never owned a car* (this would seem to be incorrect based on what Mark McKenna told reporters) *and always worried about the security of trains.'*

Howley thinks that the money was stolen from McKenna, whereas the McKenna family think it more probable that Patrick, if indeed he was the Ulsterman, would have given this to the Catholic Church. There is another school of thought that suggests McKenna passed the cash on to the IRA.

Wherever, the money ended up, the victims in this instance are Patrick McKenna's family. Whether or not he was the Ulsterman, his family will now have to live with the possibility that he was not the man they thought him to be. Others will not give them the benefit of any doubt, and the family name will be forever associated with the Great Train Robbery.

Not the legacy that Patrick McKenna would have wanted to bequeath his family.

Leonard Field

Leonard Field was what the American's call a 'Patsy', defined as a 'scapegoat' or a 'person easily taken advantage of, or manipulated.'

Field was 31 years old at the time of the robbery and was a merchant seaman working as a steward for P&O. His only previous criminal conviction was in 1951 when he was fined 40 shillings for 'intent to steal property from motorcars.'

Field was the brother of Harry Field who had been a client of solicitors James and Wheater when he was charged with horse doping and with robbing a bank in Stoke. For the last offence Harry Field was sentenced to five years in prison.

No doubt encouraged by the prospect of some quick and easy money, Leonard agreed to allow the contract for the purchase of Leatherslade Farm to be drawn up in his name for a payment of £12,000, believing Brian Field who had told him that the farm was to be used to store stolen cigarettes.

Leonard was also persuaded by Brian Field to accompany him to a viewing of Leatherslade, an action which would have given the prosecution and the jury the impression that Leonard was more than just a 'bit part' player in the planning of the robbery.

His not guilty plea at his trial was further hindered when the prosecution revealed that the 10% deposit for the purchase of the farm had been provided by Leonard. When his brother Harry was sent to prison for bank robbery, Leonard had been appointed Power of Attorney over his financial affairs, and the deposit was raised from Harry's money, probably by John Wheater.

When police confiscated Wheater's file on the purchase of Leatherslade Farm, Leonard Field's finger prints were found on a signed bank authority form, although there is every chance that Field signed this simply because he was told to do so. Solicitor John Wheater told police that the deposit had been paid in cash.

It later transpired that when contracts were exchanged, Wheater had signed the purchaser's contract on behalf of Field. Whilst this practice was not illegal, it was unusual.

It is highly likely that Leonard Field had no idea that he was being used by Brian Field, and, to a lesser extent, by John Wheater, to front the purchase of the property which was to be used as the robber's hideaway.

Believing that Leatherslade Farm was to be used as a stow for stolen cigarettes, and given that he had only one previous conviction for a minor offence 12 years earlier, Leonard would have assumed that, if caught, at worst he would be looking at a short term prison sentence.

However, the fact that he was the brother of a convicted felon would not have helped him, and both John Wheater and Brian Field talked up Leonard's role to the police, hoping to deflect attention away from much of their own involvement in the robbery - hence the reason why, when sentencing Leonard Field, the judge told him; '*Although you have but one previous conviction, which I ignore, you are a dangerous man. Not only have you perjured yourself repeatedly in this trial to save your own skin, but on your own showing at one stage you perjured yourself in an endeavour to ruin the accused Brian Field.*

I sentence you not for perjury; I sentence you solely for conspiracy. The overt act committed by you in pursuance of that conspiracy is beyond doubt. You made a vital contribution.'[22]

Leonard Field was sentenced to 25 years imprisonment for conspiracy to rob, and 5 years for conspiracy to obstruct justice and as he was being taken away his mother shouted out from the public gallery. According to the *Guardian* newspaper on 17 April 1964, '*only once was the calm of the courtroom broken. The moment came as Leonard Dennis Field - "A dangerous man" - was sentenced to 25 years. From Field's mother on the public gallery came a cry: "I am his old mother. He's innocent. They are liars. Justice has not been done." Field paused on the steps leading to the cells as she called: "Oh you poor boy." He cried back "don't worry mother, I am still young."*'

Even with maximum remission, Field was still looking at serving a minimum of 16 years, which would have made him 47 years old on release.

However, counsel for Leonard Field submitted an appeal on his client's behalf and on 13 July his appeal against the 25 year sentence for conspiracy to rob was allowed as '*No facts had been established that he knew of the intention to stop and rob the train.*' However, his appeal against the 5 year sentence for conspiracy to obstruct justice was dismissed.

Harsh as this latter decision was, the outcome was probably far better than Field had expected.

Leonard Field was paroled in May 1967 and little is known about him until he married in 1976. He is believed to have died in 2005.

Just as William Boal was manipulated by Roger Cordrey, so Leonard Field was manipulated by Brian Field. Neither William nor Leonard had any involvement in the planning and execution of the train robbery, and their sentences were harsh in the extreme.

The one difference is that, to a certain extent, justice was done on appeal for Field, even though many still considered the five year term excessive.

Frances Reynolds

Frances Allen first met Bruce Reynolds when he was going out with her elder sister Rita. However, it was Frances that took his eye and the pair were married on 7 September 1961 at St Mary Abbott's Register Office, Kensington. The following year their only child was born, who they named Nicholas Rufus Reynolds.

However, the responsibilities of having a wife and a new baby didn't change Reynolds, who already had a number of criminal convictions to his name.

Another train robber, John Daly, was married to Frances's sister Barbara, and whilst both Frances and Barbara were aware of the criminal backgrounds of their husbands, neither expected that one day their own names would feature on the front pages of newspapers across the world.

Three weeks after the train robbery, the *Miami Times* carried the headline *'Sisters Sought in Train Holdup'* and led with *'Two pretty sisters with a taste for night-clubbing went on Scotland Yard's wanted list yesterday in the hunt for the great train robbery gang.*

'The women are Mrs Frances Reynolds and Mrs Barbara Daly, both in their early 20's. Their husbands, Bruce Reynolds, 42, and John Daly, 32, are antique dealers and Scotland Yard wants to question them.' [23]

On the day of the robbery, Frances and Barbara were at a holiday campsite at Winchelsea in Sussex, along with Sheree White, the wife of robber Jimmy White who owned the caravan where they were staying.

48 hours later, all three were on the run with their respective husbands and children. However, they were soon to realise, as many had before them, that life on the run can be a miserable existence – and this applied particularly to Bruce and Frances Reynolds who managed to stay one step ahead of the police for over five years.

However, on 8 November 1968, at just after 6:00am, Bruce Reynolds was arrested in Torquay where he had been living with Frances and son Nick. He was subsequently sentenced to 25 years in prison on 14 January 1969.

Reynolds was allowed a very brief visit from his wife before he was taken away to Durham prison. He was shocked by her appearance as she had had little sleep for three weeks before the trial, and had lost almost a stone and a half in weight. [24]

In March 1969, two months after her husband had been sentenced, readers of the Australian *Women's Weekly* magazine were given an insight by Frances of her life with Bruce whilst he was one of Britain's 'most wanted.'

'For five long years every knock at the door set my heart pounding. Every time a stranger looked at me I trembled. Every time I gave my name I told a lie. When you are the wife of a man on the run...you live in a nightmare 24 hours every day. All the money in the world can't bring you peace of mind. I can honestly say that all that train money brought us nothing but misery.

'People who have always lived normal open lives can have no idea of the strain and tension of living for years on the run.

The worst thing when you are living on the run is that you haven't any real identity. You have no papers, no genuine passport, nor employment cards. You don't exist as a normal citizen.' [25]

This was a reprint of her story that had been published in the German magazine 'Stern' and then serialised in the UK by the *Sunday Mirror*. [26]

The fee she received from these publications enabled Frances to buy a flat in Queen's Road, Weybridge, in Surrey, where, to avoid being hounded by the press, she changed her name to Angela Conway. [27]

Despite a round trip of over 550 miles, Frances and son Nick made the long and arduous journey to Durham every few weeks, but it got more and more difficult as time went on and in his autobiography Reynolds describes how they tended to argue more and more. Two years in Durham, was followed by a year in Chelmsford, a year in Leicester, and three and a half years in Parkhurst on the Isle of Wight.

During that time, Frances's visits had become fairly sporadic and by the time Reynolds had completed seven years inside, he had arrived at the conclusion that his marriage was more or less over. It wasn't that much of a surprise when divorce papers arrived at Parkhurst.

However, Nick Reynolds was by now a teenager, and when his father was transferred to Maidstone Prison in Kent, Nick was a regular visitor.

Whilst Reynolds was in Maidstone, Frances had begun to suffer from severe depression triggered by the death of her brother. She was hospitalised shortly after, having taken an overdose, the result of despair at losing her brother and general long term stress, and she was eventually diagnosed as being a manic depressive.

Bruce Reynolds was finally released from prison in October 1978 having served 9 years and 9 months, and, against all the odds, he and Frances were eventually reconciled, although the couple continued to have their ups and downs. During one of those downs, Frances suffered a nervous breakdown and doctors recommended that she be admitted to the Maudsley, a well-known psychiatric hospital in Denmark Hill, South London. However, eventually she was to end up in an old Victorian hospital in Tooting Bec, Wandsworth. [28]

Although Frances was allowed home a few weeks later, things went from bad to worst. In 1983, Bruce was arrested and charged with dealing in amphetamines, a charge he always strenuously denied. However, he was found guilty and sentenced to three years in prison, and soon found himself back in Wandsworth.

Almost immediately, Reynolds began lobbying for a move, and this paid off when he was transferred to Spring Hill in Aylesbury, a Category 'D' open prison. Spring Hill was far more inviting for prisoners and their visitors, with visits permitted every fortnight and visitors allowed to stay for up to two hours - instead of the maximum 60 minute visits permitted in the higher security jails.

Whilst waiting for the date of his parole hearing at Spring Hill, Reynolds learnt from friends that Frances had succumbed to her depression yet again, going missing after having checked herself in to hospital. She resurfaced six days later and returned to hospital voluntarily.

Reynolds was released from Spring Hill in March 1985 and, at 54 years old, he realised that a return to a life of crime was not really an option if he wanted to live out the rest of his years with Frances. A life of normality, free from the stress of being the wife of an active criminal, was the best possible medicine for her.

From then on, Bruce and Frances Reynolds enjoyed a happy and peaceful life, growing old together, until Frances, by now in her late sixties, passed away on 30 December 2010. Bruce Reynolds, one of the principal architects of the Great Train Robbery, eventually passed away on 28 February 2013 aged 81.

For Frances Reynolds, her life was very much a 'tale of three parts'. The first two decades were the formative years brought up in a happy and loving family environment, and this continued into the early years of her marriage to Bruce.

But all that was to change in August 1963 when Bruce and John Daly arrived at the Winchelsea camp site where Frances and her sister Barbara Daly were staying, and told their wives that they had been part of the gang that had robbed the mail train. For Frances, this was the beginning of the second phase of her life, much of which was spent either on the run with Bruce, or battling the demons of her mental illness.

We will never know what path she and Bruce might have taken in life, had he not been a 'great train robber.' But almost certainly, it would have been better than the one Frances had to endure from 1963 through to the mid 1980's.

However, at least her story had a happy ending and from then on until she passed away in 2010, she was able to enjoy life as a normal wife and mother.

Barbara Daly

Before her marriage to John Daly, Barbara Allen, sister of Frances Reynolds, was well aware that her husband-to-be had a fairly lengthy list of criminal convictions, mainly for theft from either shops or cars. However, he was by no means a major league player in the criminal world.

However, all that changed when, a couple of days after the train robbery, Daly and Bruce Reynolds turned up at the campsite in Winchelsea where their wives were staying and admitted their involvement. Both couples chose to go on the run, but unlike his brother in law, John Daly remained at large for less than four months.

After Winchelsea, John and Barbara, together with their daughter Lorraine, booked into the Endcliffe Hotel, Cliftonville as Mr & Mrs Cox-Daly. However, once his photo started to appear in the newspapers and on the television, Daly sent his daughter to stay with friends in Cornwall, whilst he and Barbara went to stay in a basement flat in Eaton Square, Belgravia, owned by small time thief Godfrey Green.

Whilst living at Eaton Square, the couple used the names Mr and Mrs Grant, and in an effort to alter his appearance Daly lost four stone in weight and grew a beard.

On 3 December 1963, Daly was arrested by Tommy Butler and Frank Williams at the flat. Barbara was subsequently collected by her brother James who took her to stay with Mary Manson, and on 28 December, she gave birth to a little boy who weighed in at a very healthy nine pounds.

However, in his book, *The Train Robbers, Their Story*, Piers Paul Read wrote that for Barbara, '*The shock of the arrest seemed to have affected her mind; she had become silent and withdrawn – the first of the civilian casualties on the Robber's side.*' [29]

Barbara's state of mind seriously improved when, on 14 February 1964, she received the best Valentine's Day present imaginable when husband John was acquitted and was able to walk out of court a free man.

Not bad for someone who had contemplated submitting a guilty plea just a few days before the trial begun.

As to the fate of Daly's share of the robbery, the only thing that is for certain is that Daly never set eyes on it again. Speaking after the death of her husband on 10 April 2013, Barbara Daly told reporters; '*John was devastated when he learned his money had been stolen. (At first) things were tight financially and John struggled to get work.*' [30]

After his acquittal, John, Barbara and the two children set up home in Launceston, East Cornwall. There, not a soul knew about his train robbery background until after his death.

Speaking about the four months when they were in hiding from the police, and the subsequent years they spent living in Cornwall, Barbara said; '*I was pregnant and had to leave my oldest, who was a baby, with a friend. Wanted pictures of us had been released by the police and I felt like a hunted animal.* (Even after his acquittal) *the worry that he might be arrested again was making me ill. I hated the Great Train Robbery; it was like a stone on my back.*

'*John didn't have any money, but he had his freedom, his garden and his family – and that was everything. He proved that crime does not pay and that the best things in life come from hard work and honesty.*

'*We just had enough to survive and we worked long hours to make ends meet. He was a decent man who reformed and had a strong belief in God.*

'*John would get up at 5:00am and walk 17 miles a day following the dustcart* (Daly worked as a dustman and street cleaner for the local council). *Even after he retired from the council he got cleaning jobs and worked until he was 70. We had a simple life and didn't earn a lot, but we had what we needed.*' [31]

The time from the day of the robbery to John Daly's arrest, just under twenty weeks in total, was by far and away the most unsettling period during John and Barbara Daly's long marriage. Had it stretched to years rather than weeks, it is quite possible that Barbara would have gone on to suffer psychologically as her sister had.

However, John enjoyed a stroke of good fortune when he was acquitted fairly early on in the trial. And perhaps the loss of his share of the money from the robbery was a blessing in disguise. Who knows how the lives of the Daly family would have panned out otherwise?

June and Nicolette Edwards

Anyone who has seen the 1988 film Buster will remember it as a comedy drama, with rock star Phil Collins playing the title role of Ronald 'Buster' Edwards and Julie Walters cast as his wife June.

In his autobiography, Bruce Reynolds said of the film: '*I was shown the original script which I didn't like particularly. As it turned out, the final version was only mildly more appealing.*

'*When the film was finally released, I was very disappointed.........only a few commentators picked up on the fact that Phil Collins was portraying a Train Robber as being a lovable rogue.*' [32]

Ronald Edwards married June Rose Rothery in 1952, having first met her outside the Regal Cinema in Kennington, South London, when they were both in their mid-teens. Prior to their marriage, the only blot on his copybook occurred whilst doing his national service in the RAF where he was court martialled for stealing cigarettes. However, between their wedding day and the day of the train robbery, Edwards had been convicted of four fairly minor offences.

After the death of their first child at the age of six weeks, June suffered two miscarriages before giving birth to their daughter Nicolette in 1960.

In the days following the train robbery, having decided it was too risky to return to their home in Twickenham, Buster, June and Nicolette stayed at various places before moving to a house in Wraysbury, Buckinghamshire.

Whilst they were more than happy in each other's company, June was very much a home-loving bird and missed her friends and family. But she couldn't get in contact with any of them, knowing that the police would be keeping a close eye on anyone with connections to her husband.

Whilst on the run, Buster and June endlessly discussed their options, one of which was to make a deal with the police whereby he would give up his share of the robbery, in return for a lesser criminal charge than those already arrested.

However this option was blown out of the water once the trial had finished and the judge had handed out sentences totalling 307 years to the 12 convicted men.

This would have been a real blow to both Buster and June, particularly as Buster had decided that the only alternative to giving himself up was to go abroad to a country where there was no extradition agreement in place.

After a spell in Germany where he underwent plastic surgery on his face, Buster was joined by June and Nicolette and the three of them, travelling under the name of Ryan, arrived in Mexico City in April 1965 – meeting up with Bruce and Frances Reynolds who had been there since the previous summer.

The 'Ryans' were unable to settle in their new surroundings with June missing her mother, family and friends and concerned what impact a life in Mexico would have on Nicolette's schooling and upbringing. June had already been writing to her mother, and within a month of their arrival Buster had told Bruce Reynolds that he was already thinking of a return to the UK, and doing a deal with police.

After getting in touch with Frank Williams through an intermediary, it was agreed that Buster would return to the UK where he would give himself up to Williams. In return, Williams would accept Buster's claim that he was not a 'major player' and that his role was simply to clean Leatherslade Farm once it had been vacated by the robbers.

On 19 September 1966 Edwards was arrested at a pre-agreed location, near to the Elephant Castle in South East London, where he gave Frank Williams a written statement outlining his involvement with the robbery. He was arrested and taken to Cannon Row police station where he was formally charged.

The trial of Buster Edwards took place on 8-9 December 1966 and he was found guilty of both conspiracy to rob and robbery and was sentenced to 15 years for the charge of robbery, and 12 years for the charge of conspiracy to rob - significantly less than the sentences dished out to other members of the gang, but longer than what he had hoped for.

Edwards served eight and a half years in prison and was released in April 1975.

During that time, and for the first time ever, June Edwards had had to make a living for herself and Nicolette. On top of this, she had to bring up her daughter who would be without a father figure until she was in her mid-teens.

Initially, June went to work in the 'Nicolette Wig Factory', which Buster had set up with his share of the BOAC robbery with long-time friend Derek Glass as his business partner.

Unfortunately, this didn't work out and she was soon looking around for alternative employment. She eventually found work as a bar maid, working alongside Tommy Wisbey's wife Renee. [33]

The time she spent as a single parent had a considerable impact on June. No longer was she totally dependent on Buster, and she became quite self-sufficient. Circumstances had forced her to become so, and, to her surprise, she found herself thoroughly enjoying the independence.

His time in prison also had a major impact on Buster. Until he was incarcerated for his involvement in the train robbery, the longest he had spent behind bars was 42 days whilst awaiting his court martial by the RAF. The cheerful easy going guy he had been when he began his sentence, was replaced by someone who was irritable, sometimes angry, with low self-esteem and guilt for what he had put his wife and daughter through.

After his release, and now no longer the bread-winner, Edwards soon found himself back in prison that same year when he was sentenced to 6 months for shop lifting from Harrods department store in Knightsbridge.

However, when he came out of prison this time, he acquired a pitch outside Waterloo station selling flowers and continued to work at this until his death by suicide in 1994, aged 63.

According to the *New York Times*, he once told an interviewer that selling flowers was boring compared to the life he used to lead. [34]

In his autobiography, Bruce Reynolds quoted from another interview Edwards gave shortly before his death; *'I know I'm lucky to have got the chance to have this (flower) stall and be my own boss, but it's so dreary compared with the life I used to lead. It wasn't even the money. I had been on jobs that hadn't netted me a penny but, oh, does the adrenalin flow. My main excitement here is sorting out the fights between the winos.'* [35]

The body of Buster Edwards was discovered by his brother Terry who found him hanging from a metal beam in his lock-up close to Waterloo Station.

At the inquest into his death, the Southwark Coroner's Court was told that Edwards suffered from acute depression and a serious drink problem, regularly consuming a bottle of vodka a day. He had also tried to commit suicide on two previous occasions. Medical reports showed his family had 'been at the end of their tether' trying to stop him drinking, but one specialist had noted that he *'doubted that Mr Edwards really wanted to stop'*.

The coroner, Sir Montague Levine, said that a post mortem showed that he had enough alcohol in his body to kill someone unused to drink and that this enormous quantity of alcohol in his blood stream, over four times the legal drink-drive limit, cast doubt on his ability to form the intent to take his own life. However, he was certain that no other person was involved.

June Edwards was too distressed to attend the hearing, but Nicolette was there, although she left the court whilst the pathologist gave evidence. Also representing the family was Buster's brother Terry who told the court that Buster had been depressed as his flower selling business had begun to lose trade due to the extension of the Jubilee Line on the London Underground. However, he added, he believed his brother's depression and drink problem originated from the nine years he spent in prison from 1966 to 1975. [36]

All in all, this is a particularly sad story. Ronald 'Buster' Edwards knew that when he came out of prison for the last time, he had to go straight otherwise he risked losing the two people he loved most in life, his wife and daughter. And yet a life without crime, and the excitement and adrenaline rush that went with it, would seem to have ultimately been the cause of his death at the relatively young age of 63.

Buster Edwards was the one and only true love for June Edwards. She knew that Buster was a fairly small time crook when she married him, and had learned to accept this. It was probably part of his attraction and charm.

However, the Great Train Robbery changed all that as the small time crook became one of the UK's most wanted criminals. If she could have, I'm sure June would have wanted to turn the clocks back so things could go back to how they were before the robbery. I'm not sure that that is what Buster would have wanted – he had tasted the big time, and nothing else could compare with that. Ultimately, perhaps not even his love for his wife and his daughter.

Mary Welch and Jean Steel

In her book 'The Robbers' Tale, Peta Fordham described Bob Welch as '*a married man with no children with some domestic complications. Pale, tense and strained looking, he looks more like a research student than a criminal.*' [37]

After the robbery, when the police were keeping watch on the Islington home Welch shared with his wife Mary, they also kept a house in Camberwell under surveillance. This belonged to a woman called Jean Steel where Welch had been a frequent visitor over the preceding 18 months or so. This was the domestic complication Peta Fordham was referring to.

During the trial, it was revealed that Jean Steel, who had met Bob Welch when she worked at the club he owned at the Elephant and Castle, had had a baby boy by Welch, something that Mary Welch had been unable to do. Until that point in time, Mary had been unaware of her husband's infidelity.

Welch, a compulsive gambler, was sentenced to 30 years in prison, a daunting prospect for a man with just two previous convictions to his name. In 1958 he had been sentenced to 9 months for receiving stolen tea, coffee and custard powder, and in 1963 he had been fined £210 for serving and selling alcohol after hours. This latter conviction led to the closure of his club.

There is no doubt that Mary Welch and Jean Steel were both in love with Bob Welch, and, for the first few years of Welch's incarceration, both visited him at every possible opportunity, despite the difficult journey to Parkhurst on the Isle of Wight.

Their devotion to Welch caused both women to suffer from depression and psychological issues, and in Mary Welch's case this developed into paranoia, believing that everywhere she went people were pointing her out as the wife of one of the Great Train Robbers. [38]

Mary also invented a fictitious lover and asked Welch for a divorce so she could marry him. Welch was more than happy to allow a 'quickie' divorce to take place.

Her illness resulted in Mary Welch spending two months in a mental hospital in Newcastle, and on her release she returned to London and began to write to her ex-husband having clean forgotten that they had been divorced at her instigation. [39]

Having told Bob Welch that she would wait for him to be released and that she would remain faithful during that time, Jean Steel had created a rod for her own back spending most of her time at home bringing up their young son. The only other activity she looked forward to was her regular trip to Parkhurst, and yet one day when Welch was eight years into his sentence, Jean found herself at Waterloo station unable to get on the boat train to the Isle of Wight. She was suffering from a severe panic attack, but thankfully she managed to get to the home of Welch's sister in Islington.

Her doctor was called, and he immediately sent her to the local hospital psychiatric department where she was prescribed anti-depressants and tranquilisers. [40]

Welch also suffered whilst he was in prison, but his problem was physical rather than psychological. Operations to repair knee ligaments left him suffering constant pain and needing to use crutches permanently.

Far more a gambler than a criminal, Bob Welch was released in 1976, the last of the robbers tried and sentenced at Aylesbury in 1964 to be released, having served 12 of his 30 year sentence. He never returned to crime and married Jean Steel.

Their son now had a father.

John Wheater

When sentencing solicitor John Wheater to three years imprisonment for conspiracy to obstruct justice, the presiding judge, Mr Justice Edmund Davies, told Wheater; '*Your case is in many respects the saddest and most difficult of all. You have served your country gallantly in war and faithfully in peace.*

(Wheater was mentioned in dispatches and had been put forward for the Military Cross). [41]

'Why you participated in it (the robbery), *I don't know. You have not told me, and your learned counsel has been able merely to hazard a guess. Whether or not all the facts, if known, would speak in your favour or to your prejudice, I have no means of telling and must not speculate. But I am disposed to accept the view that you allowed yourself to be overborne in some manner by your more able and masterful managing clerk.'* [42]

If ever the phrase 'crime doesn't pay' applied to any of those involved in the mail train robbery, then it would be John Denby Wheater.

It is difficult to understand why Wheater, aged 42 at the time of the robbery, allowed himself to become involved in the way he did. Married to Angela, with whom he had two daughters, with a distinguished military career behind him and the owner of a solicitor's practice, many would say that he was sitting pretty with a bright future ahead for himself and his family.

However, as Bruce Reynold's put it in his autobiography; *'Field's employer, John Wheater, owned a battered old Ford and lived in a rundown neighbourhood, but Brian drove a gleaming new Jag and had a beautiful house.'* [43]

Perhaps this is one of the reasons why Wheater did what he did. Many people employing someone 15 years younger in a junior position, who already had the trimmings of success, would be more than a little envious. It is also likely that some of Wheater's criminal clients appeared to possess more wealth than he did.

For all we know, perhaps Wheater's wife Angela occasionally pointed this out to her husband. As many a parent knows, having children can be quite an expensive pastime.

Whilst this is nothing but speculation and supposition, this could have made John Wheater susceptible to his young clerk's suggestion that he 'bend the rules' a little where the purchase of Leatherslade Farm was concerned, utilising Leonard Field's name, his lack of intelligence and the money he had ready access to as power of attorney over his brother's financial affairs.

We will never know why Wheater allowed himself to end up on trial at Aylesbury in January 1964. Neither the trial judge, nor his counsel, had been able to prise this information from him, despite the fact that of all those on trial, Wheater had the most to lose. To paraphrase Sir Winston Churchill, to those that knew him, John Wheater was *'a riddle, wrapped in a mystery, inside an enigma.'*

John Wheater was released in February1966. He could not return to his former profession as whilst he had been in prison the Law Society's disciplinary process had banned him from ever again practicing law in the UK.

It is believed that Wheater eventually moved to Harrogate in Yorkshire to run the family laundry business. He died in 1985 aged 64. [44]

The Family of Tommy Wisbey

Tommy Wisbey (born in April 1930) was a self-confessed 'heavy', a member of the 'South Coast Raiders' whose role in the train robbery was to add some muscle to the gang. He had known Buster Edwards since the mid 1950's when both worked for Freddie Foreman and he was the link between the Raiders and the firm headed by Bruce Reynolds.

Wisbey's wife Renee had been a bridesmaid at Foreman's wedding and her father (Tommy's father-in-law) was a cousin of Billy Hill, who was known at the time as the 'boss of Britain's underworld'.

Freddie Foreman was also godfather to Wisbey's eldest daughter Marilyn, who years later was involved in a long term friendship with Frankie Fraser, a one-time associate of both the Kray twins and the Richardsons.

With his illustrious connections, it is surprising that Tommy Wisbey had just two criminal convictions to his name prior to the train robbery - one for breaking and entering, the other for receiving - with the latter earning him a four month prison sentence.

Sentenced to 30 years for his participation in the robbery, his appeal against his conviction was dismissed and he went to prison in 1964 facing a very lengthy stretch. Despite this, Renee Wisbey remained loyal to her husband throughout his time inside.

One benefit she did enjoy, which the families of other convicted mail train robbers didn't, was indirect access to Tommy's share of the stolen money, since this had been left in the hands of one of her husband's brothers. Her brother-in-law used part of this to buy a pleasant house in South London for Renee and her two daughters, Marilyn and Lorraine, and also paid Renee a regular income which meant that she was fairly comfortably well-off. [46]

However, Renee keenly felt her husband's absence when she discovered that her daughters were being teased mercilessly by other school children who knew that their father was one of the train robbers.

But this was just a minor issue compared to what happened in 1971. Lorraine Wisbey, who was just 16 years old at the time, was critically injured in a car accident which claimed the life of her boyfriend who was driving at the time. Tommy was allowed to travel from Parkhurst, on the Isle of Wight, to see Lorraine, but tragically she passed away a couple of days after her father's visit.

At the funeral, whilst there were floral tributes from several of the train robbers, as well as flowers from the Richardsons and the Krays, the principal absentee was Tommy Wisbey himself.

Although the prison authorities had no objection to Tommy attending his daughter's funeral, for some inexplicable reason, Home Secretary Reginald Maudling refused to give his consent.

Whilst Tommy had to grieve alone in prison, Renee and Marilyn Wisbey struggled to come to terms with their loss and, almost inevitably, both fell into a state of deep depression, with Marilyn requiring some psychiatric care.

Thankfully, both Renee and Marilyn had their spirits raised when Marilyn gave birth to a little boy in 1974, who she named Jonathan. Tommy learnt about the birth of his grandson when a thoughtful prison officer slipped a piece of paper under his cell door which read '*Your daughter's had a baby boy at 6:30 this morning.*' [47]

Tommy Wisbey was released from prison in February 1976 having served 12 of the 30 years to which he had been sentenced.

However, this was not to be his last spell in prison. Within a year of his release, Wisbey began a 15 month spell on remand whilst the police investigated a swindle involving £40,000 worth of American Express Travellers Cheques, although he was eventually released without charge. During this time Renee Wisbey suffered a minor stroke which may well have been triggered by her husband's arrest. [48]

And then, in 1989, Wisbey and fellow train robber James Hussey were sentenced to 10 years and 7 years in prison respectively after having pleaded guilty to trafficking cocaine.

Wisbey had been seen by police passing a package containing the drug to Hussey in a local park. Hussey had been tailed to Streatham by the police and arrested, although it was another year before Wisbey was arrested in Wilmslow, Cheshire.

A consequence of Wisbey's conviction was that police seized whatever assets they could find, which included a flat in Eltham, South East London, which had been bought and paid for by his daughter Marilyn, but had been registered in her father's name. [49]

Tommy Wisbey spent over two decades behind bars and there is no doubt that his absence left its mark on his immediate family. In her book 'Gangster's Moll', Marilyn Wisbey offered this advice to anyone contemplating a life of crime; '*if you are thinking of taking the road to crime, please do not have children or get married. Full stop. It is not fair to your children to grow up and visit their father in those terrible places called prisons, and it's not fair to your wife, girlfriend or mother. At the end of the day, it's not just you that suffers. Everyone does.*' [50]

CHAPTER 31
The Police and the Others

Detective Chief Superintendent Tommy Butler

Thomas Marius Joseph Butler was born in 1912, a year most notable for the sinking of the 'unsinkable' White Star Line British passenger liner *RMS Titanic*.

Known as 'one day' because of the speed he would catch criminals, Butler rose through the ranks at an incredible rate, due in no small part to his dedication to his work. During busy times, a 17 hour working day was the rule for Butler, rather than the exception. He would often sleep in his office rather than going home, and he expected those around him to do likewise.

Inevitably, his obsession with work precluded him from having a family life with a wife and children. Instead, he lived with his mother in Barnes, in the London Borough of Richmond, although he did have a lady friend who worked as a bus conductress or 'clippie' as they were known back then.

Unlike many of his contemporaries, he was a non-smoker and virtually teetotal. Those same contemporaries found Butler a difficult person to work for, as he would keep things close to his chest, was painstakingly meticulous and a perfectionist. He did not suffer fools gladly.

However, Butler's reluctance to share information was almost certainly due to the number of corrupt officers working for the Metropolitan Police at that time. When Robert Mark (later to become Sir Robert in 1973) was appointed Assistant Commissioner, corruption, particularly within the detective branches at the Met, was endemic with plainclothes officers having financial arrangements with a whole range of criminals, including bank robbers and drug dealers. At the time of his arrival, Mark announced that his ambition was to *'arrest more criminals than we employ.'* [1]

On 13 August 1963, Tommy Butler was appointed to head the police investigation into the train robbery, a task which was to dominate his life for the next five years.

Butler chose Detective Chief Inspector Peter Vibart and Detective Inspector Frank Williams to be his deputies, and appointed Detective Sergeants Slipper, Moore, Neville and Van Dyk to be the principle members of his team.

Someone from outside the police force, who got to know Butler well over the next few years, was Post Office investigator Harold Lyons.

As well as having his own men on the team, Butler wanted a PO investigator, and Lyons was selected for the role by his post office employers.

In an interview with the *Sunday Express* on 4 August 2013, just 4 days before the 50th anniversary of the robbery, Lyons, now 86 years old, said of Butler: *'He was a strange bloke. People thought he was offhand, but I thought*

he was rather shy....He told me later he was married to the job which, he
admitted, occupied his thoughts 24 hours a day.

'In all my years I never knew anybody so devoted to his work. '

Lyons travelled to different parts of the country during his time with Butler, and of this he told the *Express*: *'We stayed in hotels, but wherever we were, Tommy always had Friday nights off when he liked to go to the pictures. It had to be a cowboy film and he liked to have boiled sweets. Detectives took the mickey out of him because he was different, eccentric.*

'Tommy didn't follow the normal path, an enigma inside a mystery - that was him.'

Lyons also remembered that Butler had some health issues, including a persistent cough. [2]

The retirement age for police officers in the 1960's was 55, which Butler reached in 1967. By that time, all but Bruce Reynolds, Charlie Wilson and Ronnie Biggs were behind bars. However, such was Butler's dedication and obsession with catching the train robbers, that he was able to persuade his superiors to allow him to stay on beyond retirement so that he personally could put the handcuffs on the three still at large.

Butler never slackened his pace and it is said that any holiday he took during that time was of the busmen's variety.

On one occasion, whilst following up a lead that Bruce Reynolds was in the South of France, Butler took his holiday in the French Riviera, spending his time scanning the sun-bathers on the beach with binoculars hoping to pick out Reynolds amongst them. To much hilarity amongst his colleagues, Butler was arrested by gendarmes thinking he was a Peeping Tom(my)!

However, despite catching both Reynolds and Wilson, the powers that be at Scotland Yard would not put off Butler's retirement indefinitely, and in January 1969 he left the Yard for good, with Ronnie Biggs still enjoying his liberty.

As it happened, Biggs was not to return to the UK to complete his prison sentence until 2001, so even if he had stayed on for a while longer, Butler's ambition of putting all of the train robbers behind bars would have remained unfulfilled.

Tommy Butler sadly did not live long enough to enjoy a long and meaningful retirement. That persistent cough noticed by Harold Lyons turned out to be lung cancer, and on 8 May 1970, Thomas Marius Joseph Butler MBE passed away at the age of just 57.

Given his lifestyle, particularly working extremely long hours over a continuous period, it would not have been a surprise if the cause of Butler's death had been due to heart failure. However, his death was attributed to lung cancer, the number one cause of which was, and still is, cigarette smoking. Yet Butler was a non-smoker.

Scientists have been reporting widely on the link between cancer and smoking since the 1960's, and every study undertaken since has provided more evidence that smoking is the primary cause of lung cancer.

However, studies into the dangers of passive smoking, in effect inhaling second hand smoke, were not undertaken until the 1980's.

The air we breathed in 1960's Britain was polluted by swirling clouds of cigarette smoke in pubs, clubs, cinemas, trains, buses, shops, offices, streets, schools and, ironically, even in our hospitals.

Around 70% of men and 40% of women smoked in the 1960's and Tommy Butler almost certainly died a victim of passive smoking. His lifestyle left him little time to breathe unpolluted air.

The copper, who had worked tirelessly to put all the robbers behind bars, was himself a victim of the Great Train Robbery.

Detective Inspector Frank Williams

The appointment of Frank Williams, a former sergeant major with an army commando unit during the Second World War, as assistant to Tommy Butler was a 'no-brainer'.

In his autobiography, Williams wrote: '*Among criminals I had a reputation of being a hard man, but one who would deal fairly with anyone caught.*' [3]

But his main asset to the train robbery investigation was his extensive network of informants.

Jack Slipper described Williams as: '*a very quiet man who was always deep in thought*' and wrote that his greatest strength was: '*dealing with informants and I don't think I've ever come across anyone who was better at it.*' [4]

Throughout the years spent tracking down the various gang members, it was Williams who kept 'the back channels open,' particularly with Buster Edwards.

When Edwards finally decided to return to the UK to face the music, he negotiated through a third party (probably Freddie Foreman) that he would give himself up in return for Williams doing what he could to help him receive a much lighter sentence than the 30 year terms handed out to those already convicted.

As it was, when the case came to trial, Edwards was sentenced to 15 years.

In 1967, with Tommy Butler rapidly reaching the compulsory retirement age for police officers, Williams assumed that he would replace him as Head of the Flying Squad. However, the postponement of Butler's retirement hugely frustrated Williams, particularly as no date had been given when his boss would now eventually retire.

In view of this, Williams decided to apply for a transfer to Scotland Yard's Murder Squad. The fact that his application was approved unopposed suggested to Williams that he would now never take over the reins at the Flying Squad.

As it turned out, Williams had read the signs correctly. There was a feeling at the Yard that he had helped Buster Edwards get away with a much lighter sentence than he had deserved. If there had ever been any doubts about Williams succeeding Butler, helping Edwards had put the seal on them.

The Great Train Robbery had a major impact on the career of Frank Williams. Had the robbery not happened, Williams would almost certainly have achieved his ambition of becoming the Head of the Flying Squad.

As it was, in the early seventies, Williams left the force permanently to take up the position of Head of Security for the Australian airline Qantas.

However, there was one last 'hurrah' left for Williams.

On 12 December 1948, 24 unarmed villagers were killed by British troops during the Malayan Emergency.

Known as the Batang Kali massacre, 7th platoon, G Company of the 2nd Scots Guards surrounded a rubber plantation and rounded up civilians, separating the men from the women and children. The official report at the time was that the 24 men were found to be Communist sympathisers and were shot whilst trying to escape. All were killed, none were wounded.

In 1970, Denis Healey, the Labour Government's Defence Secretary, ordered an enquiry to be set up to investigate claims of a 'cover up' and Frank Williams was appointed to head that enquiry.

Twenty two years after the event, many of those involved and interviewed by Williams and his team had long left the army, and at least one of them told the detectives that the platoon had been ordered to shoot the civilians.

Williams decided that his investigation could only be completed by a visit to the scene of the shootings where he could carry out interviews on witnesses, and therefore he informed the Director of Public Prosecutions that he intended to travel to Malaya at the earliest possible opportunity.

By now the Labour Government of Harold Wilson had been replaced by a Conservative administration under the leadership of Edward Heath, which was very reluctant to sanction any enquiry that might shame the nation. Williams was instructed to submit his report without going to Malaya as planned, and shortly after, the Attorney General announced to Parliament that there was '*no reasonable likelihood of obtaining sufficient evidence to warrant criminal proceedings.*' [5]

However, Frank Williams, a copper used to putting behind bars those responsible for criminal acts, made it quite clear that, as far as his investigation was concerned, it was still unfinished business.

John and Grace Maris

John Maris, a local herdsman, was the source of the tip-off on Monday 12 August, which first alerted Buckinghamshire police that Leatherslade Farm may have been used as a hideout by the train robbers.

The timing of his telephone call was crucial. Another 24 hours, and it was perfectly likely that the farm would have been raised to the ground, if not by Mark, the person contracted to do it, then by some of the robbers themselves.

Angry that the farm had not yet been sanitised as arranged, Bruce Reynolds, Charlie Wilson, Buster Edwards, Roy James and John Daly had agreed that they would do the job instead. The news of the discovery of Leatherslade Farm stopped them in their tracks.

Maris was subsequently presented with a cheque for £19,000 – worth over £300,000 by today's reckoning (2015) – donated by the banks and the Post Office. Some of this was used to buy the couple their own house and a new car.

However, it wasn't all sweetness and light from then on for Maris and his wife Grace.

Whilst they received some congratulatory letters, they also began receiving threatening mail with Grace Maris once receiving a letter with a drawing of a coffin inside with her husband's name on it.

With John starting work early each day, it was usually Grace who opened the day's post.

'I felt it, but my wife felt it even more' said John. *'It was she who mainly opened the threatening letters and saw their contents. It was only recently she admitted to me that some of them she never showed me, but took to the police who said they'd deal with it.*

'She bottled it up and by doing so thought she was protecting me. I never knew she had been to the police at the time. For many years after the Great Train Robbery, wherever it was recalled, my wife Grace suffered terribly and this, we were assured, was due to the original shock to her nervous system.

'I bitterly regret that she should have suffered so much as a result of my actions. I think the first four or five months after the robbery I was particularly frightened, even though I was a young fit farmer.' [6]

And the threats were not just in letter form. On one occasion, John Maris had a call from a friend who warned him that four men in a car were asking after him.

'I was constantly scared, always worried. That fear lasted for years. I was always looking over my shoulder.' [7]

The couple became so worried that Grace even sewed a long pocket into her husband's trousers so he could carry a wooden cosh with him at all times, just in case. And John strategically placed jars of acid around the farm buildings, and hid wooden staves where they were easily accessible.

Thankfully, he never had cause to use them, although they did buy a German Shepherd puppy as additional protection for them and their children.

In hindsight, John Maris still reflects on whether it was the right decision when he called the police back in 1963.

'Yes, I did regret getting involved' he said. *'I thought at the time 'God, what have I done? But I had to accept I was involved and had to get on with it.'*

THE END OF THE LINE

CHAPTER 32
The Last Rites?

The Fascination with the Great Train Robbery

I am writing this chapter more than half a century after the Great Train Robbery took place. I was just a couple of months short of my tenth birthday when I heard news of the robbery on the radio, and still remember that day fairly well.

The initial fascination with the Train Robbery was almost certainly due more to the size of the haul, than the boldness of the crime itself. Over £2.6million was a staggering amount in 1963 when the average weekly wage was £18 and the price of a typical family home was just over £3,000.

In the first few days many marvelled at what appeared to be the perfect crime executed with military style precision and timing. Even the police were stunned at the sheer audacity of those responsible. '*You won't believe this, but they've just stolen a train*' was the message delivered into the VHF police radio by one of the first coppers on the scene, his voice a mixture of awe and amazement.

With no arrests in the first few days following the robbery, Scotland Yard made the decision to release photographs of those suspected to have been involved – against the advice of Tommy Butler and Frank Williams, who a couple of days earlier had been charged with the task of bringing those responsible to book.

The nation watched, listened and read about progress made by the police over the next few weeks and months, as one by one those suspects whose names and faces we had become familiar with, were arrested and subsequently charged.

When it came to the trial, which began in January 1964, the general view was that the accused in the dock would almost certainly be found guilty. With the normal sentence for robbery around 12 years, it was thought that those convicted could expect to receive somewhere between 10 to15 years in prison.

However, behind the scenes, members of the 'Establishment' had decided that normal sentencing would not be enough. An example had to be made in this instance to deter others. That deterrent was the 30 year prison sentences awarded to seven of the robbers by Mr Justice Edmund Davies on 16 April 1964.

If some members of the general public had been wavering in their latent or begrudging admiration for the robbers, the perceived draconian sentences handed out was to tip the balance firmly back in favour of the criminals. In the eyes of many, the robbers had, in an instant, become the underdogs to the all-powerful British Establishment, and if the British public favours anyone, it is usually the underdog.

After hearing the news of the sentences on the radio, Bruce Reynolds was stunned: '*At first I couldn't believe it. How could they do this? These sentences would throw the whole system out of kilter: at a stroke they rendered their tariffs ineffectual. What sentences could they now award to the truly savage and horrendous crimes – forty years? Fifty years? A hundred years?*' [1]

Reynolds also believed that a serious error of judgement had been made.

'*Thirty years....for a crime committed without firearms, and it should have come as no surprise to the authorities that, from that time onwards, criminals took the view that they might as well carry guns as not.*' [2]

If evidence was needed that this would be the case, tragically it was not long in coming.

On 12 August 1966, three plain clothed policemen from Shepherd's Bush police station stopped to talk to the three occupants of a car waiting near Wormwood Scrubs Prison, who they thought might be involved in a possible escape attempt. Without any warning, Harry Roberts shot Detective Constable David Wombwell and Detective Sergeant Christopher Head, whilst John Duddy shot Police Constable Geoffrey Fox. All three officers died at the scene.

The motive for this desperate crime was Roberts's fear that his criminal record would see him being returned to prison for at least 15 years if found in possession of a firearm. At the time of writing, Roberts is still in prison almost 50 years on from the shooting. [3]

The severity of the sentences also forced those train robbers still at large to make a decision about what they should do next.

'*When the sentences were handed down by Mr Justice Edmund Davies, I knew it was time to leave Britain*' wrote Bruce Reynolds [4]

Reynolds and Buster Edwards decided to quit the UK for sunnier climes, as did the imprisoned Charlie Wilson and Ronnie Biggs who began to formulate their escape plans.

Jimmy White, a former paratrooper, decided to stay in Britain, and used his military training to good effect, managing to avoid arrest for almost three years.

If interest in the robbery had begun to wane, it was revitalised by the audacious escapes from prison, first by Wilson (on 12 August 1964) and then by Biggs (8 July 1965). It was not just the fact that Wilson and Biggs escaped that captured the imagination of the public - it was the manner of their escapes.

Wilson was freed from Winson Green Prison in the early hours of the morning by three men who had acquired copies of keys that opened the doors to the high security wing where Wilson was being held. His rescuers were in and out in a matter of minutes.

If Wilson's escape was considered bold, Biggs's release from Wandsworth was positively adventurous, taking place in the middle of the afternoon in broad daylight with Biggs literally 'going over the wall'.

Wilson remained at liberty for almost four years, whereas Biggs was to enjoy his freedom for over 35 years until his voluntary return to the UK in 2001.

It is a popular misconception that Biggs was one of the leaders of the train gang. In fact, he was a very minor participant in the robbery and was not particularly popular with the other members of the gang who felt that the only reason he was there was because of his long standing friendship with Bruce Reynolds.

In 2014, Gordon Goody told the *Observer* that: '*Biggsy was an arsehole. I didn't like him, no one did. His one job was to bring a train driver and he brought a guy who couldn't do the job. They had to go and sit in the car. Even the ones who pulled him out of prison had brains way out of Biggsy's league.*' [5]

However, there is no doubt that Biggs did as much, if not more, than anyone else to keep the interest and fascination with the Great Train Robbery going throughout the 70's, 80's, 90's and into the 21st century.

Biggs's notoriety came only after he was sprung from Wandsworth, and in doing so became catapulted into the national consciousness as one of Britain's 'most wanted' criminals.

Others, such as the Krays, the Richardsons and John McVicar, had their spells at the top of the leader board as 'public enemy number one', but Biggs was up there for over three decades, surviving several attempts to bring him back to the UK from Rio de Janeiro to face the music.

Unlike the Krays, the Richardsons and McVicar, Biggs had no track record of violence, which perhaps helped to endear him more to the British public. Ask anyone today to name the members of the Great Train Robbery gang, and Biggs will be the first one they come up with, followed by Buster Edwards - thanks to the 1988 film 'Buster'.

By the end of the 1960's, Biggs was the only known gang member still at large as Jimmy White, Bruce Reynolds, Buster Edwards and Charlie Wilson had all been arrested.

Another misconception is the length of the sentences actually served by the robbers. They may have been sentenced to 30 years in 1964, but due to the 1967 Criminal Justice Act and the establishment of the Parole Board, none were to serve more than 12 and a half years.

As a consequence, there were regular reminders of the robbery on television, on radio and in our newspapers throughout the 1970's as, one by one, the principal players were released. There was also sporadic news in the 1970's and 1980's when some of those reoffended and were returned to prison.

The death of the unfortunate Jack Mills, who never recovered from the trauma of the events of 8 August 1963, quite rightly attracted much media focus in 1970.

The 25th anniversary of the robbery generated more media interest, but the biggest reminder that year was the release of the film 'Buster' to coincide with the anniversary.

The inspired choice of Phil Collins in the title role ensured that Edwards was portrayed as a 'likeable rogue', but, apart from a cameo in the 1991 Steven Spielberg film 'Hook', this was to be the beginning and the end of Collins's acting career. The film had a strong cast including Julie Walters, Larry Lamb and Sheila Hancock and was fairly popular with the general public despite many critics giving it the thumbs down.

Inevitably, as the years rolled on, the deaths of some of the train robbers guaranteed renewed media coverage, particularly when the death was not due to natural causes. In 1990 it was the apparent execution of Charlie Wilson, shot by a contract killer at his home in Spain. In 1994, it was the suicide of Buster Edwards, found hanging in his lock-up at Waterloo Station, and in 1997 it was the death of Roy James from a heart attack, less than a year after a triple bypass operation had been carried out whilst he was still in prison.

The return to the UK of Ronnie Biggs in 2001 was once again to polarise public opinion. At the age of 71, Biggs was a shadow of his former self having suffered three strokes in as many years, the third in 1999 being the most serious. He was arrested as he got off the plane and immediately taken to prison to serve out the remainder of his sentence.

As the years went by, Biggs made various parole applications, all of which were rejected. However, during this time, his health continued to deteriorate. Public opinion was divided between those who felt that Biggs should remain incarcerated until he had served out his original sentence, and those who believed it inhumane to continue to keep an 80 year old man with failing health under lock and key.

Finally, in 2009, Biggs was released on compassionate grounds and was taken to a nursing home in Barnet where he remained until his death in December 2013.

His funeral, and that of Bruce Reynolds who had passed away ten months earlier, was covered extensively by the media with appropriate obituaries in most newspapers. One endearing memory is of a wheel-chair bound Biggs giving a two fingered salute to photographers at the funeral of his old pal Reynolds.

There was also a significant amount of media interest in the 50th anniversary of the Robbery in August 2013, and in 2014 two DVD's were released – '*The Great Train Robbery, a Robbers Tale, and a Copper's Tale*' and '*The Great British Train Robbery, A Tale of Two Thieves*'.

The second DVD was brought out to coincide with an interview given by Gordon Goody to *The Observer* in September 2014 during which Goody revealed the true identity of the person only previously known as the 'Ulsterman'.

However, Goody continued to remain coy about the identity of the person who coshed the train driver Jack Mills. Whilst he confirmed that it wasn't James

Hussey, who had made a deathbed confession in 2012, Goody refused to go into any detail as to who actually did deliver the blow. [6]

The release of Goody's autobiography '*How to Rob a Train*' in November 2014 would have seemed an appropriate time to lay this particular matter to rest, but disappointingly, there were no further revelations from the former train robber.

So, have we now reached the end of the story and are we witnessing the last rites of the Great Train Robbery, particularly as just three of the known robbers, Goody, Bob Welch and Tommy Wisbey, are still alive.

Personally, I think not and the flurry of DVD's and printed words about the robbery in the last couple of years suggest that I may be right.

And, as recent as 16 June 2015, evidence that the Great Train Robbery has no intention of going quietly into the night was demonstrated with the holding of yet another auction of train robbery memorabilia. Almost 400 items went under the hammer, many of these hand-signed by Bruce Reynolds and Ronnie Biggs, attracting telephone and internet bids from across the globe.

We still remember Robin Hood and His Merry Men some 800 years after their exploits captured the imagination of the good folk of Nottingham. What is there to stop the Great Train Robbery having a similar longevity?

CHAPTER 33
The Flawed Plan?

So, was the Great Train Robbery a masterpiece of criminal planning, or was it doomed to fail because the plan they followed was fatally flawed?

The catalyst for the robbery was the introduction of the Ulsterman (Patrick McKenna) to Gordon Goody by Brian Field, and the motivation was the size of the potential jackpot. According to Bruce Reynolds, a figure of £6 million was first mentioned by the Ulsterman.[1]

Even the final count of £2,631,784 represented a vast amount of money in 1963 and also involved a huge number of banknotes - probably around a million in total given that the notes in the mail bags were a mixture of £5, £1 and 10 shilling denominations. With each gang member walking away with around £150,000, hiding away upwards of 50,000 banknotes required a significant amount of space.

It is not known whether Bruce Reynolds, Buster Edwards, Charlie Wilson, Roy James or Gordon Goody, the principal architects of the plan, carried out any background checks on the Ulsterman. They may well have taken his word that the information he shared with them had come from a relative employed by the post office. It is almost certain that they wanted to believe everything he said because of the size of the prize that awaited them if all went according to plan.

'*This prospect excited me enormously. What set it apart from the other possibilities was the inside information*' wrote Reynolds. [2]

The exact amount on the train would not be known until the cash was counted after the robbery. Until then, it was, at best, a 'guesstimate' based on the number of mail bags loaded onto the train at Glasgow Central at the beginning of its journey, and the number of other bags it would pick up on route.

Whatever the final figure, the gang's expectations were that it would be a significant amount.

As experienced felons, they would have been well aware that the higher the amount, the more likely it was that other criminals would be drawn towards them, working out ways they could either become involved, or how they might relieve the gang of some of their plunder. It is a fact that several of the gang were swindled out of their share of the loot by so-called friends offering to mind their money or carefully invest it whilst they were serving time in prison.

In addition, if the take from the robbery was as large as they hoped, it would be standard procedure for the banks involved, together with the Post Office in this instance, to offer a fairly sizeable reward for '*such information as will lead to the apprehension and conviction of the persons responsible for this robbery*', as the posters put it. The actual reward offered was £260,000, equivalent to almost £5,000,000 in 2015, and such a huge sum of money acted as a magnet attracting a vast number of calls to The Flying Squad from both members of the public and police informants, the majority of which were hoaxes and red herrings.

The core of the gang itself was made up of men who had worked together previously. However, one stumbling block was that the train had to be stopped at a specific point during its journey and no one could come up with a fool proof way to do this.

The planners came to the conclusion that they needed outside help, and in this instance it meant joining forces with the South Coast Raiders, led by Roger Cordrey. The Raiders were known by reputation, but it helped that Buster Edwards knew one of the gang, Tommy Wisbey, fairly well.

Yet, the fact that most of the robbers knew each other well was both a strength and a weakness. On the plus side they knew what to expect of each other particularly if they should find themselves in a tight corner. The downside was that if one of them was arrested, the police would have a pretty good idea who his friends and known associates were, resulting in other gang members being pulled in for questioning – like a row of dominoes, you knock one down and the rest will follow.

Charlie Wilson, Gordon Goody and Roy James had all been arrested within 24 hours of the BOAC robbery in November 1962, whilst Bruce Reynolds had been listed as a suspect. Wilson and Goody were both charged, but ultimately neither man was convicted.

The four of them must have realised that they would be high up the list of suspects, and that they were certs to be interrogated by the police as they 'shook London until it rattled.'

As part of the planning process, the gang weighed up the options available to them once they had loaded the Land Rovers and the lorry with the mail bags – those options being either a quick return to London, or go to ground somewhere, a sensible distance from the scene of the robbery.

Roy James was against using a hideaway, suggesting instead that they return to London *en masse* in a fleet of Jaguars, with the back seats removed to make room for the money which would still be in the mail sacks. The major drawback here was the loss of the back seats which meant only two people per car, and they would therefore need a minimum of 8 cars.

Apart from James, nobody really liked that idea. For a start a convoy of eight cars on the road early in the morning would be pretty conspicuous, and as no one would know exactly how much money was in each bag in each car, what was to stop the odd bundle of cash disappearing before all the bags were counted?

A second objection to using getaway cars was that if, somehow, the police got an early warning of what was going on at Bridego Bridge, road blocks could be set up fairly quickly to seal off the immediate surrounding area. And, after all, not everyone could handle a 3.8 litre Jag the way Roy James could.

So, overall, the consensus was to locate an appropriate hideaway, and this turned out to be Leatherslade Farm.

Having picked up a copy of the property details for Leatherslade Farm from a local estate agent, Bruce Reynolds decided to have a look at it from the outside. However, not content with this, he let his enthusiasm get the better of him and decided to knock on the door to speak to the owner.

'*It was then that I made a major blunder – we stopped and knocked on the door*' wrote Reynolds in his autobiography. '*By talking to the owner, I was creating a potential link between myself and the crime.*' [3]

Yet, this error was compounded when Brian Field and Leonard Field also called at the farm a couple of days later – this time the pair were shown around by the owner's wife. Not the brightest thing to have done.

The various members of the gang arrived at Leatherslade Farm in dribs and drabs on Tuesday 6 August on the assumption that the robbery would take place in the early hours of the following day.

However, the robbery had to be deferred for 24 hours when the gang received the news, via the Ulsterman, that the train hadn't taken on board a sufficient number of mail bags at Glasgow Central to make the holdup worthwhile.

Because of this, they had time to kill, and, despite Reynolds constantly urging everyone to wear their gloves at all times, mistakes were made, and finger and palm prints were left on an array of items, which would subsequently be discovered by the fingerprint experts from Scotland Yard.

One of those killing time was Pop, the substitute engine driver. Including him in the robbery team not only turned out to be a waste of time, but it could have become a major security risk if he had at any stage been apprehended by the police. It was more by luck than judgement that his presence did not end up biting them all on the backside.

Fortunately, Pop had no criminal record, and any prints that he might have left at the farm were useless to the police as they had nothing to compare them with.

Several of the gang had been totally against Pop being there. Roy James in particular was confident that he could drive the train if it became necessary. But ultimately it came down to a show of hands, and it was agreed to go ahead with Pop's recruitment.

As it turned out on the night, Pop was unable to move the train as its braking system had lost vacuum pressure when the engine and the first two carriages had been uncoupled from the rest of the train. Warning signs that he might have difficulties were already there when Pop admitted to Biggs several weeks before the robbery that he had never driven a D-type diesel before. Whilst the old chap subsequently told Biggs that he had cadged a lift in the cab of a D-type with an old mate, so he would be 'alright on the night', Biggs did not bother to check up on this – probably because he knew that if Pop was told he wasn't needed, the gang would almost certainly exclude him as well.

Fortunately for Pop and Biggs, when Jack Mills was brought back to the driver's cab, he was able to get the train moving. But what would they have done if Mills had refused to move the train, or, worse still, if he had been seriously injured when the robbers stormed his cab? Would Roy James have been able to move it? We will never know.

In total, 120 of the 128 mail bags on the train were unloaded and taken back to Leatherslade Farm, where they were opened and the vast amount of money counted.

In hindsight, Roy James's view that the money should be taken straight back to a safe house in London to be counted was almost certainly the best option.

When the farm was eventually examined by the police forensic and fingerprint teams, they took a total of 243 photographs of scene of crime marks made up of 311 fingers and 56 bits of palm. They also took 1,534 bank envelopes back to the Yard for further examination. All this potential evidence because the robbers had been unbelievably slack with regard to wearing gloves, particularly while counting the money.

Whether this was due to post-robbery euphoria, or because they believed someone was going to clean the farm after they had left, will never be known. Quite possibly it was a combination of both. Whatever the reasons, for many of them, their cavalier attitude was to cost them dearly since ultimately it was fingerprint evidence that would lead to the conviction of the majority of the gang.

The plan had been to remain hidden at Leatherslade Farm for several days, whilst waiting for the initial fuss to die down. Had that happened, that too could have turned out to be a serious error of judgement.

Tommy Butler and Frank Williams had independently compiled a list of suspects fairly soon after the robbery had taken place. Both men believed there were only a limited number of criminals who could pull off such a major heist and consequently their lists included Goody, Wilson, Reynolds, White, Welch, James and Daly. [4]

Had Butler sent out men to check on the whereabouts of all seven, and discovered that none of them were home nor could they be located, this would certainly have had alarm bells ringing back at Scotland Yard.

As it was, the robbers decided to quit the farm early the day after the robbery, when they heard on the radio that police had asked the public to be on the lookout for the 'army vehicles' that had been used in the robbery.

This caused immediate concern since the plan had been for the robbers to return to London in the two Land Rovers and the lorry, on Sunday 11 August. That part of the plan now had to be abandoned, and instead it was left to each gang member to organise their own transport as quickly as they could.

This helps to explain the bizarre behaviour of Roger Cordrey who first turned to his friend William Boal for help in hiding away his share of the robbery, and then used some of that money to buy two cars in Oxford (a Rover and a Wolseley) the day following the robbery, and to purchase another two in Bournemouth (a Ford Anglia and a van) two days later. To be fair to Cordrey, it was just bad luck that he should rent a garage in Bournemouth from the widow of a policeman, who then alerted her late husband's former colleagues.

The normally ultra-cautious Jimmy White was also forced to act out of character when he bought an Austin Healey car from a garage in Chelsea and then a static caravan in Boxhill, Surrey, using money from the robbery.

With other members of the gang having to do the same as Cordrey and White, this would suggest that there was no contingency plan in place to fall back on should they not be able to use the Land Rovers or the lorry, the only form of transport they had available to them at Leatherslade Farm. After all, if, say, the lorry had suffered a major mechanical break-down, they could hardly have called out the RAC or the AA!

However, perhaps the biggest flaw in the planning was the failure to clean up the farm after the robbers had left. Almost certainly this task had been given to the man they knew only as Mark, the same man that Goody and Edwards had met at Brian Field's office, who then took them to meet the Ulsterman for the first time.

The gang's unplanned early departure could well have been the main reason why the cleaning never took place. After all, if they were not due to leave the farm until three days after the robbery, Mark would probably have been planning to do the necessary a day or so after they left, either on Monday 12th or Tuesday 13th August.

Back in 1963, long before the advent of mobile phones and all the other communication tools we take for granted today, the only way to contact someone quickly was by telephone, by telegram or in person, and it is quite possible that Mark was totally unaware that he was needed far sooner than originally intended. It is also possible that Mark got cold feet due to the media frenzy surrounding the robbery.

Unless he was going to burn down the farmhouse and the outbuildings, a thorough clean of a property that size would have taken time, time during which the police could have arrived on the scene at any moment.

According to Bruce Reynolds, before they left the farm; '*People began clearing up, disposing of all combustible evidence in the stove and wiping down every surface and object.*' [5]

However, they must have done a pretty poor job considering the large number of finger and palm prints subsequently found throughout the farm and the outbuildings. This would certainly suggest that getting rid of all the prints would have taken Mark a considerable amount of time if the farm was to be comprehensively cleaned by hand. He would certainly have needed help.

Again in hindsight, the farm and the outbuildings should have been burnt to the ground once the bulk of the robbers had left on the Friday. Certainly it would have brought attention to Leatherslade Farm, and the police would have discovered the hideout several days sooner than they actually did. However, with most if not all of the finger and palm prints destroyed, the police would have had far less evidence to work with, and what they would have been left with, would have been circumstantial at best.

To summarise, the robbery itself was fairly well planned and executed, the one exception being the recruitment of Pop, and even that caused no major damage to the overall operation.

However, not enough thought was given to contingency planning – there did not appear to be any plan 'B' to turn to as evidenced when they were forced to leave the farm far earlier than they had originally intended. A lack of alternative transport which they could have used once the public had been asked to be on the lookout for army type vehicles created an 'every man for himself' culture amongst the robbers.

As a result, many of the gang ended up at Brian Field's house on the Friday night/Saturday morning, while each made arrangements to be picked up by friends or family, and many of Field's neighbours mentioned this when questioned by the police.

Individually, many members of the gang appear to have been ill-prepared to cope with the large number of banknotes they had to pack away in bags and suitcases, as well as being uncertain what they would do, and where they would go, once they quit the farm.

Those, such as Gordon Goody, who had attempted to arrange an alibi for themselves, seem to have gone about this in a fairly amateurish way. For example, Goody's alibi that he was in Ireland on 8 August was soon disproved by the police.

Another major error was the decision to purchase Leatherslade Farm, a decision which, it must be said, only Roy James had tried to resist to any great extent.

We will never know what the eventual outcome would have been if the robbers had agreed to James's suggestion that they return to London immediately they had finished loading the mail bags onto the lorry. Almost certainly, this would have presented them with a different set of problems which, no doubt, they would have needed contingencies for.

But the use of Leatherslade Farm had serious consequences for the gang right from the very start.

Bruce Reynolds, on his own admission, made a fundamental error by calling on the vendors before any sort of offer to purchase the farm had been made. His visit and his face would be remembered by Mr and Mrs Rixon.

Shortly after this, John Wheater was instructed to act for the gang in the purchase of the farm, with Leonard Field used to front that purchase. A few days later, Brian Field and Leonard Field also called on the vendors, compounding the error committed by Reynolds.

Had there been no farm to purchase, John Wheater and Leonard Field almost certainly would not have become involved with the robbery, and their lives would have followed completely different paths to the ones they chose.

Having excluded a quick return to London after the robbery, the need for a base is understandable. However, once Leatherslade Farm had been acquired, it is inevitable that mistakes would be made.

When the message came through via the Ulsterman, that the robbery was to be postponed for 24 hours, the 16 strong gang was cooped up in a four bedroom farmhouse for over 36 hours, and it was almost inevitable that not everyone would remember to wear their gloves at all times.

That same slackness was again evident once the mail bags had been unloaded from the lorry into the farm house, some of it understandable – after all it is almost impossible to count banknotes whilst wearing gloves.

On the day following the robbery, television and radio announcements were made asking people in the area to keep a look out for army vehicles, and to immediately report any sightings. Had the gang already been back in London by this time, there would have been nothing to report. Roger Cordrey would have been back on his home turf by then and probably would never have made his telephone call to William Boal. As a consequence, Boal and his family would have been spared the nightmare they endured over the next six years, although William would still sadly have passed away in 1970 from a brain tumour.

But the biggest mistake of all was the failure to sanitise Leatherslade Farm once everyone had left the scene. Had the robbers gone straight back to London as Roy James had urged, there would have been no farm to clean up, and the police would never have had the *'one big clue'* that led to the convictions of at least half of the gang.

It is always easy to pontificate and pass judgement with the benefit of hindsight. However, the decision to acquire Leatherslade Farm was a fundamental flaw in the planning process for the robbery, and this was compounded by the failure to thoroughly clean the property once the robbers had vacated it. These errors were to set in motion a sequence of events which would leave all but a lucky few facing lengthy sentences behind bars.

CHAPTER 34
The Unanswered Questions

Fifty one years after the event, and there are still unanswered questions. These include; Was Patrick McKenna really the fabled 'Ulsterman'? Who struck driver Jack Mills? Who were the three unknown train robbers whose identities have never been revealed? Who was Mark, the man contracted to clean Leatherslade Farm?

Until September 2014, the name Patrick McKenna, who passed away in 1992 after suffering a heart attack, was remembered only by friends and family. That changed when the *Observer* published their interview with Gordon Goody. [1]

In his fictional book *'The Men Who Robbed The Great Train Robbers'*, published in December 2013, some nine months before the *Observer* article appeared, author Mick Lee has the Ulsterman as an IRA fundraiser who he calls Eddie Maloney. [2]

According to the *Irish Times*, Goody told them that the Ulsterman had been introduced to him as 'Barry' (although Goody states in his autobiography that he was actually introduced as Freddie!).

'When I saw his name on his glasses case and discovered he wasn't Barry, he wasn't at all happy about it. He threatened to walk away. Buster (Edwards) *and I had to promise we would never say anything. And we never did until now.'* [3]

Whilst there is no reason to doubt what Goody told the *Observer*, it is a fact that only Goody, Buster Edwards and Brian Field had face to face contact with the Ulsterman, and as Edwards and Field are both dead, Goody's claim that McKenna was the Ulsterman is uncorroborated.

Patrick McKenna's family were said to be shocked and flabbergasted that he could have had any involvement with the train robbery, particularly since he had just £3,000 to his name when he died.

They believe that if McKenna had been involved in some way, his conscience may have got the better of him, and that he could well have donated his share to the Catholic Church.

However, if McKenna was involved in raising funds for the IRA as Mick Lee's book suggests, this could also explain why the McKenna family never saw a penny of the robbery money.

Verdict: It may be uncorroborated, but Patrick McKenna was a real person who was born in Belfast and worked for the Post Office. He would certainly fit the profile of the Ulsterman.

But why did Gordon Goody wait so long to reveal the identity of the Ulsterman if he was indeed Patrick McKenna?

The answer may lie in the *Observer* interview where Goody says that he has decided to write a book saying '*I suppose it was time to put a few things straight.*'

As Adam S. McHugh once said, '*the work of promoting the book requires just as much work as writing the book, if not more so.*'

Two months after the Observer interview, in November 2014, Goody's autobiography '*How to Rob a Train*' was released.

Gordon Goody may have revealed the true identity of the Ulsterman, but he continues to remain reticent about the identity of the man who struck train driver Jack Mills. Despite James Hussey making a deathbed statement in November 2012 that he hit Mills, it is by no means certain that Hussey was the culprit.

Goody is adamant that it wasn't Hussey, and John Mills, the son of Jack, has said that his father had told him who did it, and that it wasn't Hussey.

Another candidate is Buster Edwards who died in 1994, and in Piers Paul Reads book '*The Train Robbers, Their Story*', Edwards is said to have struck Mills twice whilst the driver was being restrained by Gordon Goody. [4]

However, this is unlikely as, by all accounts, when the blow was struck, Edwards was in the process of taking care of assistant driver David Whitby some distance away from the engine.

There is a strong possibility that the person responsible was one of the three unnamed members of the gang, despite Jack Mills having given his son the name of his assailant.

In his autobiography, Bruce Reynolds wrote that the person who hit Mills '*could not be charged because of the lack of evidence………he had left no fingerprints or identifiable marks elsewhere.*

'None of those arrested informed on him, although he had completely disobeyed instructions and used violence during the robbery.' [5]

Verdict: This is almost a case of *'you pays your money and you takes your choice'* as it could be any one from five – Hussey, Edwards or one of the three robbers who have never been named nor prosecuted.

Almost certainly, we will never know the answer, but if I was a betting man, I would go for one of three who have been known only by the aliases they used - Bill Jennings, Alf Thomas or Frank Munroe.

But, in this instance, I will leave the last words on this matter to Gordon Goody; *'I'm not going to make a suggestion. It should never have happened. It wasn't our intention to do any harm to anyone. A lot of people came in the door into the cab. So I'll give it to the person who was behind me. But we were all wearing balaclavas. And it was dark'* [6]

Whilst never named, it is indisputable that there were four men present during the robbery whose true identities have remained a secret for over 51 years; Pop, the train driver recruited by Ronnie Biggs, and the three men known only by the aliases Bill Jennings, Alf Thomas and Frank Munroe.

Bill Jennings had worked with Buster Edwards for a few years before he became a regular member of the gang that robbed the BOAC offices in November 1962, so it was nailed on that he would also have taken part in the train robbery nine months later.

In his autobiography, Bruce Reynolds, who referred to Jennings by the nickname 'Flossy', wrote that *'he had no previous convictions and stayed well out of contact with the group. A shadowy figure, nobody knew exactly where he lived or even what his real name was. All we knew was that he was one hundred per cent.'* [7]

It is difficult to believe that they appeared to know so little personal detail about someone they trusted implicitly, and who they had worked with on numerous earlier jobs.

However, it is possible that Reynolds was making sure that he simply shut the door early on in his book on the possibility of giving away clues to the real identity of Bill Jennings.

Alf Thomas was a friend of Jimmy White's and was said to be in the gang to provide extra muscle if needs be. It was Thomas and White who had bought the lorry and one of the Land Rovers at auction, and it was Thomas who drove the lorry to and from Bridego Bridge on the night of the robbery. He was also part of the team that smashed its way into the HVP coach.

There is a lot of speculation that the money left in a telephone box in South East London on 10 December 1963, was put there by Thomas, or someone acting on his behalf, after banknotes stolen during the train robbery were traced back to some of his friends who were now being held for receiving.

So the story goes, the money left in the phone box, which totalled £47,245, was being 'returned' by Thomas so that police would abandon attempts to link him to the money found on his friends, and to drop any further investigations into whether it was he who struck Jack Mills.

In his book, A Detective's Tale, George Hatherill, former Head of CID at Scotland Yard, wrote that the money was returned by '*one about whom extensive inquiries had been made....But in spite of our strong suspicions, nothing could be proved against him, and so no charge could be brought. My belief is that he thought we knew more about him than we did, and thinking things were getting hot, he decided to get rid of the money to avoid being found in possession of it.*' [8]

Frank Munroe came to the train robbery gang as one of the South Coast Raiders, being described by Bruce Reynolds as their 'motivator'. His role during the robbery was to add muscle, and, like Alf Thomas, to be part of the assault team on the HVP coach.

And, like Thomas, he went to ground in the immediate aftermath of the robbery, thus escaping the attentions of the police, and would never be brought to justice.

In later years, Frank Munroe is believed to have become a movie stunt man for a while, before setting up a recycling and scrap metal business. It was as the boss of this that Munroe offered Bruce Reynolds a job, although this was more 'for old time's sake' than anything else, and would only last for a few months.

Whilst the identities of Bill Jennings, Alf Thomas and Frank Munroe have never come into the public domain, there is no doubt that their real names were known to the police, and almost certainly they would have been interviewed at one time or another.

It is possible that all three were far more careful during their stay at Leatherslade Farm than the other robbers and that no finger or palm print evidence linking them to the robbery was ever found.

It is also likely that their names appeared on the list of suspects drawn up by the Flying Squad as soon as they assumed responsibility for tracking those that carried out the robbery.

Names that have cropped up from time to time as possible members of the gang are Terry Hogan, Henry (Harry) Smith, Danny Regan and Daniel Pembroke.

Hogan, who Bruce Reynolds refers to as Harry Booth in his autobiography, was a long-standing friend of Reynolds, and could have been the robber known only as Bill Jennings.

Bruce Reynolds described Hogan, who was a member of the gang that robbed the BOAC offices, as being; '*involved in most of the major crimes of the time and, although he was not much older than me, he was very much my mentor. 'Lucky' Harry never got caught. In fact, he only ever served a short sentence for a matter unrelated to the many robberies he took part in.*'

'*Soon afterwards* (the train robbery), *married and with a family, Harry decided to quit crime completely. He went into the textile business and lived a respectable life in West London.*' [9]

Was it just a coincidence that Hogan gave up crime and went straight soon after the train robbery, even though he had an alibi which put him in Cannes on 7/8 August?

More likely to be Bill Jennings was Henry Smith, who was known to have worked with Charlie Wilson. On 5 May 1964, Smith was interviewed by Tommy Butler and Frank Williams and two days later attended an identification parade. Despite being brought before 10 people, none of these picked Smith out and he was released from custody.

However, Butler still believed Smith to be involved; '*there was not the slightest doubt in our minds ..... that Smith....was one of the robbers actually at the scene and taking a very active part in the commission of the offence......We have been defeated on the question of physical identification, whilst any palm and finger impressions he may have left at the farm were erased before the arrival of officers from the Fingerprint Department.*' [10]

It was also recorded that '*there is the house in Barking Road in which Smith has been living and which has now been sumptuously furnished.*' [11]

In his autobiography, Bruce Reynolds wrote of Alf Thomas that he '*was a notable recruit. A mate of Jimmy's* (White), *we were going to need some hard men and Alf fitted the bill.*'

A betting shop that was next door to a café owned by Jimmy White was one of several owned and run by Danny Regan and his brothers. Regan was also a friend of Henry Smith.

In a report to Commander George Hatherill, Tommy Butler wrote; '*On 27 September 1963, Regan was brought to this office and closely interrogated concerning the offence. He staunchly denied all knowledge of it. His palm prints were taken and compared with those left at the farm, but no identification was made. Regan admitted knowing White and Smith and several of the other persons who at the time had been arrested for complicity in the offence, but said that he had not seen any of them for many weeks.* [12]

When Detective Sergeants Slipper and Suter travelled to Hampshire to search a couple of properties Danny Regan had purchased, they found details of other properties purchased by Regan and his associates which included '*thirty two houses (including a row of eleven), a drinking club and a hotel in the Portsmouth and Gosport districts.*' [13]

Daniel Pembroke, who was known to be friends with Tommy Wisbey and Bob Welch, was arrested on 6 September 1963 by Frank Williams and Jack Slipper and taken back to Scotland Yard. Whilst being interviewed at the Yard by Tommy Butler and Williams, his palm prints were taken as was a sample of hair. None of these were a match for those found at Leatherslade Farm.

Pembroke was also one of those that had accompanied Bob Welch to Beaford, North Devon, in the middle of September where they were kept under constant surveillance by the local police. Could Pembroke have been Frank Munroe?

Verdict: Over 50 years have passed since the Great Train Robbery, during which time the true identities of Bill Jennings, Alf Thomas and Frank Munroe have not been revealed. It is now highly unlikely that their real names will ever become known, although Henry Smith's file in the police archive will become available in 2036 - so there's something to look forward to! [14]

It is evident, given the extracts above, that Tommy Butler firmly believed that Henry Smith and Danny Regan were two of the three who were never caught.

However Butler, who was notorious for keeping his cards close to his chest, is no longer with us, and his passing in 1970 no doubt enhanced the chances of Jennings, Thomas and Munroe remaining anonymous for posterity.

Not much is known about Mark, the multi-tasker who took Buster Edwards and Gordon Goody to meet the Ulsterman, and who then failed to clean Leatherslade Farm as arranged after the robbers had left early and in somewhat of a hurry.

For someone about whom so little is known, Mark played two very pivotal roles in the Great Train Robbery. However, the likelihood is that Mark was not the first choice to do the clean-up.

In her book 'the Robber's Tale, Peta Fordham wrote; '*the truth was that a very close associate had originally been entrusted with the job, which he would undoubtedly have carried out faithfully. Unfortunately, a 'brush' with the police, a few days before the robbery, kept him tailed so closely that the robbers considered him too risky to use. They had, however, considered that they would have plenty of time themselves.*' [15]

The original cleaner was almost certainly William Still, who was well known to both Bruce Reynolds and John Daly.

However, contrary to Peta Fordham's understanding, Still was arrested on 25 June, some 6 weeks before the robbery, after police found him and three others to be in possession of explosives, detonators, drills, putty, a pick axe handle, jemmy and nylon stockings – not items that were readily available from the local corner shop in 1963. [16]

When a bail application for Still was not admitted, Brian Field stepped in and said he would arrange for a cleaner, on payment, of course, of the money that Still was to have received – believed to be in the region of £30,000. The cleaner in question was Field's associate Mark.

A few days after the robbery some of the gang began to get edgy that such an important job as removing all traces of their stay at Leatherslade Farm, had been entrusted to someone Goody and Edwards had only met the once – this being Mark.

Charlie Wilson contacted Field to make sure that Mark had done the business. Despite receiving Field's reassurances, Wilson was less than convinced, and he had every right to be concerned.

Not long after, news broke that Leatherslade Farm had been discovered and it soon became obvious to everyone that the mysterious Mark had let them down and had failed to fulfil his part of the bargain.

Verdict: No doubt the police would have asked why the farm hadn't been cleaned when interviewing all of those arrested for the train robbery. However, not only would they have remained silent since they would not 'grass' anybody up, the robbers genuinely wouldn't have known Mark's true identity.

All that was known at the time was that he was someone connected to Brian Field. And I'm not certain that the police were particularly interested in knowing who Mark was since, virtually single-handedly, he had placed the heads of most of the robbers on a platter for them.

Many of the robbers would have held a deep-rooted grudge against both Brian Field and Mark, and may well have wanted to exact some degree of vengeance on their release.

This, no doubt, was one of the reasons why Brian Field completely changed his identity after his release from prison, and he did this so well, that, to all intent and purposes, he vanished off the face of the earth.

In *'The Autobiography of a Thief'*, Bruce Reynolds wrote of Field that; *'I...discovered that someone had been waiting for him on the day he was released from prison – a character called Scotch Jack Buggy, who'd just done eight or nine years for shooting someone at Club Pigalle. Buggy was a heavy and I knew his opening line: 'I know you got money from the train, give me some or else'.*

I don't know what happened to Brian, but I'm sure it was no picnic. He probably got roughed up, maybe tortured; whatever the case, he went to ground.' [17]

With this acting as an incentive, Mark almost certainly would have done the same as Field and disappeared. He had the added advantage that none of the robbers had known his true identity in the first place, so there was no real trace for them to follow, nor could anyone but Gordon Goody and Buster Edwards put a face to his name.

The true identity of Mark, as with Pop, Bill Jennings, Alf Thomas and Frank Munroe, will almost certainly never become known.

CHAPTER 35
The Curse, or just bad luck?

There are a number of so-called 'curses' which have become very well-known over the years such as; 'the Curse of the Hope Diamond', 'the Curse of the Kennedy Family' and, perhaps the most famous of them all, 'the Curse of Tutankhamen's Tomb'.

In the first edition of his autobiography, Bruce Reynolds wrote that the Great Train Robbery *'proved a curse that followed me around'*.

If indeed the robbery itself was cursed, then those that committed it have only themselves to blame.

But what about their families, and those people who were just going about their normal daily business, yet found their lives blighted forever by just being in the wrong place at the wrong time?

Was the Great Train Robbery truly cursed, or was it just bad luck that affected many of those who were both directly and indirectly connected to this crime in some way? Common sense tells us that curses only exist in science and fantasy fiction. On that basis, the following must simply be a fairly lengthy catalogue of bad luck.

Or is it?

After serving his time in prison for the train robbery, **Bruce Reynolds** was finally released in 1978. However, he found himself back in prison in 1983 having been arrested and charged with dealing with amphetamines.

Whilst her husband was in prison for the first time, **Frances Reynolds** began to suffer from severe depression triggered by the death of her brother. She was hospitalised shortly after, having taken an overdose, and suffered from further bouts of severe depression over the course of several years, until Bruce was released in 1985.

Charlie Wilson was also released from prison in 1978. He had further brushes with the law in 1984 when accused of a VAT fraud along with **Roy James**, and the following year when he spent four months in jail awaiting trial for the alleged armed robbery of a security van. He was freed amid allegations of police corruption.

In 1990, Wilson was gunned down at his villa in Spain, apparently a victim of a feud between rival drug dealers.

Buster Edwards found himself back in prison within a few months of being released in April 1975. His crime this time was shoplifting goods worth £66 from Harrods department store - a far cry from walking away from the train robbery with nigh on £150,000.

Edwards found it very difficult to adapt to a life without crime and the adrenaline rush that went with it. He suffered from depression and a serious drink problem, regularly consuming a bottle of vodka a day. One can only imagine the agonies Edwards put his wife June and daughter Nicolette through.

In 1994, he was found hanging from a metal beam in his lock-up close to the flower stall he worked from at Waterloo Station. He was 63 years old.

Roy James left prison in 1975, optimistic that he would be able to pick up his career as a racing driver. Sadly, this was not to be the case as too many years had passed, and a serious crash put paid to his dreams.

In 1984 he was charged along with **Charlie Wilson** of being involved in a £2.4 million VAT fraud. He was acquitted after a retrial.

In 1994 James was sentenced to six years in prison for shooting his father-in-law and for assaulting Anthea James, his wife. In 1996, whilst still in prison, he underwent a triple bypass operation, and was released early the following year as his heath continued to deteriorate. A few months later, he died of a heart attack aged 62.

In January 1971, **Nicholas**, the eldest son of **Ronnie** and **Charmian** Biggs, was killed in a motor accident in Kilsyth, Australia. He was just 10 years old.

Farley, their youngest son, also suffered injuries, and with Biggs on the run and living in Rio de Janeiro at the time, the news took almost a month to reach him.

In 1971, **Lorraine Wisbey**, the sixteen year old daughter of **Renee** and **Tommy Wisbey**, was killed in a car accident. Despite the prison authorities having no objections to Tommy attending his daughter's funeral, for some inexplicable reason, Home Secretary Reginald Maudling refused to give his consent.

Renee Wisbey and her daughter **Marilyn** struggled to come to terms with their loss and both fell into a state of deep depression, with Marilyn requiring psychiatric care.

Tommy Wisbey was released from prison in February 1976, but within a year began a 15 month spell on remand during which his wife suffered a minor stroke, triggered by her husband's arrest.

In 1989 Wisbey and **James Hussey** were sentenced to 10 years and 7 years in prison respectively after having pleaded guilty to trafficking cocaine.

Bob Welch was released in 1976 and never returned to crime. Whilst in prison he was divorced by his wife **Mary**, who spent two months in a mental hospital in Newcastle, as she discovered Welch had had a child by a woman named **Jean Steel** prior to his arrest in October 1963. Steel also suffered from psychiatric problems including depression and panic attacks.

Whilst in prison, Welch was left partially crippled by a botched operation to repair knee ligaments which resulted in him needing to use crutches at all times.

A grave miscarriage of justice resulted in **William Boal** being sentenced to 24 years imprisonment in 1964, which was reduced to 14 years on appeal. However, Boal should have been sentenced to no more than a couple of years on three counts of receiving, leaving him a free man to enjoy the remaining years of his life.

Sadly, William Boal died from a brain tumour on 8 June 1970 after having been admitted to hospital on 29 May. Right up to the end, he was still protesting his innocence.

Boal's son **David** said that his father's conviction '*virtually destroyed his life*' and those of his mother **Renee**, his brother **Anthony** and his sister **Debbie**.

Renee was to lose her own battle with cancer in 1992. [1]

Whilst her husband was acquitted of robbery and conspiracy to rob on 14 February 1964 on the instructions of the trial judge, **Barbara Daly** had started suffering from severe depression almost immediately after **John Daly's** arrest on 3 December 1963. Speaking shortly after John's death in April 2013, Barbara told the *Cornish Echo* that the pair had lived in fear of his being re-arrested, and that 'she hated the train robbery which had become like a millstone on her back'.

Having been recruited by Ronnie Biggs, **Pop**, the back-up train driver, would have begun living on his nerves immediately he heard that Biggs had been arrested by the police. Not only that, he feared that some of the other robbers might come looking for him with a view to silencing him forever.

His **wife** hadn't known that he had been part of the gang at first, since Biggs had concocted a story that he and Pop were going on a tree felling job somewhere in Wiltshire.

When author Piers Paul Reid managed to track down Pop, who he called 'Stan Agate', some dozen or so years after the robbery, he found that the name Ronnie Biggs still got an angry reaction from Pop's wife.

It was solicitor's clerk **Brian Field** who introduced **Gordon Goody** and **Buster Edwards** to **Patrick McKenna**, the Ulsterman, and in so doing set The Great Train Robbery's wheels in motion.

In his relatively short life, Field managed to marry three times. His first wife, **Brenda**, also worked for James and Wheater, and the pair married in 1958. However, the marriage didn't last that long, and Brian and Brenda were divorced three years later. Brian married his second wife, **Karin**, the following year, whereas Brenda left it a little longer before tying the knot again. She married for a second time in 1966, ironically to another man named Brian. Sadly, Brenda died in 1979 aged just 45. [2]

Field's second wife, Karin, gave birth to a baby girl who was 16 weeks premature, with doctors blaming this on the stresses and strains of her husband's arrest. Sadly, the baby did not survive and 18 months later the couple divorced.

Brian Field was released in April 1967, and fell off the radar until 1979 when he and his third wife, **Sian**, were killed in a car accident on the M4. Brian Field was 44 years old at the time of his death; his wife was only in her late twenty's.

Patrick McKenna died of a heart attack in 1992 aged 72. He went to his grave never having shared with his family that, as the fabled Ulsterman, he had played a pivotal role in The Great Train Robbery. When **Gordon Goody** revealed the true identity of the Ulsterman in September 2014, it came as a complete and utter shock to McKenna's family who will now forever be associated with the train robbery.

Of the others involved with either the planning or the execution of the robbery, **James Hussey** was back in prison in 1989 having been sentenced to 7 years after pleading guilty to drug-trafficking charges. He passed away in 2012 having suffered from cancer.

Gordon Goody was released in 1975 and went to work in the furniture business after which he went into the wholesale Vegetable trade. His biggest regret, so he said, was the grief and all the upset he caused his **mother** – on one arm he has the tattoo 'Dear Mother'.

On his release he immediately went back to live with his mother who had had a stroke while he was in prison, and was now suffering from cancer.

After she died, Goody moved permanently to Spain and ran a bar before retiring. At the time of writing, he lives with his partner and their five dogs in the Spanish countryside.

Roger Cordrey's bad luck (or was he the first victim to the curse?) began a couple of days before he took part in the train robbery, when his wife left him, taking their children with her. After his release, and after having tried to help Tommy Wisbey's daughter Marilyn to break into show business, [3] Cordrey went to live in the West Country and resumed his career as a florist. He retired to Swanage and passed away in 2005.

Jimmy White moved to Sussex and became a roofing contractor using one of his old aliases, James Patten. White died in November 2012 aged 84.

After his release in 1965, **John Wheater** moved to Harrogate to run the family dry cleaning business. He died in 1985 at the relatively young age of 64.

And finally, **Leonard Field** kept his nose clean after his release in 1967, and is believed to have passed away in 2005.

Jack Mills was never the same man again after the robbery due to a combination of the physical injuries and the psychological trauma he suffered on 8 August 1963. He made several unsuccessful attempts to return to work and sadly passed away in 1970, aged 64, from chronic lymphocytic leukaemia.

Mills is often referred to as 'the forgotten man' of the Great Train Robbery, due to the fact that the robbers attracted far more attention because of the amount of money they stole, and the length of the prison sentences they received.

Even more forgotten than Mills is his assistant that night, **David Whitby**, who was just 25 years old when the robbery occurred. His family also say he was never the same after the robbery, and David died in 1972 after suffering a heart attack. He was just 34 years old.

Frank Dewhurst was one of the five post office workers inside the HVP coach subjected to the 'shock and awe' attack by several of the train robbery gang. Dewhurst was struck five or six times during that attack as the robbers looked to quash any hint of retaliation from within.

Frank Dewhurst died from a heart attack 28 months after the raid on the train. He was just 51 years old.

Having devoted his life to putting criminals behind bars, **Tommy Butler** had to accept the compulsory retirement his superiors 'offered' him in 1969. By far, he would have preferred working until he dropped.

Sadly, Butler died just 16 months into his retirement, a victim of lung cancer, even though he was a non-smoker. The cancer was almost certainly caused by passive smoking. Having completed decades of public service, if anyone deserved a long and healthy retirement, it was Tommy Butler who was just 57 years old when he passed away.

Butler's deputy during the years spent tracking down the robbers, was **Frank Williams** who everyone expected to eventually succeed Butler as Head of the Flying Squad. However, Butler's extended service gave the hierarchy at Scotland Yard more time to consider who should succeed him, and a general feeling that he had helped Buster Edwards receive a shorter sentence than he deserved probably scuppered Williams's chances. He would eventually leave the force to take up a position with the airline Qantas as Head of Security.

Of the other members of the police force involved with the train robbery, **Jack Slipper** died in 2005, aged 81, after a long battle with cancer; **Malcolm Fewtrell** also passed away in 2005, aged 96; **George Hatherill** was 87 when he passed away in 1986; **Ernie Millen** was 77 when he died and **Gerald**

MacArthur, who became renowned for breaking the infamous Richardson gang, died in 1996 aged 70.

John Maris was a herdsman who received a reward for contacting the police and telling them that he thought Leatherslade Farm had been used as a hideaway by the train robbers. This call prevented the farm from being cleaned and cleared of all the evidence that was eventually used by the prosecution to convict the majority of the robbers.

However, his actions were not without recriminations, and for years after, Maris and his wife **Grace** were subjected to hate mail and the occasional sinister visitor to the area asking locals where they lived. Thankfully, words spoke louder than actions and Mr and Mrs Maris lived to tell the tale.

So there you have it. Was the Great Train Robbery cursed, or did many of those involved in some way or another, merely enjoy some rank bad luck mixed in with a helping of serious misfortune? For what it is worth, I believe it is the latter – but what do you think?

I end this book as it began, leaving the last words to Ronnie Biggs; *'The people who paid the heaviest price for the Great Train Robbery are the families. And that is the families of all the people involved with the Great Train Robbery. The Robbers families, the families of Old Bill, the families of the rail men and the post office workers, and even the families of the people that have helped us over the years. All have paid a price, one way or another, for our collective involvement in the robbery.'*

POSTSCRIPT
'Not a lot of people know that'

It is believed that Bruce Reynolds was the inspiration for Michael Caine's portrayal of the fictional spy Harry Palmer, created by writer Len Deighton, in the films 'The IPCRESS File', 'Funeral in Berlin' and the 'Billion Dollar Brain.'

At the end of August 1963, the *Daily Mirror* held a competition inspired by the Great Train Robbery when it asked readers to submit their suggestions as to how they would hide £250,000 in five pound notes. The prize for the best suggestion was £50, equivalent to over £900 today.

The winner was a Mr McBride from Doncaster in Yorkshire who said he would give it to his wife as she had a talent for losing things around the house. McBride told the *Daily Mirror 'I feel that she is capable of concealing a herd of elephants in the cupboards which would defy all the resources of Scotland Yard to find.'* [1]

To celebrate the 50th anniversary of the Great Train Robbery, the Luton Model Railway Club created a miniature replica of the scene of the heist which included bags of cash being unloaded from the HVP carriage and fifteen robbers making their escape with their ill-gotten gains. Begun in 2013, it took the modellers a year to complete and went on display at the National Festival of Railway Modelling in Peterborough in October 2014.

A spokesman for the club said *'We do not condone the actions of the event, but it is a fact that the Great Train Robbery has become a part of the national consciousness for many people over a certain age. We have tried to portray this event in a sensitive way, taking due regard for the injuries sustained by the locomotive crew on the night.'*

In the 1988 film 'Buster', Buster Edwards (played by Phil Collins) and Bruce Reynolds (played by Larry Lamb) are portrayed as supporting Charlton Athletic Football Club. In the first reference, 'Harry', a member of the Reynolds gang, tells Buster Edwards *'I was unlucky. I done the 18 months. You went off to watch Charlton Athletic'* to which Buster responds *'Yeah, well they got beat 4-0. See I told you we were both unlucky.'*

In the second reference, Edwards, reading an English newspaper whilst lounging in a swimming pool in Acapulco, Mexico, turns to Reynolds and says *'Bloody Hell. Bruce, Bruce! Charlton Athletic won at Manchester City. Eddie Firmani scored twice.'* To which Reynolds replies *'Fantastic.'*

The connection with Charlton continued, according to the great Sir Stanley Matthews, when Ronnie Biggs invited him to his apartment in Rio de Janeiro after hearing that Matthews was in the city.

According to the footballer in his autobiography; *'We had tea on the small balcony at the rear of his home, and one of the first things he asked was 'how are Charlton Athletic doing?' It turned out he had supported Charlton from being a small boy and had often seen me play at The Valley.'* [2]

On 4 February 1969 an auction was held of items belonging to some of the Great Train Robbers. 128 items went under the hammer at the event in Measham, in Staffordshire raising £9,837 – equivalent to around £130,000 today. As well as household items belonging to Bruce Reynolds, the Austin-Healey sports car which he bought for £835 in 1963 went for £930.

46 years later, on 18 February 2015, at an auction in Northamptonshire, an eclectic range of items were sold, including a watch and signet ring worn by Ronnie Biggs which fetched £900, and parts of the Monopoly set used by some of the gang during their stay at Leatherslade Farm, which sold for £400.

Other items that went under the hammer included a £1 and a 10 shilling note stolen during the robbery as well as a piece of wire used to tamper with the railway signalling and a key from one of the getaway cars.

Auctioneer Jonathan Humbert told the Northampton News: *'This proves the enduring appeal of this most audacious robbery and we are delighted with the result and the 100% sale rate.'* [3]

The author Graham Greene wrote to the *Daily Telegraph* asking *'Am I one of a minority in feeling admiration for the skill and courage behind the Great Train Robbery? More important, am I in a minority in being shocked by the savagery of the sentences?'*

During his short spell in Winson Prison, before his escape on 12 August 1964, prison authorities put Charlie Wilson to work sewing mail bags. Quite ironic, considering he was in prison for stealing 120 of them!

Dubbed Alec in Blunderland, the Chief Constable of Durham, Alec Muir, once said that violent criminals should be disposed of, and the Great Train Robbers should have been shot. He followed this up by saying Durham Prison, which at the time held several of the Great Train Robbers, should be prepared for an attack by criminals in tanks and armed with small nuclear weapons to blast their way into prison in an attempt to free them!

The house that Bruce Reynolds rented in Torquay, where he was living when arrested by Detective Chief Superintendent Tommy Butler, had once been rented by Carry On star Sid James. [4]

Somewhat bizarrely, Buster Edwards was the victim of a crime in 1991 when actor Dexter Fletcher ran past his flower stall outside Waterloo Station and snatched two bunches of flowers. As it happened, Edwards had seen Fletcher in a film the previous evening and so was able to tell police precisely who had robbed him!

According to *Life Magazine*, 'at least one gang wife was incensed last year to hear that Liz Taylor and Richard Burton hoped to do a movie about the crime: *"Fancy a tart like 'er playing a respectable woman like Frances Reynolds."'* [5]

In July 2015, Ian Mills, the grandson of Jack Mills, unveiled a street sign as part of the launch of Jack Mills Way, a £7million road linking the A500 at Shavington with Gresty Road in Crewe.

NOTES

THE STORY

Chapter 1 – The Planning

1. Bruce Reynolds, *The Autobiography of a Thief*, Page 204
2. Bruce Reynolds, *The Autobiography of a Thief*, Page 206
3. Piers Paul Read, *The Train Robbers, Their Story*, Page 42
4. Piers Paul Read, *The Train Robbers, Their Story*, Page 45
5. Bruce Reynolds, *The Autobiography of a Thief*, Page 212
6. Piers Paul Read, *The Train Robbers, Their Story*, Page 48
7. Jim Morris, *The Great Train Robbery, a New History*, Page 17
8. Bruce Reynolds, *The Autobiography of a Thief*, Page 201
9. *North Wales Daily Post*, 18 December 2013
10. The *Observer*, 28 September 2014
11. Bruce Reynolds, *The Autobiography of a Thief*, Page 226
12. Chris Pickard, Nick Reynolds, *The Great Train Robbery*, Page 19
13. Piers Paul Read, *The Great Train Robbers, Their Story*, Page 83
14. Nick Russell Pavier & Stewart Richards, *The Great Train Robbery, The Definitive Account*, Page 59
15. Jim Morris, *The Great Train Robbery, a New History*, Page 24
16. Bruce Reynolds, *The Autobiography of a Thief*, Page 229
17. Daily Post, 18 December 2013 – www.dailypost.co.uk/
18. Piers Paul Read, *The Train Robbers, Their Story*, Page 85
19. Piers Paul Read, *The Train Robbers, Their Story*, Page 85
20. Piers Paul Read, *The Train Robbers, Their Story*, Page 85
21. Bruce Reynolds, *The Autobiography of a Thief*, Page 237
22. Nick Russell Pavier & Stewart Richards, *The Great Train Robbery, The Definitive Account*, Page 17
23. Nick Russell Pavier & Stewart Richards, *The Great Train Robbery, The Definitive Account,* Page 62
24. Bruce Reynolds, *The Autobiography of a Thief*, Page 228
25. *Moments of History, The Great British Train Robbery*, 1963, Page 67
26. Piers Paul Read, *The Train Robbers, Their Story*, Page 99
27. Nick Russell Pavier & Stewart Richards, *The Great Train*

Robbery, The Definitive Account, Page 405-7

Chapter 2 – The Robbery

1. Bruce Reynolds, *The Autobiography of a Thief*, Page 242
2. Ronnie Biggs, *Odd Man Out*, Page 22
3. Jim Morris, *The Great Train Robbery, a New History*, Page 30
4. Peta Fordham, *The Robbers Tale*, Page 74
5. Bruce Reynolds, *The Autobiography of a Thief*, Page 246
6. Ronnie Biggs, *Odd Man Out*, Page 27
7. Piers Paul Read, *The Train Robbers, Their Story*, Page 115
8. Nick Russell Pavier & Stewart Richards, *The Great Train Robbery, The Definitive Account*, Page 32
9. Nick Russell Pavier & Stewart Richards, *The Great Train Robbery, The Definitive Account*, Page 36
10. Ronnie Biggs, *Odd Man Out*, Page 28
11. *Moments of History, The Great British Train Robbery*, 1963, Page 31
12. *Moments of History, The Great British Train Robbery*, 1963, Page 32

Chapter 3 – The First Few Days

1. Bruce Reynolds, *The Autobiography of a Thief*, Page 248
2. Ronnie Biggs, *Odd Man Out*, Page 29
3. *Moments of History, The Great British Train Robbery*, 1963, Page 35
4. *Moments of History, The Great British Train Robbery*, 1963, Page 53-54
5. Nick Russell Pavier & Stewart Richards, *The Great Train Robbery, The Definitive Account*, Page 81
6. *Moments of History, The Great British Train Robbery*, 1963, Page 55
7. Bruce Reynolds, *The Autobiography of a Thief*, Page 252
8. Nick Russell Pavier & Stewart Richards, *The Great Train Robbery, The Definitive Account*, Page 98
9. Ronnie Biggs, *Odd Man Out*, Page 34
10. Peta Fordham, *The Robbers Tale*, Page 85
11. Robert Ryan, *Signal Red*, Page 379
12. *Moments of History, The Great British Train Robbery*, 1963,

Page 57

13. *Moments of History, The Great British Train Robbery*, 1963, Page 60

14. Andrew Cook, *The Great Train Robbery*, Page 45

15. Bruce Reynolds, *The Autobiography of a Thief*, Page 255

Chapter 4 – The Breakthrough

1. *Moments of History, The Great British Train Robbery*, 1963, Page 70

2. *Daily Mirror*, 3 August 2013

3. www.bbc.co.uk/news/uk-england-beds-bucks-herts-23572717

4. Chris Pickard, Nick Reynolds, *The Great Train Robbery*, Page 39

5. Ronnie Biggs, *Odd Man Out*, Page 38

6. Chris Pickard, Nick Reynolds, *The Great Train Robbery*, Page 39

7. Chris Pickard, Nick Reynolds, *The Great Train Robbery*, Page 38

8. Peter Guttridge, Crime Archive – *The Great Train Robbery*, Page 60

9. Nick Russell Pavier & Stewart Richards, *The Great Train Robbery, The Definitive Account*, Page 116

10. Nick Russell Pavier & Stewart Richards, *The Great Train Robbery, The Definitive Account*, Page 117

11. *Moments of History, The Great British Train Robbery*, 1963, Page 74

12. Piers Paul Read, *The Train Robbers, Their Story*, Page 137

Chapter 5 – The First Arrests

1. Nick Russell Pavier & Stewart Richards, *The Great Train Robbery, The Definitive Accoun*t, Page 143

2. *Moments of History, The Great British Train Robbery*, 1963, Page 82

3. Jim Morris, *The Great Train Robbery, a New History,* Page 71

4. Nick Russell Pavier & Stewart Richards, *The Great Train Robbery, The Definitive Account*, Page 148

5. Nick Russell Pavier & Stewart Richards, *The Great Train Robbery, The Definitive Account,* Page 149

6. Piers Paul Read, *The Train Robbers, Their Story*, Page 154

7. Moments of History, *The Great British Train Robbery*, 1963, Page 88

8. *Moments of History, The Great British Train Robbery*, 1963, Page 104

Chapter 6 – The Net Closes

1. Andrew Cook, *The Great Train Robbery*, Page 65
2. Ronnie Biggs, *Odd Man Out*, Page 40
3. Peter Guttridge, Crime Archive – *The Great Train Robbery*, Page 37
4. Nick Russell Pavier & Stewart Richards, *The Great Train Robbery, The Definitive Account*, Page 139
5. Piers Paul Read, *The Train Robbers, Their Story*, Page 156
6. Peter Guttridge, Crime Archive – *The Great Train Robbery, Page 35*

Chapter 7 – The Key to the Farm

1. Piers Paul Read, *The Train Robbers, Their Story*, Page 159
2. Nick Russell Pavier & Stewart Richards, *The Great Train Robbery, The Definitive Account,* Page 180

Chapter 8 – The Arrests Continue

1. Piers Paul Read, *The Train Robbers, Their Story*, Page 169
2. Nick Russell Pavier & Stewart Richards, *The Great Train Robbery, The Definitive Account,* Page 185
3. Piers Paul Read, *The Train Robbers, Their Story*, Page 157
4. Andrew Cook, *The Great Train Robbery*, Page 119
5. Andrew Cook, *The Great Train Robbery*, Page 121
6. Andrew Cook, *The Great Train Robbery*, Page 122
7. Nick Russell Pavier & Stewart Richards, *The Great Train Robbery, The Definitive Accoun*t, Page 129
8. *Moments of History, The Great British Train Robbery*, 1963, Page 93
9. *Moments of History, The Great British Train Robbery*, 1963, Page 93
10. Nick Russell Pavier & Stewart Richards, *The Great Train Robbery, The Definitive Account*, Page 198

Chapter 9 – The Absent Friends

1. Bruce Reynolds, *The Autobiography of a Thief*, Page 260-264

2. Nick Russell Pavier & Stewart Richards, *The Great Train Robbery, The Definitive Account*, Page 158-159
3. Piers Paul Read, *The Train Robbers, Their Story*, Page 170
4. Bruce Reynolds, *The Autobiography of a Thief*, Page 264-267
5. Andrew Cook, *The Great Train Robbery*, Page 118-119
6. Chris Pickard, Nick Reynolds, *The Great Train Robbery*, Page 52-53
7. Bruce Reynolds, *The Autobiography of a Thief*, Page 273
8. Piers Paul Read, *The Train Robbers, Their Story*, Page 168

Chapter 10 – The Tale of Goody's Two Shoes

1. Bruce Reynolds, *The Autobiography of a Thief*, Page 257

Chapter 11 – The Search Continues

1. Andrew Cook, *The Great Train Robbery*, Page 133
2. *Moments of History, The Great British Train Robbery*, 1963, Page 95
3. Chris Pickard, Nick Reynolds, *The Great Train Robbery*, Page 53
4. Piers Paul Read, *The Train Robbers, Their Story*, Page 168
5. Andrew Cook, *The Great Train Robbery*, Page 141

Chapter 12 – The Review of the Evidence

1. Nick Russell Pavier & Stewart Richards, *The Great Train Robbery, The Definitive Account,* Page 216
2. Nick Russell Pavier & Stewart Richards, *The Great Train Robbery, The Definitive Account*, Page 222
3. Andrew Cook, *The Great Train Robbery*, Page 168
4. *Moments of History, The Great British Train Robbery*, 1963, Page 104

Chapter 13 – The Early Christmas Presents

1. Andrew Cook, *The Great Train Robbery*, Page 148
2. Nick Russell Pavier & Stewart Richards, *The Great Train Robbery, The Definitive Account*, Page 240
3. Moments of History, *The Great British Train Robbery*, 1963, Page 106-107
4. Piers Paul Read, *The Train Robbers, Their Story*, Page 170
5. Piers Paul Read, *The Train Robbers, Their Story*, Page 171

6. Andrew Cook, *The Great Train Robbery*, Page 152
7. Andrew Cook, *The Great Train Robbery*, Page 153

Chapter 14 – The Trial

1. Bruce Reynolds, *The Autobiography of a Thief*, Page 270
2. Andrew Cook, *The Great Train Robbery*, Page 148
3. Nick Russell Pavier & Stewart Richards, *The Great Train Robbery, The Definitive Account*, Page 245
4. The *Observer* 28 September 2014
5. Ronnie Biggs, *Odd Man Out*, Page 55
6. Nick Russell Pavier & Stewart Richards, *The Great Train Robbery, The Definitive Account*, Page 264
7. *Moments of History, The Great British Train Robbery*, 1963, Page 143
8. Piers Paul Read, *The Train Robbers, Their Story*, Page 187-188
9. Nick Russell Pavier & Stewart Richards, *The Great Train Robbery, The Definitive Account*, Page 271
10. Nick Russell Pavier & Stewart Richards, *The Great Train Robbery, The Definitive Account*, Page 285

Chapter 15 – The Verdicts and Trial of Ronnie Biggs

1. Ronnie Biggs, *Odd Man Out*, Page 57

Chapter 16 – The Sentencing

1. Ronnie Biggs, *Odd Man Out*, Page 50
2. Ronnie Biggs, *Odd Man Out*, Page 61
3. The *Observer*, 28 September 2014
4. *Daily Sketch*, 17 April 1964
5. Bruce Reynolds, *The Autobiography of a Thief*, Page 282

Chapter 17 – The Appeals

1. Nick Russell Pavier & Stewart Richards, *The Great Train Robbery, The Definitive Account*, Page 307

Chapter 18 – The Great Escaper

1. Paul Buck, Prison Break – *True Stories of the World's Greatest*

Escapes
2. Bruce Reynolds, *The Autobiography of a Thief*, Page 282
3. Bruce Reynolds, *The Autobiography of a Thief*, Page 302
4. Bruce Reynolds, *The Autobiography of a Thief*, Page 302

Chapter 19 – The Second Great Escaper

1. Andrew Cook, *The Great Train Robbery*, Page 210
2. Piers Paul Read, *The Train Robbers, Their Story*, Page 209
3. The Guardian, 9 July 1965
4. Ronnie Biggs, *Odd Man Out*, Page 81

Chapter 20 – The First to be Released

1. The *Observer*, 28 September 2014

Chapter 21 – The End of the Road

1. Piers Paul Read, *The Train Robbers, Their Story*, Page 233
2. Nick Russell Pavier & Stewart Richards, *The Great Train Robbery, The Definitive Account,* Page 336
3. Piers Paul Read, *The Train Robbers, Their Story*, Page 234

Chapter 22 – The Change of Scenery

1. Bruce Reynolds, *The Autobiography of a Thief*, Page 318

Chapter 23 – The Sweet Smell of Success

1. Bruce Reynolds, *The Autobiography of a Thief*, Page 333
2. Bruce Reynolds, *The Autobiography of a Thief*, Page 340
3. Nick Russell Pavier & Stewart Richards, *The Great Train Robbery, The Definitive Account,* Page 342

Chapter 24 – The End of the Beginning

1. Ronnie Biggs, *Odd Man Out*, Page 108
2. *Gettysburg Times*, 7 January 1969

Chapter 25 – The 1970's

1. Nick Russell Pavier & Stewart Richards, *The Great Train Robbery, The Definitive Account,* Page 352

2. *MotorSport Magazine*, December 1998, Page 68
3. The *Observer* 28 September 2014
4. Marilyn Wisbey, *Gangster's Moll*, Page 96
5. Marilyn Wisbey, *Gangster's Moll*, Page 96 – 97
6. Jim Morris, *The Great Train Robbery, a New History*, Page 196

Chapter 26 – The 1980's

1. Jim Morris, *The Great Train Robbery, a New History*, Page 190
2. Bruce Reynolds, *The Autobiography of a Thief*, Page 400
3. *Daily Mail*, 5 August 1989

Chapter 27 – The 1990's

1. Peter Guttridge, Crime Archive – *The Great Train Robbery*,
   Page 96
2. *The Independent*, 30 November 1994
3. *The Independent*, 9 February 1995
4. Bruce Reynolds, *The Autobiography of a Thief,* Page 410

Chapter 28 – The 21ˢᵗ Century

1. Bruce Reynolds, *The Autobiography of a Thief*, Page 412
2. http://www.thamesvalley.police.uk
3. *The Independent*, 15 November 2012
4. *The Guardian*, 29 January 2008
5. *Daily Mirror*, 3 January 2014
6. *The Observer*, 28 September 2014
7. *The Crewe Chronicle*, 2 December 2014
8. www.abc.net.au/news 30 December 2014

THE VICTIMS

Chapter 29 – The Workers on the Train

1. Andrew Cook, *The Great Train Robbery*, Page 26
2. http://www.dailystar.co.uk/news/latest-news/288166/Thug-who- battered-my-dad-got-away-with-it
3. http://www.railstaff.co.uk/2013/10/15/robbery-staff-remembered/
4. *Crewe Chronicle*, 18 December 2013
5. Andrew Cook, *The Great Train Robbery*, Page 171

Chapter 30 – The Robbers and their Families

1. Ronnie Biggs, *Odd Man Out*, Page 50
2. Bruce Reynolds, *The Autobiography of a Thief*, Page 279
3. Ronnie Biggs, *Odd Man Out*, Page 19
4. Ronnie Biggs, *Odd Man Out*, Page 22
5. Piers Paul Read, *The Train Robbers, Their Story*, Page 126
6. Nick Russell Pavier & Stewart Richards, *The Great Train Robbery, The Definitive Account*, Page 350
7. Piers Paul Read, *The Train Robbers, Their Story*, Page 157
8. Piers Paul Read, *The Train Robbers, Their Story*, Page 315
9. Peta Fordham, *The Robbers Tale*, Page 78
10. Ronnie Biggs, *Odd Man Out*, Page 31-32
11. Ronnie Biggs, *Odd Man Out*, Page 16
12. *The Observer* 28 September 2014
13. Nick Russell Pavier & Stewart Richards, *The Great Train Robbery, The Definitive Account*, Page 214-216
14. Ronnie Biggs, *Odd Man Out*, Page 14
15. Ronnie Biggs, *Odd Man Out*, Page 82
16. Ronnie Biggs, *Odd Man Out*, Page 120
17. Ronnie Biggs, *Odd Man Out*, Page 139
18. Chris Pickard, Nick Reynolds, *The Great Train Robbery*, Page 25
19. Chris Pickard, Nick Reynolds, *The Great Train Robbery*, Page 25
20. The Observer, 28 September 2014
21. Nick Russell Pavier & Stewart Richards, *The Great Train Robbery, The Definitive Account*, Page 98
22. *Moments of History, The Great British Train Robbery*, 1963, Page 139
23. *The Miami News*, 1 September 1963
24. Bruce Reynolds, *The Autobiography of a Thief*, Page 350
25. http://trove.nla.gov.au/ndp/del/article/43201146
26. Bruce Reynolds, *The Autobiography of a Thief*, Page 356
27. Chris Pickard, Nick Reynolds, *The Great Train Robbery*, Page 89
28. Bruce Reynolds, *The Autobiography of a Thief*, Page 387
29. Piers Paul Read, *The Train Robbers, Their Story*, Page 170
30. *The Cornish Guardian*, 1 May 2013
31. *The Cornish Guardian*, 1 May 2013
32. Bruce Reynolds, *The Autobiography of a Thief*, Pages 399-401
33. Piers Paul Read, *The Train Robbers, Their Story*, Page 278
34. *New York Times*, 5 December 1994

35. Bruce Reynolds, *The Autobiography of a Thief*, Page 407
36. *The Independent*, 10 February 1995
37. Peta Fordham, *The Robbers Tale*, Page 24
38. Piers Paul Read, *The Train Robbers, Their Story*, Page 266
39. Piers Paul Read, *The Train Robbers, Their Story*, Page 267
40. Piers Paul Read, *The Train Robbers, Their Story*, Page 268
41. Nick Russell Pavier & Stewart Richards, *The Great Train Robbery, The Definitive Account*, Page 390
42. *Moments of History, The Great British Train Robbery*, 1963, Page 142-143
43. Bruce Reynolds, *The Autobiography of a Thief*, Page 212
44. Jim Morris, *Great Train Robbery, a New History*, Page 203
45. Nick Russell Pavier & Stewart Richards, *The Great Train Robbery, The Definitive Account*, Page 383
46. Piers Paul Read, *The Train Robbers, Their Story*, Page 268
47. Marilyn Wisbey, *Gangster's Moll*, Page 80
48. Marilyn Wisbey, *Gangster's Moll*, Page 192
49. Marilyn Wisbey, *Gangster's Moll*, Page 196
50. Marilyn Wisbey, *Gangster's Moll*, Page 296

Chapter 31 – The Police and the Others

1. *The Guardian*, Obituaries, 1 October 2010
2. *The Sunday Express*, 4 August 2013
3. Frank Williams, *No Fixed Address: Great Train Robbers on the Run*
4. Jack Slipper, *Slipper of the Yard*
5. *Hansard*, 9 July 1970
6. *Daily Mirror*, 3 August 2013
7. *Daily Mail*, 3 August 2013

THE END OF THE LINE

Chapter 32 – The Last Rites

1. Bruce Reynolds, *The Autobiography of a Thief*, Page 280
2. Bruce Reynolds, *The Autobiography of a Thief*, Introduction
3. Jon Fordham, *Thanks for the Memories*, Page 43
4. Bruce Reynolds, *The Autobiography of a Thief*, Page 284
5. *The Observer*, 28 September 2014
6. *The Observer*, 28 September 2014

Chapter 33 – The Flawed Plan

1. Bruce Reynolds, *The Autobiography of a Thief*, Page 223
2. Bruce Reynolds, *The Autobiography of a Thief*, Page 224
3. Bruce Reynolds, *The Autobiography of a Thief*, Page 228
4. Nick Russell Pavier & Stewart Richards, *The Great Train Robbery, The Definitive Account*, Page 344
5. Bruce Reynolds, *The Autobiography of a Thief*, Page 251

Chapter 34 – The Unanswered Questions

1. *The Observer*, 28 September 2014
2. Mick Lee, *The Men Who Robbed The Great Train Robbers*
3. *The Irish Times*, 4 October 2014
4. Piers Paul Read, *The Train Robbers, Their Story*, Page 114
5. Bruce Reynolds, *The Autobiography of a Thief*, Page 281
6. *The Irish Times*, 4 October 2014
7. Bruce Reynolds, *The Autobiography of a Thief*, Page 273
8. George Hatherill, *The Detective's Tale*
9. Bruce Reynolds, *The Autobiography of a Thief*, Page 407-8
10. Andrew Cook, *The Great Train Robbery*, Page 199
11. Andrew Cook, *The Great Train Robbery*, Page 200
12. Andrew Cook, *The Great Train Robbery*, Page 126
13. Andrew Cook, *The Great Train Robbery*, Page 200
14. Nick Russell Pavier & Stewart Richards, *The Great Train Robbery, The Definitive Account*, Page 347
15. Peta Fordham, *The Robbers Tale*, Page 85
16. Andrew Cook, *The Great Train Robbery*, Page 66
17. Bruce Reynolds, *The Autobiography of a Thief*, Page 325

Chapter 35 – The Curse, or just Bad Luck?

1. Jim Morris, *Great Train Robbery, a New History*, Page 197
2. Jim Morris, *Great Train Robbery, a New History*, Page 196
3. Marilyn Wisbey, *Gangster's Moll*, Page 245

THE POSTSCRIPT

1. *The Miami News*, 1 September 1963
2. Sir Stanley Matthews, *The Way It Was, My Autobiography*

3. *Northampton News* 19 February 2015
4. Jim Morris, *Great Train Robbery, a New History*, Page 171
5. *Life Magazine*, 8 April 1966

Lightning Source UK Ltd.
Milton Keynes UK
UKOW06f0622290416

273214UK00007B/93/P